HARVARD STUDIES IN ENGLISH

VOLUME I

COURTLY LOVE
IN CHAUCER AND GOWER

BY

WILLIAM GEORGE DODD

COURTLY LOVE
IN CHAUCER AND GOWER

BY

WILLIAM GEORGE DODD

GLOUCESTER, MASS.

PETER SMITH

1959

Reprinted, 1959

By Permission of

HARVARD UNIVERSITY PRESS

PREFACE

This work is a revision of a study originally made by the writer while a student in the Graduate School of Harvard University. The limitation of the consideration to the so-called "love paramours" made necessary the omission of much of Chaucer's best and most interesting work. But even so, in what is left, there is abundant opportunity for observing the poet's genius. The romantic love in Chaucer, although it differs in no essential respect from that treated by his predecessors and contemporaries in France, becomes in his hands the material for an artistic product of an entirely new sort. The very artistic excellence of the work has sometimes led critics, the writer believes, to wrong impressions of the love itself, and hence to wrong assumptions not only as to the poet's purpose but also as to his achievement. This fact may perhaps be considered sufficient reason for the present study.

Readers nowadays, as a matter of course and, it would seem, often conventionally, complain of the dullness of Gower. His treatment of love does not make it possible for us to deny the justice of such a complaint. At any rate, to the reader of early erotic literature, he serves the useful purpose of showing by contrast how brilliant may be a real poet's treatment of romantic love. Some such purpose, it is hoped, the chapter on Gower will serve in this study.

It is a pleasure to express my appreciation of the interest shown in the progress of my work by my friends and teachers of the Graduate School of Harvard University. In an especial way, I am under obligation to Professor Kittredge. I began the study at his suggestion, and while working at it I had the opportunity of consulting him freely, and of receiving his criticisms and suggestions. Students who have done work under Professor Kittredge's direction, and perhaps only they, will realize all that this means. In helping to revise the work and to arrange it for the press, both he and Professor Robinson have been most kind. They have made many valuable suggestions which I have gladly adopted, and which I here gratefully acknowledge.

W. G. D.

TALLAHASSEE, FLORIDA, July 1, 1913

CONTENTS

CHAPTER I

CHAPTER II

CHAPTER III

CHAPTER IV

CHAPTER V

COURTLY LOVE IN CHAUCER
AND GOWER

CHAPTER I

THE SYSTEM OF COURTLY LOVE

It is in the south of France and at a very early period that we must look for the origin of the system of Courtly Love. Gathered about several small courts, there existed, as early as the eleventh century, a brilliant society, in which woman held the supreme place, and in which, under her influence, vast importance was attached to social etiquette and decorum. Definite rules governed the sexes in all their relations, and especially in matters of love. It was to this society that the troubadours belonged, and it was love, chiefly, that was the inspiration of their songs.[1] In the troubadours, therefore, we find the earliest expression of the ideas of courtly love.

In time, these ideas were introduced into northern France, largely through the influence of Eleanor of Aquitaine. This amorous duchess took a lively interest in the doctrines, as well as the practices, of courtly love. Before leaving her southern home to become queen of France, she received, and, it seems, encouraged, advances of a very familiar nature from the troubadour Bernart de Ventadorn. At the northern court, also, she lent her authority to the new doctrines. In this she was followed by her daughter, Marie of Champagne, and other noble ladies,

---

[1] *Romania*, 1883, p. 521 ; G. Paris, *La Littérature Française au Moyen Age*, 3d ed., Paris, 1905, p. 199.

who amused themselves and the fashionable society about them by rendering decisions on difficult questions which were argued before the mock Courts of Love.[1] Naturally, such decisions soon came to be regarded as definite rules and regulations of the courtly system. Thus, in northern France, the new ideas of love received from the first the sanction and support of women of high rank, through whose influence they found their way into contemporary literature. Marie of Champagne, for instance, impressed them upon Chrétien de Troies, and he, in turn, introduced them into the romances of the Round Table.[2] Under his hands, the Arthurian romances became the representatives *par excellence* of the chivalrous and courtly ideal of twelfth-century society.[3] His *Conte de la Charrette*, which reflects in an especial manner the conceptions of the courtly love, owes its existence, as he himself tells us,[4] to Marie of Champagne.

The ideas of love in the romances of Chrétien are the ideas found in the lyrics of the troubadours; but in many instances the genius of the French poet has transformed them into something peculiarly his own. The fancies and conceits of the earlier poetry he elaborates highly; mere hints he develops into formal doctrines. He subjects the emotions of the human heart to delicate and subtle analysis, and philosophizes upon them with astonishing minuteness. The result of this process of refinement was the formulation of certain doctrines, the observance of which became equally obligatory upon courtly lovers and upon later writers who dealt with the subject.

As the system was left by Chrétien, so it was to remain. It would be wrong, however, to suppose that the crystallizing of the courtly sentiments was due to him alone. The process had begun in the poetry of the troubadours. Even for them love

[1] Mott, *The System of Courtly Love*, Boston, 1896, p. 57.
[2] Paris, p. 202.   [3] Ibid., p. 103.
[4] Chrétien de Troies, *Conte de la Charrette*, ed. W. Förster, Halle, 1899, ll. 1–30.

was an art to be practised rather than a passion to be felt. It was largely a matter of behavior. To regulate his conduct in strict accord with the rules and restrictions with which the art was hedged about, became the lover's chief concern. Naturally, the literature which drew its inspiration from such love was devoid of spontaneity and real feeling. In the poetry of Bernart de Ventadorn, it is true, there is to be found what seems to be earnest passion; but the writings of the troubadours after Bernart are to a great extent characterized by artificiality and monotony of sentiment. Through each poet's imitation of his predecessor, the very emotional experiences of lovers became stereotyped.[1] The exaggerations employed to give a semblance of intensity to an artificial passion became poetical conventions. It was with such material that Chrétien worked. His contribution to the courtly system was the fixing of ideas already present in twelfth-century literature, the development of others, and the introduction of them all into the romances of the Round Table.

The interest in courtly love is nowhere more clearly manifested than in certain works roughly contemporary with Chrétien, which treat of love as an art, setting forth in a scientific manner the principles of the system and codifying the laws upon which it was based. This method of treatment had its origin in the erotic writings of Ovid,[2] the favorite poet of the mediaeval· schools.[3] His *Ars Amatoria* was several times translated into French, curiously altered to suit the manners and customs of mediaeval society, the sensualism of the original being newly interpreted in accord with the chivalrous spirit.[4] Of the works of this period which, following the plan of Ovid, treat of love as an art, the most important is the *De Arte Honeste Amandi* by Andreas Capellanus.[5] Here we have fully worked out the

---

[1] Mott, p. 16.   [2] Paris, p. 167.   [3] Ibid., p. 83.
[4] Paris, *La Poésie du Moyen Age*, 1st Series, Paris, 1887, pp. 189 ff.
[5] Ed. E. Trojel, Havniae, 1892.

jurisprudence of that courtly system which is exemplified in the romances of the Round Table.[1] Andreas treats with scholastic precision the following questions : What is love ? What are its effects ? Between whom can it exist ? How is it acquired, retained, augmented, diminished, terminated ? What is the duty of one lover when the other proves unfaithful ?[2] He is chiefly concerned, however, with showing whom the lover should choose for his *amie*, how he may win her, and how her favor may be retained. This threefold division was common with the mediaeval imitators of Ovid,[3] and is manifestly copied from the plan of the *Ars Amatoria*.[4] The second of his three questions Andreas answers by means of eight imaginary conversations between model lovers of various ranks. He also deals with the love of clerks, monks, courtesans, and rustics ; he condemns love which is acquired by means of money, as well as that obtained with too little difficulty. Chapter seven of the second book contains twenty-one decisions rendered by noble ladies, on disputed points of love.[5] Chapter eight gives the thirty-one

[1] Paris, *La Litt. Fr. au M. A.*, p. 167.   [2] Andreas, p. 3.

[3] Paris, *La Poésie du M. A.*, pp. 189 ff.

[4] W. A. Neilson, *The Origin and Sources of the Court of Love*, Boston, 1899, p. 177.

[5] These decisions have been used as an argument in favor of the reality of the so-called courts of love, by those who maintain that the courts were judicial bodies, before which disputed points of love were carried for settlement. The question was debated for many years after Diez disputed their reality in his *Ueber die Minnehöfe* in 1825. The principal scholars of recent times who held in favor of the reality of the courts, were E. Trojel in his *Middelalderens Elskovshoffer* (Copenhagen, 1880) and P. Rajna in *Le Corti d'Amore* (Milan, 1890). Cf. also *Tre Studi per la Storia del Libro di Andrea Cappellano* in *Studj di Filologia Romanza*, V, 193–272). The opposing view was strongly maintained by G. Paris in the *Journal de Savants*, 1888, pp. 664 ff. and 727 ff., and in *Romania*, XIX, 372. See also Neilson, pp. 240 ff. The latest contribution to the discussion (which has flagged of late) is an article by G. Zonta, *Rileggendo Andrea Cappellano*, in *Studi Medievali*, 1908, Fasc. 1, in which he argues with G. Paris against the reality of the courts of love. For a good summary of the history of the controversy, see the article in Johnson's Encyclopedia, V, 375–376, by A. R. Marsh, entitled " Courts of Love."

statutes which bear the stamp of authority of the god of Love himself. Besides the thirty-one rules, there is also in the work a short code of twelve which purport to have been revealed to a knight in a vision of the Palace of Love. These two codes sum up the whole doctrine of Andreas. His third and last book is entitled *De Reprobatione Amoris*, and is modeled on Ovid's *Remedia*. Throughout the work there are references to Eleanor of Aquitaine, Ermengarde of Narbonne, and the Countess Marie of Champagne, oftenest to the last named. Obviously it was her theories which, to a large degree, inspired Andreas to write his treatise.[1]

The book of Andreas furnishes us a ready means of understanding the abstract principles and the laws underlying the courtly system.[2] These principles, which are few in number, are:

1. *Courtly love is sensual.* Andreas makes this clear at the outset by defining love as a passion arising from the contemplation of beauty in the opposite sex, and culminating in the gratification of the physical desires thus awakened.[3] On this definition the whole system rests. The insistence with which the sensual element is dwelt upon throughout the book, contrasts strangely with the high ideals of conduct and character presented at the same time. For this incongruity, however, Andreas is not responsible. The love which was practised by the courtly society of southern France, and which spread to the North, though essentially impure, was yet exalted as uplifting and ennobling and productive of every virtue.

2. *Courtly love is illicit and, for the most part, adulterous.* Indeed, in the courtly system marriage has no place. The Countess Marie is reported by Andreas to have decided, in a disputed case, that "love cannot

---

[1] *Romania*, 1883, pp. 521 ff.

[2] A résumé of the principles of the courtly love may be found in J. Bédier, *De Nicolao Museto*, Paris, 1893, pp. 23 ff. He makes the statement: "All the mediaeval lyric poetry takes its rise in a few principles." He then proceeds to tell what these principles are, and, in so doing, mentions, in the main, the points which appear in the following pages of this chapter.

[3] "Amor est passio quaedam innata procedens ex visione et immoderata cogitatione formae alterius sexus, ob quam aliquis super omnia cupit alterius potiri amplexibus et omnia de utriusque voluntate in ipsius amplexu amoris praecepta compleri." — Andreas, p. 3.

exist between two people joined together in the conjugal relation."[1] The idea is again expressed, on the authority of the same Countess, in the excuse which a certain lover offers for seeking love out of wedlock, although he has a beautiful wife whom he professes to love " totius mentis affectione maritali."[2] In accord with these opinions, and probably based upon them, is the first law of the longer code, which frankly states that a woman cannot plead marriage as a sufficient excuse for denying a lover's petition.[3]

3. *A love, sensual and illicit, must needs be secret.* The shorter code lays this down as a law;[4] and the longer adds, as the reason, that a love which is divulged, rarely lasts.[5] No article of the code is so important as this, and none is insisted upon so much. " Qui non celat, amare non potest."[6] He who reveals the secrets he should keep, is branded as a traitor to the god of Love. Nothing is so despicable as to blab after having received favors. But not only must love be secret; it must also be furtive. It was the element of furtiveness, largely, that made the courtly love incompatible with the legal relations between husband and wife. The necessity of secrecy gives rise in the literature to a constant fear of spies: a fear exaggerated, no doubt, but not without foundation, if we may accept the romances as reflecting contemporary life. In these stories, it is often the rôle of the false steward to spy upon lovers and to report their actions to the lady's father or husband.

There were grounds of a very practical nature for the insistence upon secrecy. Chaucer, describing the violation of Lucretia, tells us:

> Thise Romain wyves loveden so hir name
> At thilke tyme, and dredden so the shame,
> That, what for fere of slaundre and drede of deeth,
> She loste bothe at ones wit and breeth,
> And in a swough she lay.[7]

Fear of slander has disturbed the mind of many a woman far less chaste than Lucretia. As the Wife of Bath aptly puts it,

---

[1] " Dicimus enim et stabilito tenore firmamus, amorem non posse suas inter duos iugales extendere vires." — Andreas, p. 153.

[2] Ibid., p. 172.

[3] " Causa coniugii ab amore non est excusatio recta." — Ibid., p. 310.

[4] "Amoris tui secretarios noli plures habere."—Ibid., p. 106.

[5] "Amor raro consuevit durare vulgatus."—Ibid., p. 310. Cf. also " Qui suum igitur cupit amorem diu retinere illaesum, eum sibi maxime praecavere oportet, ut amor extra suos terminos nemini propaletur, sed omnibus reservetur occultus." — Ibid., p. 238.

[6] Ibid., p. 310.

[7] *Legend of Good Women : Lucretia*, ll. 133–137.

" For be we never so vicious withinne,
We wol been holden wyse, and clene of sinne." [1]

Despite the moral laxness of the society out of which the courtly love grew, there were some, perhaps many, to whom its ideas were abhorrent. However this may be, the women of that society felt it necessary to protect their good name. Chastity might be dispensed with without scruple, but a sullied reputation was unbearable. Once the lady had satisfied herself that the aspiring lover would be true to her, her greatest fear was that their *liaison* should become known, and that she might be subjected to the aspersions of talebearers.

Another reason for secrecy may be found in the peculiar relations between husband and wife among the higher classes of mediaeval society. Marriage was rarely a matter in which the heart was concerned. Business affairs and political considerations often brought about unions in which no affection could exist.[2] Yet the integrity of the tie and the exclusive rights pertaining to the married state seem to have been insisted upon by husbands. By the theory of courtly love, jealousy could not exist between a man and his wife,[3] and since jealousy was a requisite of love,[4] no love could exist between them. As a matter of fact, jealous husbands are execrated in love poetry from the early carols of the peasant girls of Poitou and Limousin [5] to Chaucer. Criseyde says:

" Shal noon housbonde seyn to me ' Chekmat! '
For either they ben ful of jalousye,
Or maisterful, or loven novelrye." [6]

What action the husband of an unfaithful wife was expected to take, in case her infidelity was discovered, we may infer from the summary and severe punishment dealt out to such offenders, as it is pictured in romances, ballads, and chronicles.[7] Due precaution for the maintenance of strict secrecy would therefore be dictated by wisdom and common sense.

[1] *Wife of Bath's Tale*, ll. 87–89.
[2] Langlois, *Origines et Sources du Roman de la Rose*, Paris, 1891, p. 3.
[3] Andreas, p. 154.
[4] " Ex vera zelotypia affectus semper crescit amandi." — Ibid., p. 154.
[5] Paris, *Origines de la Poésie Lyrique en France au Moyen Age*, Paris, 1892, p. 51.
[6] *Troilus and Criseyde*, bk. ii, st. 108.
[7] See the ballad of *Sir Aldingar*, and the romances *The Erl of Tolous* and *Sir Triamour;* also the romance of *The Knight of Curtesy and the Fair Lady of Faguel*. The story of the lover's heart being served by the husband to his wife while eating, is told also of the troubadour Guillem de Cabestaing; see *The Lives of the Troubadours*, translated by Ida Farnell, London, 1896, pp. 41 ff.

4. *Love, to meet the requirements of the courtly system, must not be too easily obtained.*[1] This idea receives great stress because of the lofty position which woman held in the courtly society. The concrete working of the rule is seen in the coldness and capriciousness of the lady, which are the cause of all the lover's woes as they are pictured in the poetry of the troubadours.

We have already observed that courtly love was exalted under the system as a virtue which ennobled those who practised the art. In theory, love is the fount and origin of every good.[2] It is constantly associated in the literature with courtesy and "largess." Andreas declares that love is " ever banished from the domicile of avarice."[3] In another passage, he states specifically that love makes the rude and uncouth excel in every grace; that it enriches those of low birth with real nobility of character; and that it makes the true lover show a becoming complaisance to all.[4] And then he breaks out rapturously: "O, how wonderful is love, which causes a man to be effulgent in virtue, and teaches every one to abound in good manners!"[5] It was to achieve these virtues that the courtly lover sought his lady's favor. Strangely enough, the "good" was all on one side. If this love was like mercy, which "blesseth him that gives and him that takes," it is not so stated in the manual of Andreas. This again is due to the high position held by woman in the society of the time, and the reverence with which she was regarded. From her lofty place, as the perfect being, she dispensed favors which were at the same time the reward of noble deeds and the incentive to further effort.

It must be noted that the ideals of the courtly system, if we disregard the element of sensualism, were high. This was true,

---

[1] "Facilis perceptio contemptibilem reddit amorem, difficilis eum carum facit haberi." — Andreas, p. 310.

[2] The iteration of this idea in Andreas becomes tiresome. See pp. 29, 63, 69, 81, 86, 87, 88, 162.

[3] Rule 10, Andreas, p. 310.   [4] Andreas, p. 9.   [5] Ibid., p. 10.

not only in matters of decorum, but of honor as well. Constancy was of the utmost importance.[1] No more grievous fault could be committed, no breach of the canons could be more serious, than for a lover, man or woman, to be unfaithful. This idea is insistently dwelt upon by Andreas, and it appears conspicuously in the other erotic literature of the period and of the following centuries. " Supplanting " also was strictly forbidden.[2] To choose for his mistress one whom he would be ashamed to marry, was thought unworthy of a lover.[3] Though sensual love lay at the bottom of the system, voluptuousness was regarded as fatal to real love.[4] Indeed, though according to the courtly ideas love is in essence sensual, and should be secret and furtive, yet it incited the lover to worthy deeds ; it demanded of him nobility of character and moderation in all his conduct. It is a love evil at the heart of it, yet it is a love which " loses half its evil, by losing all its grossness."

Such was the theory of the courtly system. For its practical side, we turn to the poetry of the troubadours. Inspired, professedly, by real and actual love affairs, their lyrics present the concrete workings of the sentiment which afterward became the basis of the erotic philosophy not only of Chrétien de Troies but of Andreas himself. In the poems of the troubadours, therefore, we find portrayed the birth and progress of their love, their emotional experiences, their relation and attitude toward the ladies whose favor they sought, and their behavior as affected by their passion.

---

[1] " Nemo duplici potest amore ligari." "Verus amans alterius nisi sui coamantis ex effectu non cupit amplexus."— Rules 3, 12, Andreas, p. 310. Cf. Rule 7, same code.

[2] " Alterius idonee copulatam amori scienter subvertere non coneris." — Rule 3, Andreas, p. 106.

[3] " Eius non curis eligere, cum qua naturalis nuptias contrahere prohibit tibi pudor."— Rule 4, Andreas, p. 106.

[4] " Non solet amare, quem nimia voluptatis abundantia vexat."— Rule 29, Andreas, p. 311. Cf. also Rule 8, ibid., p. 106.

The lady is regularly represented as perfect in all her attributes. The basis of this idea is, of course, the high social position of woman. Her good qualities were doubtless exaggerated, however, because of her rank; for the poet was often politically her subject, as well as her humble lover. Her perfection is pictured in her physical beauty, her character, and her influence upon others. Her physical beauty, when portrayed, accords with the mediaeval ideal. Her hair is blond or golden; her eyes beautiful; her complexion fresh and clear; her mouth rosy and smiling; her flesh white, soft, and smooth; her body slender, well formed, and without blemish. In character, she is distinguished for her courtesy, kindness, refinement, and good sense. In short, all that makes the perfect woman, in soul or in manners, the poet's love possesses. Her influence on others is always ennobling. Her goodness affects all who come near her, making them better. One poet fondly sings: "There is not in the whole world a vile person so ill-bred that he will not become courteous, if he speaks a word with her."[1] Another declares: "The most ignorant man in the company, when he sees and gazes at her, ought at parting to be wise and of fine bearing."[2]

As a perfect being, the lady occupies a position of exalted superiority in respect to the lover. He becomes her vassal and

---

[1] Qu' el mon non es vilas tan mal apres,
Si parl' ab lieys un mot, non torn cortes.

G. de Saint-Didier.

See Raynouard, *Choix des Poésies Originales des Troubadours*, Paris, 1816, III, 301. The translations of the passages from the troubadour lyrics are taken from Mr. Mott's work, *The System of Courtly Love*.

[2] Lo plus nescis hom del renh
Que la veya ni remir
Deuria esser al partir
Savis e de belh captenh.

Raimond de Miraval, Raynouard, III, 359.

protests absolute submission and devotion to her.[1] " Good lady," begs Bernart de Ventadorn in his humility, " I demand nothing more of you than that you take me for a servant, for I will serve you as one serves a good master, whatever be my reward."[2] Even power of life and death is in the lady's hands. The same poet says : " In her pleasure may it be, for I am at her mercy : if it please her to kill me, I do not complain of it at all."[3] His love for her surpasses all other things in value ; the slightest token from her makes him rich. " She, whose liegeman I am without recall, kills me so sweetly with desire, that she would make me rich with a thread of her glove, or with one of the hairs that falls on her mantle."[4] The service which he professes is often carried to the extreme of worship, and he adores her as a divinity, giving and commending himself to her with hands joined and head bowed.[5]

[1] This feature, of course, reflects the relation of the contemporary vassal to his lord under the feudal system. On the parallels in this poetry between the love-service and that of the political vassal, see Wechssler, *Frauendienst und Vasallität* (*Zeitschrift für französische Sprache und Litteratur*, XXIV, 159 ff.).

[2]   Bona domna, plus no us deman
      Mas que m prendatz per servidor,
      Qu' ie us servirai cum bon senhor,
      Cossi que del guazardon m'an.
                    Bernart de Ventadorn, Raynouard, III, 45.

[3]   En son plazar sia,
      Qu' ieu sui en sa merce ;
      S'il platz que m'aucia,
      Ieu no m'en clam de re. — Raynouard, III, 64.

[4]   Tan belhamen m'aucira deziran
      Selha cui sui hom liges ses revelh,
      Que m fera ric ab un fil de son guan,
      O d'un dels pels que 'l chai sus son mantelh.
                    G. de Saint-Didier, Raynouard, III, 300.

[5] Mas juntas, ab cap cle,
     Vos m'autrei e m coman. — Raynouard, III, 60.

The lady rarely appears as a personality in the poetry of the troubadours, but remains indistinct in the background. From the poet's portrayal of his own feelings, however, her attitude toward him is clear enough. We have seen that she possesses every good quality; her kindness, however, the lover seldom experiences. To him she is cold, disdainful, capricious, and domineering. In vain does he implore pity; in vain does he complain of her cruelty and beg for mercy; her rigor is unabated. This coldness of the lady is the keynote of by far the larger part of the poetry which we are now considering. Originating in the instinctive hesitancy of the woman to yield too easily, it is here exaggerated beyond all naturalness. In later erotic literature it becomes a convention and is the motive of almost all the love-poetry of France for the next four centuries.

Nobility of rank was not a requisite in the troubadour-lovers of Provence. Poetry seems to have been a common meeting-ground for knight and burgher, for prince and peasant. The first troubadour whose work is extant is William IX, Count of Poitiers. Piere Vidal, one of the most prolific writers, was the son of a furrier. Alphonso II of Aragon, one of the great rulers of his age, like Richard the Lion-Hearted, was not only the friend and patron of the troubadours, but a maker of verses himself. Bernart de Ventadorn, who loved and was loved by Eleanor of Aquitaine, was " of low degree, son, to wit, of a serving man, who gathered brushwood for the heating of the oven wherein was baked the castle bread." [1] All who sang of love, however, agreed as to the ennobling effect of love on the character of the lover. Specifically, because of his love, he becomes courteous, gentle, humble, generous, and courageous. As one lover proudly says, " Happy is he whom love keeps joyous, for love is the climax of all blessings, and through love, one is gay and courteous, frank and gentle, humble and proud."

[1] Farnell, *The Lives of the Troubadours* (translated), London, 1896, p. 27.

I have spoken of the absolute devotion of the lover to the lady, of his service, and his submission to her will. In their efforts to emphasize these features of their love and the power which that love exerted over them, the troubadours made use of as extravagant fancies as their imaginations could invent. The effects of love, which Professor Neilson aptly speaks of as "symptoms," are described as suffering, or a severe sickness; sleeplessness; confusion and loss of speech in the lady's presence; trembling and pallor when near the loved one; fear to make an avowal to the lady; and dread of detection by others.[1]

Certain other ideas and conceits, though frequent in the poetry of the troubadours, are important rather because of the elaborate treatment of them by Chrétien de Troies. Three especially are to be mentioned: the idea that love is caused by the beauty of the opposite sex; the conceit that through the eyes, beauty enters the heart, inflicting a wound which only the lady can heal; and the fancy that, though absent from the loved one, the lover leaves his heart with her. Because of Chrétien's subtlety in dealing with these ideas, they may be regarded as his particular contribution to the conventional stock.

The idea that love is caused by beauty is illustrated in the *Cligès*, where Alexander is represented as thinking of the charms of Soredamors. "Love pictures to him her beauty, on

[1] The place of secrecy in the courtly system has been noticed in considering the work of Andreas. It may be added that secrecy was a quality which the troubadour-lovers prized very highly in themselves; they seldom omit it from the list of their virtues, when recommending themselves to their ladies' favor. Yet, the maintenance of secrecy was a difficult matter. Slanderers and talebearers are constantly execrated. Apparently the talebearer did not confine himself to mere tattling. Misrepresentation of the lover's actions to the lady herself furnished to unscrupulous persons an easy means of "supplanting," and the lover sometimes had to warn his lady not to believe such reports. Thus Rambaut de Vanqueiras says: "Beautiful worthy lady, courteous and well-bred, do not believe calumniators nor evil-speakers about me, for I am constant to you." See Mahn, *Die Werke der Troubadours*, Berlin, 1846, I, 374.

account of which he feels himself *fort grevé*. It has robbed him of his heart, nor does it allow him to rest in his bed : so much is he delighted to remember the beauty and the countenance of [Soredamors]." [1]

More subtlety is displayed in the poet's use of the second idea, in the passage from the same poem where Alexander undergoes a rigid self-examination on the manner in which love has attacked him. He says : " It has wounded me so severely, that even to the heart his (Love's) dart has penetrated. . . . How then does it penetrate the body when the wound does not appear on the outside ? . . . Through what has it penetrated ? Through the eye. Through the eye ? And yet it has not put out the eye ? In the eye it has not hurt me at all, but in the heart it hurts me grievously. Tell me then : how has the dart passed through the eye so that it is neither wounded nor destroyed ? If the dart enters through the eye, why does the heart suffer, and not the eye which received the first blow ? " —And so he continues to analyze this all-important question until he hits upon the explanation that, as the sunlight penetrates glass without breaking it, so the light of beauty pierces the eye without harming it, and reaches the heart.[2]

Chrétien's treatment of the third idea is quite as subtle. When Ivain found it necessary to leave Laudine and to accompany Sir Gawain and the king to Britain, the poet tells us, the lover departed from his lady very unwillingly, although his heart did not depart from her at all. " The king can take away the body, but the heart not a bit; for it is so joined and holds so fast to the heart of her who remains behind, that he has not the power to take it. While the body is without the heart, it can in no wise live ; and if the body does live without the heart, such a wonder no man has ever seen. This wonder has come to pass ;

---

[1] Chrétien de Troies, *Cligès*, ed. W. Förster, Halle, 1910, ll. 618–625.
[2] Ibid., ll. 692 ff.

for the body [of Ivain] has kept its life without the heart which used to be there, and which does not wish to follow it more." [1] The quotations given illustrate the minuteness of Chrétien's philosophizing on questions of love, and his process of refinement, which later poets regarded with delight, and which, as far as they were able, they imitated in their own work.

In general, then, we have seen that the ideas of the troubadours, derived in the main from Ovid, but developed and exaggerated in the south of France, became in the north the principles and requirements of a fixed code. Chrétien made certain conceits into formal doctrines, which were accepted as such by later writers. Still other fancies became rules of conduct in matters of love. The coldness of the lady is reflected in Andreas's law: "The easy attainment of love renders it contemptible; difficult attainment makes it to be held dear." [2] The idea of fear in the lady's presence became a philosophical principle: "Amorosus semper est timorosus." [3] The same is true of the trembling: "In repentina coamantis visione cor contremescit amantis." [4] Sleeplessness, at first a result of love, became a requirement imposed upon lovers: "Minus dormit et edit, quem amoris cogitatio vexat." [5] In short, the ideas of the troubadour lyrics are the basis of the whole courtly system; and Andreas's book is but a quasi-scientific attempt to reduce to laws the practices of the troubadours and other courtly lovers of the time.

Besides the elements thus far treated, which belong to the essential theory of courtly love, certain incidental features of the courtly literature must be briefly mentioned. A number of conventional devices were of such frequent occurrence in mediaeval

---

[1] Chrétien, *Ivain*, ed. W. Förster, Halle, 1906, ll. 2639–2654.
[2] "Facilis perceptio contemptibilem reddit amorem, difficilis eum carum facit haberi." — Andreas, p. 310.
[3] Ibid., p. 311.   [4] Ibid., p. 311.   [5] Ibid., p. 311.

love-poetry that they became characteristic of the tradition with which this study is concerned. Many erotic poems, for example, were cast in the form of dreams or visions, doubtless in imitation of the apocalyptic writings of the Church. Thus the love-vision came to constitute a distinct literary type, and for a long time was perhaps the prevailing mode of expression of courtly sentiment. Poems of this class commonly tell the story of the experience of a hero in the service of love. The events are usually assigned to the springtime, in keeping with an old and lasting association between love and that season of the year. The hero is often conducted by a guide to the god of love, whose habitation is more or less fully described. Allegorical figures abound, exhibiting various phases of love or the virtues and faults of lovers; and the person of the divinity himself is conceived in accordance with certain definite traditions.[1]

The personification of love as a god is an inheritance from classical times, and a good example may be found in the first elegy of Ovid's *Amores*. The poet, about to sing of "arms and the violent wars," is compelled by Cupid to change his subject:

> Questus eram, pharetra cum protinus ille soluta,
>   Legit in exitium spicula facta meum,
> Lunavitque genu sinuosum fortiter arcum,
>   " Quod " que " canas, vates, accipe " dixit, " opus ! "
> Me miserum ! certas habuit puer ille sagittas :
>   Uror, et in vacuo pectore regnat Amor.[2]

Love triumphs over the poet, and he confesses himself vanquished :

> Sic erit : haeserunt tenues in corde sagittae,
>   Et possessa ferus pectora versat Amor.[3]

---

[1] The love-vision as a literary type is well described and illustrated by W. O. Sypherd in his *Studies in the "Hous of Fame,"* Chaucer Society, 1907, pp. 6 ff.

[2] Ovid, *Amores*, i, 1, 21–26.

[3] Ibid., i, 2, 7–8.

This personification of love as a god, with the appurtenances of quiver and arrows, is in constant use in the mediaeval love literature. The hero of the *Pamphilus de Amore*,[1] which is in the spirit of Ovid throughout, suffers from a wound inflicted by the god's arrows. It is a shot from his bow that brings Chrétien's hero, Alexander, low. Yvain, too, is a victim of the deadly dart. Without the accompaniment of his weapons, Love is frequently depicted as an all-powerful deity, to express the idea that to all suitable young persons love is not only a duty, but a fate which they cannot escape. In the early poetry of the troubadours, Love is a goddess whose power is irresistible, whose command is law to the lover, who at times is cruel, at others, neglectful of her servants. Bernart de Ventadorn sings : " I have no power at all that can defend me against Love ; . . . when I think to free myself, I cannot, for Love holds me." [2] He says of himself, " I alas ! whom Love forgets," [3] and addresses the cruel goddess thus : " Whatever you command me to do, I shall do, for so it is fitting, but you do not well always to make me suffer." [4] Chrétien also personifies love to express the same idea of a resistless god. Soredamors is helpless in his hands ; against Love she thinks to defend herself, but it is useless.[5] He brings her to grief and avenges himself upon her for her great pride and indifference.[6]

---

[1] Ed. by A. Baudoin, Paris, 1874.

[2] Mas ieu non ai ges poder
Que m puesca d'amor defendre ; . . .
Ans quant ieu m'en cug estraire
No pues ges, qu' amors mi te. — Raynouard, III, p. 47.

[3] Ieu las ! cui amors oblida . . . — Ibid., III, p. 91.

[4] Que que m comandetz a faire
Faral, qu' en aissi s cove,
Mas vos non o faitz ges be
Que m fassatz tot jorn maltraire. — Ibid., p. 47.

[5] Chrétien, *Cligès*, ll. 528–529.   [6] Ibid., ll. 456–459.

The classical conception of the god of Love is still familiar
in literature. In mediaeval writings, however, the deity often
took on special characteristics borrowed from the religious conditions of the time. Thus in the *Concile de Remiremont*,[1] a
Latin poem of the twelfth century, a council is assembled by
one who acts under the commands of the god of Love. Its
members are all enlisted in his service, and they regulate their
lives in accordance with his precepts and wishes. The meeting
is opened with a ceremony of worship; but the form of procedure is clearly borrowed from the service of the Church, and
is inconsistent with the worship paid to a heathen divinity. The
Concile is representative of a large class of erotic literature in
which a systematic religion of love is set forth, modelled on that
of the Church. The New Jerusalem of the Apocalypse became
the Paradise in which dwelt the god of Love, and in which were
reserved places for his disciples. There was also a Purgatory
where those who refused to bow to his commands were punished.
In the book of Andreas, both these places are elaborately described.[2] The new religious system had its gospel, its commandments, its apostles and teachers; examples of the two
former we have seen in the codes of Andreas's book. In short,
adaptations of all the important features of the mediaeval
Christian worship may be found in the erotic literature of the
time.[3]

Alongside the conception of the god of Love just noticed,
there appears another in which the characteristics of the deity
reflected rather social than religious conditions. To him were
given the attributes of a feudal lord, to whom, as to their chief,
lovers swear loyalty and obedience. In return for faithful service, the god, who now often becomes a king, acts as their pro-
tector and has at heart the welfare of his vassals. Disputes are

[1] Printed by G. Waitz in *Zeitschrift für deutsches Alterthum*, VII, 160 ff.
[2] Andreas, pp. 91 ff.   [3] Langlois, *Origines*, pp. 220 ff.

carried to him for arbitration; and in his court, surrounded by his barons, he administers justice. This conception of the god of Love was well known to Chrétien. Alexander remarks: "A servant ought to tremble with fear when his lord calls him or sends for him. And whoever commends himself to Love, makes him his lord and master, and it is right that such a one hold him in reverence and fear him and honor him much, if he indeed wishes to be of his court." [1] The same ideas appear in varying degrees in many documents of the period. In the Old French *Florance and Blancheflor*,[2] in particular, the feudal character of the god is made prominent. He here becomes a king, with a court of bird-barons, to whom a case is referred for settlement. The "inconsistency in the use of 'king or god,'" as Professor Neilson has remarked with reference to this poem, ". . . is suggestive of the process by which the classical divine court took on a feudal character. The birds are just about to be brought in, not merely as attendants on the god of Love, but as barons with deliberating power, and almost unconsciously, it might seem, the poet begins to speak of a king instead of a god." [3] An interesting example of the same process is also furnished by two other French pieces, *Li Fablel dou Dieu d'Amours* [4] and *Venus la Deesse d'Amour*,[5] which are in reality only different versions of a single story. In the former, there is no suggestion of the judicial character of the god; he is simply the classical divinity who comes to the aid of one of his worshippers in trouble. In *Venus la Deesse*, his rôle as judge is brought out with distinctness and in detail. He holds his court, before which the case of the lover is argued, and renders the decision which restores to the hero his lady.

---

[1] Chrétien, *Cligès*, ll. 3879–3892.
[2] Barbazan et Méon, *Fabliaux et Contes*, Paris, 1808, IV, 354–365.
[3] Neilson, *Origins*, p. 38.
[4] Ed. by A. Jubinal, Paris, 1834.
[5] Ed. by W. Förster, Bonn, 1880.

In the consideration of the love deity in the literature which
it is the purpose of this study to examine, the three conceptions
pointed out in the preceding paragraphs will be distinguished
by the terms " classical," " ecclesiastical," and " feudal." It is
clear, however, that, since the classical deity took on the peculiar attributes consistent with the ecclesiastical and feudal conceptions, there may appear a blending of the classical with the
ecclesiastical, or of the classical with the feudal. In any given
case where the nature of such added features is clear, the term
" ecclesiastical " or " feudal " will be used : the former, when
the religion of the deity in question reflects some phase of the
Christian religion or of the worship of the mediaeval Church ;
the latter, when the deity exercises the powers of a feudal lord
whom the lover serves in the capacity of a vassal or a subject.
The term " classical " will be reserved for those cases in which
the deity appears with the characteristics given him in the
classical literature, but without any of the attributes peculiar to
either the feudal or the ecclesiastical conception.

Care has here been taken to employ the word " deity " or
" divinity," because, instead of a god, or along with him, a
goddess often appears, to whom is attributed the same power
and authority. Venus as the goddess of Love is frequently
found with Cupid the god of Love, as was seen in *Venus la
Deesse*. Often she appears alone, either as the goddess or as
the queen of Love. In general, poets do not consistently dis-
criminate between Venus and Cupid as the love deity.

CHAPTER II

COURTLY LOVE IN THE *ROMANCE OF THE ROSE* AND LATER FRENCH WORKS

In the foregoing chapter have been presented the principles of the courtly love system, with some illustrations of its treatment in literature. It has been shown that the conduct of lovers was prescribed by laws which arose from conventionalizing real and spontaneous, although exaggerated, sentiments of the poets ; the personification of love appearing in the erotic literature has been noted ; and attention has been called to certain forms in which a large class of the love-poetry was cast. All these ideas and characteristics appear, in one way or another, in Guillaume de Lorris's part of the *Romance of the Rose*, the most important French love document of mediaeval times. Although it was written to delight its readers by the story of the author's love affair, one important purpose, hinted at by the poet in the familiar lines,

> Ci est le Roman de la Rose
> Ou l'art d'amour est tote enclose,

entitles it to be considered, as Paris calls it, "un véritable *Art d'Amour*." [1] The character of the work, therefore, and also the influence it exerted upon later literature in both French and English make a rather full summary of its contents desirable at this point.

The *Romance of the Rose* [2] is the story of a dream of a young man of twenty years. He rises on a May morning and goes

---

[1] Paris, *La. Litt. Fr. au M. A.*, p. 178.
[2] The quotations are from the Middle English translation of the *Romance*, and from the French edition of P. Marteau, Orléans, 1878.

out to hear the songs of the birds. He wanders over a lovely
meadow watered by a river. Following the course of the stream,
he sees before him a high wall, which encloses a spacious
garden. He draws closer and sees painted on the outside of the
wall ten hideous figures of Haine, Felonie, Vilennie, Couvitise,
Avarice, Envie, Tristesse, Viellesse, Papelardie, and Poverté.
As he contemplates these paintings, he longs to enter the
garden. Finally he knocks boldly at a small wicket in the wall,
and is admitted by a charming maiden called Oyseuse. She tells
him that she is the friend of Deduit, the master of the garden,
who has just now come thither with his companions to enjoy
the beauties of the place and to hear the music of the birds.

The hero greatly desires to see Deduit, and follows a little
path until he comes upon him and his merry companions dancing. In the party are the god of Love and his squire, Dous-
Regard, who carries two bows, the one crooked and gnarled, the
other well shaped and finely carved. He also has two quivers,
the one containing five beautiful gold-tipped arrows, the other
as many which are hideous to behold. Courtoisie, who is of the
god's party, perceives the hero, and invites him to take part in
the dance, which he gladly does. The dance over, the company
disbands, and the hero continues his wanderings.

As he walks along he is aware that he is being followed by
the god of Love, who holds the fair bow and the five golden
arrows. He is fearful lest the arrows are intended for him, but
he keeps on his way until he comes to a marble fountain, on
the border of which he sees the inscription: "Here died the
beautiful Narcissus." In the waters of the fountain are reflected
all the wonders of the garden. He especially admires, however,
a magnificent bush of roses, one of which, more lovely than
all the rest, he desires to pluck. While he is contemplating
the beauty of the rose, the god approaches and, drawing his
bow, shoots the arrow Biauté, piercing the lover's eye. He

immediately draws again, and shoots in rapid succession the other four darts, Simplece, Franchise, Compaignie, and Biau-Semblant. The god now tells him that all resistance is vain, and advises him to acknowledge his conqueror for his lord and master. To this the lover agrees, and offers, in token of submission, to kiss the god's feet; but he is graciously allowed to kiss his lips instead. Thus the hero becomes Love's vassal. After receiving from him assurances of his submission, Cupid proceeds to lay down his commandments and to teach him all the art of love. He shows all the joys, sorrows, and perils that a servant of Love must experience. The courage of the lover is somewhat dashed at this recital; but the god reassures him by telling him that the hope of winning his lady will sustain him in his trials, and he promises to leave with his new disciple three comforters, Dous-Penser, Dous-Parler, and Dous-Regard, who will bring him consolation if he but remain faithful. Having completed his instructions, the god leaves him alone.

The lover now desires above everything else to possess the Rose. But it is surrounded by a hedge, and his efforts to surmount the barrier would be vain. At this juncture, he sees a youth coming, Bel-Acueil, who offers to assist him over the hedge and to lead him to the Rose. He accepts the offer; but he perceives that the tree is guarded by the sleeping Dangier and his companions Male-Bouche, Honte, and Paor. The lover attempts to pluck the Rose, but Dangier suddenly awakes and drives both Bel-Acueil and him from the enclosure. While he wanders about the garden in despair, Raison approaches and advises him to give up the folly of love. He rejects this advice, however, and goes in search of Ami, to whom he confides his grief. Ami comforts him by telling him that Dangier is not so terrible as he seems; a little flattery will overcome his harshness and enable the lover to see his Rose again. The lover follows Ami's advice, and is successful in appeasing the anger of his enemy. Bel-Acueil now returns and leads the lover into the enclosure, where he is permitted to kiss the Rose. But Male-Bouche and Honte are watching, and they arouse Jalousie, who builds a high tower, in which he shuts up Bel-Acueil after soundly berating him. He places as guards at the tower, Paor, Dangier, and Male-Bouche. The lover weeps at the loss of his friend; in the midst of his plaints, the story breaks off.

The form of the *Romance* is that of the love-vision. It has several of the features already noted as characteristic of the type : the story is in the dream setting; the time is May; the place, a meadow with the usual abundance of flowers and of trees filled with singing birds; the narrative is the experience of a servant of Love, — at least, of one who in the story becomes his servant. Love himself, who is often represented in the vision-poems as enthroned in a gorgeous palace, here follows the hero in his wanderings about the garden. For the author's purpose is to tell of his own subjugation by means of the gold-tipped arrows, and there would have been an incongruity in the god's discharging the arrows from his throne. But in spite of the change of situation, the three usual conceptions of the love deity all appear clearly in the *Romance*.

In his first appearance to the hero, Love is the classical god, with his quivers and arrows. Guillaume de Lorris has employed the Ovidian fancy of giving two kinds of arrows to the god,[1] but he has elaborated it, as indeed he has most of the ideas which he borrowed.

In his encounter with the lover, the feudal characteristics of the god are brought out clearly. In order to vanquish the hero, he discharges the gold-tipped arrows in rapid succession, in accordance with the classical conception. But the figure then changes, as is shown in the god's demand that the lover do him homage (l. 1998), and later, that he give him hostages (ll. 2043 ff.).

[1] Neilson, p. 54.

The lover gives himself to the god's service (ll. 1947, 2105, 2115, 2130); puts his life and death into Cupid's hands; binds himself to the god (ll. 1955–1956); offers to kiss the god's feet (l. 1981); and becomes, in the technical sense, his "man" (l. 2035).

Though the ecclesiastical conception is not so prominent as the feudal, traces of it are seen in the general idea of giving commandments to the lover; in the idea of sin against the god, appearing in the lines:

> In thank thy servis wol I take,
> And high of gree I wol thee make,
> If *wikkednesse* ne hindre thee;

in the reference to the god's power to curse:

> I curse and blame generally
> Alle hem that loven vilany;

and in the god's imposing penance upon the lover:

> First I joyne thee, here in penaunce, . . .
> Thou set thy thought in thy loving.

The personification of carnal love as Venus should be noted. This is seen in the passage where she is described as always making war on chastity (l. 3699), and where she inflames Bel-Acueil with her blazing brand, and thus secures for the lover the coveted privilege of kissing the Rose (ll. 3697–3757).

Two methods are employed by the author to set forth the art of love: direct instruction given by the god, and the use of personified abstractions. As the personifications do little more than elaborate certain features of the formal doctrine, the interview of the god with the lover is of chief importance as a statement of the author's ideas.

The god's instructions, after he has received the lover's homage, may be divided into two parts: the first dealing with the personal qualities a lover should have; the second portraying his pains and pleasures. The commands, coming under the first head, are:

1. Leave villainy.

> Vilany at the begining,
> I wol, sayd Love, over alle thing,
> Thou leve, if thou wolt not be
> Fals, and trespasse agaynes me.

"Villainy," in the Old French poetry, was a blanket word used to cover the undesirable qualities a knight or lover should not have.[1] As the god says, "vilayns arn without pitee, friendship, love, and all bountee." After issuing this general order the god mentions two of the specific faults which, coming under the head of "villainy," the lover must avoid : speaking evil (ll. 2203–2215), and speaking words of ribaldry (ll. 2223–2228). He also mentions some specific virtues, which, as a courteous gentleman, the lover would be expected to practise : to salute those whom he meets (ll. 2216–2222) ; to serve and honor all women ; to defend their good names and endeavor to please them, that they may be well disposed toward him (ll. 2229–2238).

2. Keep yourself from pride ;

> For pryde is founde, in every part,
> Contrarie unto Loves art.

But the god reminds the lover that to dress well is not pride ;

> For fresh array, as men may see,
> Withouten pryde may ofte be.

Therefore he commands him to array himself with elegance ; to live within his income, but to have his raiment in good style and always becoming (ll. 2255–2274). He further instructs the lover as to neatness and cleanliness of person : to keep his hands, teeth, and nails clean ; to keep his hair combed. The influence of Ovid is clearly seen in the instructions in regard to cleanliness and neatness.[2]

---

[1] S. L. Galpin, *Cortois and Vilain*, New Haven, 1905, pp. 95–96.
[2] Ovid, *Ars Amatoria*, i, 505–524.

3. Be as merry and joyful as possible.

> Love hath no joye of sorrowful man.

The more detailed instruction is, to be ready to entertain others with his accomplishments of riding, feats of arms, singing, playing on instruments, dancing, or whatever they may be (ll. 2305–2324); also to make songs and complaints for his lady's sake, in order that she may be moved to pity his pain (ll. 2325–2328).

4. Be generous in giving and spending. Here may be included the later advice of the god, to give gifts freely to the lady's maid and to her other servants (ll. 2695–2716), which is taken from Ovid.[1]

These commands are all summed up " in wordes fewe compendiously " :

> Who so with love wol goon or ryde
> He mot be curteys and void of pryde,
> Mery and fulle of jolite
> And of largesse alosed be.

As a penance the lover is enjoined to set his thought on loving without repentance, and to think upon future happiness, which shall come when he meets his lady (ll. 2355–2360). This idea is elaborated in the personification of Dous-Penser :

> Thought in absence is good to thee,
> It maketh lovers have remembrance
> Of comfort, and of high plesaunce,
> That Hope hath hight him for to winne.

Dous-Penser shall bring before him, as in a mirror, all the physical charms of his lady, and so shall not only assuage the pains of love, but double the joys.[2]

---

[1] *Ars Amatoria*, i, 351–374.
[2] Cf. also :
> And thogh thou go, yet must thee nede
> Thenke al-day on hir fairhede (ll. 2483–2484).

5. To these commands the god adds a fifth, which is concerned with the relation of the lover to his lady:

> I wol and eek comaunde thee,
> That in oo place thou sette, al hool,
> Thyn herte, withouten halfen dool
> For trecherie, in sikernesse.

That is, he enjoins upon the lover constancy. The qualities which the god demands in his servant are: courtesy, humility, gaiety, generosity, and constancy. With the exception of gaiety, these are the cardinal virtues of the courtly lover, as we have seen them in the work of Andreas Capellanus.

The god now proceeds to lay before the lover the pains and pleasures which are inseparable from his service. In doing this, he enumerates the conventional symptoms of love, which have become established as principles firmly enough to be put in the form of injunctions:

1. He must keep in solitude, in order to hide from others his love sorrows (ll. 2390–2396).

2. He must suffer changes of temperature, alternate heat and cold (ll. 2397–2402).

3. He must often forget himself utterly, and be dumb and motionless (ll. 2403–2418).

4. He must be restless and ill at ease when absent from his lady (ll. 2419–2452).

5. He must have an insatiable longing for a sight of his lady (ll. 2453–2482).

The idea of this observation is elaborated in the use of the personification Dous-Regard, one of the three comforters whom the god promises to the lover. In speaking of him Cupid repeats substantially the same admonition that he gives here:

> Wherfore thou prese alwey to be
> In place, where thou mayst hir se.
> For it is thing most amerous,
> Most delitable and saverous,

For to aswage a mannes sorowe,
To sene his lady by the morowe.
For it is a ful noble thing
Whan thyn eyen have meting
With that relyke precious,
Wherof they be so desirous. . . .
For than the herte is al at ese,
Whan they seen that [that] may hem plese.

6. He must reproach himself for having been too timid to tell his lady of his love when opportunity presented itself (ll. 2483–2502).

7. He must find occasion to be near the lady's abode ; but he must go and come secretly (ll. 2503–2522).

8. He must become pale, tremble, and lose his speech in the lady's presence (ll. 2523–2552).

9. He must be sleepless and suffer agonies at night (ll. 2553–2567).

10. He must dream of happiness with her, and awake in sorrow to find it but a dream (ll. 2568–2640).

11. He must go secretly and early to her house, no matter how bad the weather (ll. 2641–2680).

12. He must grow lean and pale (ll. 2681–2694).

One of the most important principles of the courtly love, as given by Andreas, is not made the subject of especial command by Guillaume de Lorris : this is the necessity of secrecy. The idea is brought out, however, in connection with several of the symptoms of love just enumerated, and also in the god's advice to the lover to choose a discreet confidant (l. 2856).

The idea of laying down a set of laws for observance by the lover was borrowed by Guillaume from Andreas Capellanus,[1] and his precepts, so far as they correspond to those of Andreas, need only to be mentioned. A good number of the doctrines of the courtly love, as set forth by Andreas in form of statutes, arc

[1] Paris, *La Lit. Fr. au M. A.*, p. 180.

found in the *Romance* in other forms. The doctrine that love, to be prized, should not be too easily obtained,[1] is stated by the god :

> Freend, by the feith I owe to thee,
> May no man have good, but he it by.
> A man loveth more tendirly
> The thing that he hath bought most dere.
> For wite thou wel, withouten were,
> In thank that thing is taken more,
> For which a man hath suffred sore.

The possession of a confidant which is implied in Andreas's law, "Amoris tui secretarios noli plures habere,"[2] and which indeed was often a necessity in the real life of courtly lovers, is strongly advised by the god in the *Romance*, in his promise of Dous-Parler to the lover :

> Therefore I rede thee that thou get
> A felowe that can wel concele
> And kepe thy counsel, and wel hele,
> To whom go shewe hoolly thyn herte,
> Bothe wele and wo, joye and smerte.

"For it is a noble thing," he says, "to have a man thou darst say thy prive counsel." From this friend the lover can seek comfort, and with him he can talk of the pains and joys of his love. The idea is further carried out by the use of the personification Ami, who advises the lover in his time of need.

The ideas which have been noted as the especial favorites of Chrétien de Troies, and which he developed with such minuteness, are also present in the *Romance*. Beauty was the first arrow which the god shot at the hero, and piercing his eye the point remained in his heart, inflicting a wound which was curable only by the lady whose beauty was the cause. The conceit of sending the heart to the lady appears in the lover's complaint :

---

[1] Andreas, Long Code, Rule 14, p. 311.
[2] Andreas, p. 106.

> And if such cause thou have, that thee
> Bihoveth gon out of contree,
> Leve hool thyn herte in hostage,
> Til thou ageyn make thy passage.

And again,

> God what may this be,
> That I ne may my lady see?
> Myn herte aloon is to her go,
> And I abyde al sole in wo,
> Departed from myn owne thought
> And with myne eyen see right nought.

Something like Chrétien's subtlety in treating the heart and eyes appears in the passage which sets forth the virtues of Dous-Regard :

> For whan thyn eyen were thus in blis,
> Yit of hir curtesye, y-wis,
> Aloon they can not have hir joye,
> But to the herte they [it] convoye;
> Part of hir blis to him they sende,
> Of al this harm to make an ende.
> The eye is a good messangere,
> Which can to the herte in such manere
> Tidyngis sende, that [he] hath seen,
> To voide him of his peynes cleen.

The position of the lady with respect to the lover, in the system of love which the god expounds to the hero, is clearly that which we have already seen in the troubadours' poetry. The lover's attitude of humility before her, his preference for one smile of hers to having

> al utterly
> Of another al hool the pley,

his longing for her favor, his confusion, loss of speech and memory, and trembling in her presence, his complete devotion to her — all these are present in the god's exposition of love. In the development of the poet's own love story, the idea of the

lady's exalted position does not seem to be carried out. Translated into plain language, the elaborate allegory of the *Romance*
becomes a simple tale. The lover " has beheld his beautiful lady
and been charmed by her beauty, her grace, her courtesy ; she
has received him with gentleness, but when he declares his love,
she grows alarmed. He gains at last the kiss which tells of her
affection ; but her parents, intervening, throw obstacles between
the lovers." [1] This gives a hint of the difference which must
have obtained often between the theory and practice of courtly
love. However much the art taught the lover to tremble
and to be confused in the presence of his mistress, the underlying meaning of the allegory shows that she was not cold and
disdainful, that she was not moved by the lover's passion only.
Measures of prudence on her part, and precautions taken by
her parents, were the influences which restrained her from
granting her favor to the lover when asked.

The sensual element in the *Romance* is minimized. The
thought of marriage, it is true, does not enter the mind of the
author ; in this the work is in accord with the courtly ideas of
the time of Marie of Champagne. But the love here is not
avowedly sensual, though indications of its carnal nature are not
wanting.[2] Such indications, however, are little more than hints.
Very little that is gross can be found in the work. Written for
the diversion of the aristocratic circle,[3] in its delicacy, refinement, and gentleness of sentiment, the *Romance* admirably represents the side of mediaeval society to which it was addressed.[4]

---

[1] Dowden, *A History of French Literature*, New York, 1903, p. 35.

[2] Tex fois sera qu'il t'iert avis
   Que tu tendras cele au cler vis
   Entre tes bras tretoute nue,
   Ausinc cum s'el ert devenue
   Du tout t'amie et ta compaignie (ll. 2525–2529).

[3] See l. 34 : Por vos cuers plus fere esgaier.
[4] Paris, *La Lit. Fr. au M. A.*, p. 182.

But it was written at a time when the courtly love ideas, as expressed in the romance of love and adventure, had reached their full development; when, as has been seen, all spontaneity had ceased, and the desire to codify knowledge, present in all fields of learning, was displayed also in the work of erotic writers. Viewed as an art of love, the *Romance of the Rose*, therefore, may be considered as culminative, in the sense that it brings to completion sentiments before prominent in the literature, — that, if not the last, it is the best, example in poetry of the codifying process which found its expression in prose in the work of Andreas Capellanus.

The successors of Lorris in French poetry were long dominated by his influence, and the *Romance of the Rose* thus perpetuated the use of conventions which were already worn threadbare before it was written. Throughout the thirteenth and fourteenth centuries love-visions and love-lyrics in various forms were widely composed; love-allegory was enormously cultivated; and a vast mass of insipid, conventional verse, devoid of real sentiment or passion, was the result. It would not be profitable to examine this literature here at any length. Such a study would serve only to multiply examples of the ideas and devices of which we have noted the origin in earlier writers, and of which we shall later see masterly use in the hands of Chaucer. It is important, however, to observe that the courtly tradition was well represented by several poets — Machaut, Deschamps, Froissart, and Granson — by whom Chaucer was certainly influenced,[1] and who must have been well known to Gower. None of these later French writers adds anything really new to the courtly theory. They all praise the same beauties, inculcate the

---

[1] Recent research shows that Chaucer's relation to these writers was much closer than was formerly suspected. See the Chaucer *Manual* of Miss Hammond, under the authors named; and cf. *Modern Philology*, I, 1 ff.; VII, 465 ff.; VIII, 165 ff.; and *Modern Language Review*, Jan. 1910, pp. 33 ff.

same virtues, and sing the same familiar joys and sorrows. In the course of time they perhaps develop greater ingenuity in their allegory, and achieve a finer grace of style and metrical form. A kind of originality, too, is claimed for Machaut by virtue of the personal tone which he introduces into his erotic writings, though it is doubtful how far they are descriptive of actual experience.[1] But on the whole the courtly system of this later generation differs little from that of the age of Marie de Champagne. The love they celebrate, like that of their predecessors, is illicit and sensual at bottom, although described mostly with refinement or restraint. It is therefore still condemned by the Church, and various documents of the time contrast it with the higher love of conjugal life.[2] But that the courtly sentiment itself was sometimes capable of purity and elevation is shown by an important work of Chaucer's own lifetime, with which we may properly conclude our discussion of his French predecessors.

Les Cent Balades,[3] written by Jean le Seneschal and several of his friends in 1389, has been described as a " vrai bouquet de grâce et de courtoisie, dernier sourire de la société chevaleresque." [4] It tells of a young man, himself a lover, who receives from an old knight advice as to how to conduct himself in his love. The knight, who when young had been endowed by the

[1] See the *Œuvres de Guillaume de Machaut*, ed. E. Höpffner, for the Société des Anciens Textes Français, Paris, 1908, Introduction, p. ii; Chichmaref's edition of the *Poésies Lyriques* of Machaut, Paris, 1909, Introduction, p. lxvii; and Hanf, *Zeitschrift für Romanische Philologie*, XXII, 195. Compare also the remarks on autobiographical material in the love-poems of Chaucer and Gower, p. 100, n., below.

[2] Compare, for example, the *Chastiement des Dames* of Robert de Blois, published in Barbazan's *Fabliaux et Contes*, II, 184 ff.; and the *Book of the Knight of La Tour Landry*, ed. Thomas Wright for the Early English Text Society, rev. ed., 1906.

[3] Ed. by G. Raynaud, for the Société des Anciens Textes Français, 1905.

[4] G. Paris, *La Poésie du Moyen Age*, Second Series, p. 229.

god of Love with the gifts Doulce Penseé, Plaisance, Amoureux Désir, and Esperance, relates how he had given his heart wholly to the best and fairest lady in the world, and how life had been beautiful to him ever since. This great happiness had come to him because he faithfully performed the commands of Love and had remained loyal to his lady. Loyalty always brings such rewards. The knight dwells at length on the effect wrought by true love on the character of a lover; and he warns the youth of the evil consequences of disloyalty and pretense. The young lover thanks him for his good counsel, and declares that his desire is always to be loyal and true.

Not long after this, the lover happens to be near a company of "gracious and pleasing folk," in a garden bordering upon the river Loire. He does not speak to them, but keeps himself apart, his eyes upon the water, his thoughts upon his love. While he is standing there, one of the ladies in the merry company approaches him, and asks if he is in the service of the god of Love. Upon his replying that he is, she volunteers to give him some advice, by following which he will be happy and joyous. "Certainly," she says, upon hearing his determination to remain loyal to his lady, "you have need of counsel; for now I see that you will never obtain the great good which you desire. I pray you, do not persist in this foolish thought." Her good counsel is to this effect: Look to the good things in love: declare your passion to your lady, and if then you can come to your "fait," good; if not, do not be so much hers that you take no account of others. Do not let love overcome you. If love of your lady grows in your heart so that she holds you entirely in her "danger," you had better be dead. Throw off your bonds, and divide your attentions. Only, work secretly. This is all the loyalty you need observe. Always see how your "fait" can be accomplished before you ask. Conduct yourself humbly among the ladies; serve each one, praise their deeds and their beauty. If one receives your " raison " favorably, accomplish your desire quickly.

Vent au faucon, vent au heron !

The fair ones you entreat, pursue humbly to the end, and you will succeed. Solicit them morn and even, day and night. Let no long interval go by without entreating them. Be quiet; say nothing of yourself, and speak no evil of another. But swear no vows unless you must. If one repulses you, ask her pardon. Tell her she is so beautiful and good that you must love her whether you will or not; it is no use to strive against it. Then embrace her secretly. If she takes it ill, she is too nice, or wishes to play the wise woman. To love is natural: keep it up; the ladies will give in. Though you have your troubles, you will obtain your desires in the long run.

The young lover still persists in his determination to remain faithful; and so they decide to submit to all lovers the question: Which brings the more joy in love, to maintain loyalty or to practice falsity ? The book ends with thirteen *balades*, which are given in reply to the question by different knights. Some are favorable to the lady, but most of them agree with the old knight in advocating loyalty.

" In this book, we have very clearly opposed two different kinds of love, of both of which we have had abundant indications in the two preceding centuries. . . . That of the lady is the old attitude which is most clearly represented by Ovid and his mediaeval imitators, with some of the grossness left out, but with an essentially immoral element at the heart of it. It is lower than the usual troubadour ideal, inasmuch as that made much of the virtue of loyalty to one woman at a time. That of the old knight, on the other hand, is loftier than the troubadour's, since it is clearly honorable love with a view to marriage, which he recommends and praises. It includes all the noble attributes

of the mediaeval ' gentle ' knight, and all the reverential devotion to woman which characterizes the chivalrous youth of all
times. It is, on the whole, the finest ideal to be found in the
. . . twelfth, thirteenth, or fourteenth century." [1]

[1] Neilson, *Origins*, p. 198. I cannot see, as Professor Neilson does, anything in the knight's remarks to indicate that the love of which he speaks
leads to marriage. His ideal in this respect is no higher, for instance, than
that of the knight in Machaut's *Le Jugement dou Roy de Behaigne*, in which
there is nothing to indicate that marriage is the end of the love discussed.
Notwithstanding this, the tone of all the knight's considerations in *Les Cent
Balades* is a very lofty one; and the words quoted above, with the exception
noted, fittingly characterize the love-element in the work.

CHAPTER III

THE ELEMENT OF LOVE IN GOWER'S WORKS

In the *Mirour de l'Omme*, Gower's great moral work, occur the lines:

> Jadis trestout m'abandonoie
> Au fol delit et veine joye;
> Dont ma vesture desguisay
> Et les fols ditz d'amours fesoie,
> Dont en chantant je carolloie.[1]

Only two, however, of the poet's extant works are devoted to love, the *Cinkante Balades* (in French) and the English *Confessio Amantis*. We have no way of knowing whether or not the "fols ditz" of the lines quoted comprise a part of the *Cinkante Balades*. But it is probable that the collection contains poems written at various times throughout the poet's life, and selected and arranged by him on the occasion of presenting the book to Henry IV for the entertainment of the court.[2] The *Confessio Amantis*, as the author tells us, was composed at the command of King Richard II, who, in asking the poet to write something new, furnished the theme and promised to accept and read the book when finished.[3] The date of the poem in its earliest form has been placed at 1390.[4]

---

[1] *Mirour de l'Omme*, ll. 27337–27341. The references are to *The Works of John Gower*, ed. G. C. Macaulay, Oxford, 1899.

[2] Kittredge, *The Date of Chaucer's Troilus*, Chaucer Society Publications, 1909, Appendix IV, p. 76. Note the poet's Dedication to the King, ii, st. 4:

> O noble Henri, . . .
> Por desporter vo noble court roial
> Jeo frai balade.

[3] Prologue to *Confessio Amantis*, First Version, ll. 51–53.

[4] *Works*, II, xxi.

CINKANTE BALADES

The *Cinkante Balades* have been roughly divided by their author into two parts. The first division includes *Balades* 1–5, which are made especially for those who expect their love affairs to be perfected in marriage.[1] They are addressed to ladies, and express the happiness of the accepted lover, his vows of continued service, loyalty, and truth. The remainder of the fifty-one (there are fifty-one instead of fifty, as the title indicates) are "universal," and set forth the feelings of lovers in general, whether the course of their love runs smooth or not.[2] The second group may be further divided as follows :

1. *Balades* 6–40, 45, 47, are addressed by lovers to their ladies. Of these, numbers thirty-two to thirty-seven are expressions of devotion intended for certain occasions of the year : numbers thirty-two and thirty-three for the New Year, thirty-four and thirty-five for Saint Valentine's Day, thirty-six and thirty-seven for May Day. All except number forty are of the same nature : the lover complains of the lady's indifference and of his own woes, assures her of his desire to serve her, and begs for her favor. In number forty, the lover takes the lady to task for her fickleness.

2. *Balades* 41–44, 46, are addressed by ladies to their lovers. Number forty-one expresses the lady's doubts as to the truth and loyalty of her wooer. Numbers forty-two and forty-three are more outspoken, and openly accuse him of treachery. Number forty-four, on the other hand, is addressed to a lover in whom she places her entire confidence, and whose love she would rather be than to be Empress of Rome.

3. *Balades* 48–50 discourse on the nature of love in the abstract.

---

[1] " Pour ceaux q'attendout loura amours par droite mariage." I, 342.

[2] "Sclonc les propretés et les condicions des Amantz qui sont diversement travailez en la fortune d'amour." I, 343.

4. *Balade* 51 is addressed by the author to the Virgin. He declares himself the servant of all ladies, but especially of her, to whom none in life may compare. With all his heart he loves and prizes her

> q'est florie
> De bien, d'onour, de joie et de plesance.

This *balade* is an excellent example of the mystical expressions of love and devotion to Christ and Our Lady in which the language of chivalrous love was employed.[1]

The *Cinkante Balades* are written on the French models, and it is hardly necessary to say that the sentiments expressed are the conventional ones. Cupid is alluded to as a neglectful god :

> Ore est yvern, qe soloit estre Maii ;
> Ne sai pour quoi Cupide me desdeigne.[2]

The classical conception of the god with his dart occurs in the lines :

> Ma dame, quant jeo vi vostre oill vair et riant,
> Cupide m'ad ferru de tiele plaie
> Parmi le coer d'un dart d'amour ardant,
> Qe nulle medicine m'est verraie
> Se vous n'aidetz.[3]

In these lines appears also the conceit of the baneful influence of the lady's eyes, as well as the fancy that she is the only physician who can heal the lover's wounds. The superior position of the lady is pictured in almost every *balade ;* in the following, the idea is presented by means of the feudal figure :

> Pour un regard au primere acqueintance,
> Quant jeo la bealté de ma dame vi,

---

[1] For other instances of this in Middle English, see Böddeker, *Altenglische Dichtungen des Ms. Harleian 2253*, Berlin, 1878, pp. 191, 192, 198, 218 ; *Richard Rolle and His Followers*, ed. Horstmann, London, 1896, II, 354–366 ; *Ancren Riwle*, ed. Morton, London, 1853, p. 338 (the story of the lady besieged in an earthen castle and released by a king) ; *Woohing of Our Lord*, ed. Morris for Early English Text Society, pp. 268 ff.

[2] Balade 40.   [3] Balade 27.

> Du coer, du corps trestoute m'obeissance
> Lui ai doné, tant sui d'amour ravi :
> Du destre main jeo l'ai ma foi plevi,
> Sur quoi ma dame ad resceu moun hommage
> Com son servant. . . .[1]

The perfection of the lady, her coldness, and the lover's unworthiness are so often mentioned that quotation is unnecessary. Of the *balades* devoted to the nature of love (48–50), number forty-eight has for its refrain :

> En toutz errours amour se justifie.

Love is the treacherous faith ; it promises much, but it brings little in its hand. The idea is further expressed by an extended list of the contradictory characteristics attributed to the passion of love, — a device which was a favorite with the poets. In number fifty we have the convention of love's uplifting power :

> De l'averous il fait franc et loial,
> Et de vilein courtois et liberal,
> Et de couard plus fiers qe n'est leoun :
> De l'envious il hoste tout le mal.

Further details may be spared.[2] The observation of a critic that the *Balades* "add another block of the polished commonplace to his [Gower's] literary monument,"[3] is just; for there is nothing but conventionality in the sentiment of the poems from beginning to end ; and the conventions are those to be met with over and over in the French poets. The noticeable feature of the *Balades* is their finish. Lifeless as they are, they prove the poet's ability to rival his French contemporaries in giving expression to the courtly love ideas with grace and elegance. This is as much as can be said for them. They are what we should expect from a careful and painstaking poet,

---

[1] Balade 23.
[2] For an interesting summary of the *Balades*, see Works, I, lxxvi–lxxvii.
[3] W. P. Ker, *Essays on Medieval Literature*, London, 1905, p. 131.

endowed with talent, but not with genius, and perforce content to fall in with the mode and make his erotic work " one more concession to the ' tune of the time.' " [1]

Confessio Amantis

The large use of conventional ideas in the *Cinkante Balades* shows us what to expect in the *Confessio Amantis*. In so long a poem, frequent repetition of such ideas is natural. No attempt will be made, therefore, to list all the examples of the different conventions found ; enough of the more striking illustrations only will be cited to show the extent of the author's dependence upon earlier love literature in the composition of his great erotic work. The plot of the *Confessio* is as follows :

One day in May, when every bird has chosen his mate and sings for pure joy of love, the poet fares forth to walk in the fields and woods. But the joy of birds and the beauties of nature accord but little with his feelings, for he is farther from his love

> Than erthe is fro the heven above.

In the midst of the wood he finds a fair plain ; here he begins to lament the sorrows which love has brought upon him. After a time, he falls to the earth and wishes for death ; but he recovers somewhat from his pain, and looking up to heaven, he prays to the god and goddess of Love to show him some grace. Soon he sees them ; the king of Love is angry and passes him by with a glance ; first, however, the poet is pierced to the heart by the fiery dart of the god. Venus the queen remains and asks him, though with " no goodly chere," who he is, and bids him tell his malady. He replies that he is a man of hers who has served long in her court, and that he now asks as reward some weal after his long woe. She frowns, and replies that there are many who pretend to be her servants, yet have

---

[1] W. P. Ker, *Essays on Medieval Literature*, London, 1905, p. 131.

done nothing for her. Still she bids him show her all his sickness, and he promises to do so if life lasts long enough. She
commands him first, however, to confess to Genius, her own
priest. Genius is called, and the confession begins, the lover
telling all he has felt for love's sake, both of joy and of sorrow.

After this lengthy ordeal, the lover asks the priest for advice
as to what course he shall pursue in his love affair. Genius
rather unfeelingly counsels him to labor no more in things
which bring no profit, and to give up love and be subject to the
law of Reason. At the lover's request, however, the priest
carries to Venus and Cupid a petition written with the suppliant's
tears. While the lover awaits the result, Venus suddenly appears at his side, and falling upon his knees he prays her for
grace. She asks his name and half scornfully advises him to
make a "beau retrete" while he can, for his age and hoary
locks clearly show that he is unfit to be a lover. At this the
poet grows suddenly cold and falls in a swoon. While he lies
there, all the world of gentle folk who have formerly been
lovers pass before his eyes. There were Tristram and Isolde,
Lancelot and Guinevere, Jason and Creusa, Hercules and Iole,
and many others. Conspicuous were

> the four wyves
> Whose faith was proeved in her lyves,

Penelope, Lucrece, Alceste, and Alcyone. Cupid, who heads
all this wonderful procession of lovers, then presses forward and
draws out the fiery dart. Venus applies a cooling ointment to
the wound. Reason now returns to the lover, and he is once
more sound and whole. He receives absolution from the priest ;
the queen presents him with a "pair" of black beads on which
are written in gold the words "Por reposer." She advises him
to remain no more in her court, and bidding him adieu, she
is taken away, enveloped in a starry cloud. And so, with his
beads, the poet walks slowly homeward.

The setting of the *Confessio Amantis*, as it here appears, is that of the conventional May Day poems. It should be noted that no mention is made of a dream or vision, except that which the lover had of the companies of lovers while in a swoon. Something of the effect of a vision is produced, however, by the sudden appearance of the god and goddess of Love while the lover lies in agony on the ground, and the equally sudden disappearance of Venus at the end of the poem. Except for the omission of the dream or vision, the setting conforms to the love-vision type.

Certain incidental features Gower has borrowed from other writers. The contrast of the joyousness of the spring season with the lover's sorrow goes back to the troubadours' lyrics. The device of making famous lovers of old appear to the poet was probably taken from the Prologue to the *Legend of Good Women*.[1] The lovers themselves, as well as the four faithful wives, are among the most familiar figures of mediaeval poetry. The name of the priest, Genius, comes probably from the *Romance of the Rose*, although it appears in the *De Planctu Naturae* of Alain de l'Isle.

The particular scheme of a confession was doubtless suggested to the poet by the mediaeval manuals of confession, whose object was to present in condensed and convenient form for the use of laymen and clergy the teachings of the Church with regard to repentance.[2] In such manuals, designed for edification,

[1] For the relations between Gower's work and the Prologue in question, see Bech, *Anglia*, V, 365–471. Cf. also *The Works of Chaucer*, ed. by Skeat, Oxford, 1894–1897, III, xl–xliii.

[2] Mr. Macaulay states (Gower's Works, II, xi) that the idea of the confession was doubtless taken from the *Romance of the Rose*. In a later article (*Cambridge History of English Literature*, II, 150) he modifies this statement, suggesting the influence of such works as William of Wadington's *Manuel des Pechies* and its English translation by Robert of Brunne, and such other combinations of stories as were used for the illustration of a moral truth. The later suggestion certainly is the more nearly correct. There is little in the

the Seven Deadly Sins were the natural topic for treatment, and the works which used them as a framework are numerous. Such treatises as *Le Somme des Vices et des Vertus* of Friar Lorens (translated by Dan Michel under the title of the *Ayenbite of Inwit*), the *Prick of Conscience*, and Chaucer's *Persones Tale*, occur at once to our minds. Differing from all these were the *Manuel des Pechies* and Robert of Brunne's English version of the same, the *Handlynge Synne*.[1] This work is interspersed with tales designed for the illustration of the particular sin under discussion.

The employment of *exempla* or illustrative tales was extremely common in the mediaeval pulpit. So also in the confessional, the priest often needed some anecdote to explain the nature of the sins concerning which he questioned his penitent, and it was to meet his need that such manuals as Robert of Brunne's were compiled. What these manuals, with their stories, were to the Church, the *Confessio Amantis* would have been to priests of Love, if any such priests had really existed. The parallel must have been part of the poet's intention and cannot have escaped the notice of his readers.

Romance of the Rose to suggest the situation in the *Confessio Amantis* except the name of the priest, and the fact that there was a confession. The shrift which Nature there makes to the priest, Genius, has nothing in common with the confession of the lover in Gower's poem. The first part of the interview between Nature and her confessor, in the *Romance*, is a savage attack, not by Nature at all but by the priest, upon womankind; and the second part, which is the confession proper, is made the medium through which Jean de Meung displays his learning, and conveys his ideas on such subjects as astronomy, optics, natural phenomena, free will, necessity, destiny, and what makes a gentleman. This, of course, gives no suggestion of Gower's confession, which proceeds in the orderly fashion of a real shrift before a real priest, with its alternate questions and replies.

[1] " The *Handlynge Synne* forms a sort of prototype to the *Confessio Amantis*, inasmuch as in both cases a large number of tales are narrated in exemplification of the Deadly Sins, albeit the wrongdoing is of a different character, and the tales for the most part are of a different style " (Schofield, *English Literature from the Norman Conquest to Chaucer*, New York, 1906, p. 416).

The plan of the work, then, is a lover's confession of his sins against Love; the prevailing general conception of the love deity is, therefore, the ecclesiastical one. In the setting, a double personification is used, and Venus and Cupid appear together, a feature frequently found in the French love-visions. The part which Cupid plays, however, is subordinate to that of Venus throughout. It is her priest who hears the lover's confession; it is her court in which he serves; and she it is who heals the wounds made by Cupid's dart. She is

> the source and welle
> Of wel or wo, that schal betide
> To hem that loven.

It is to her, therefore, that the lover appeals for grace. Cupid does nothing of any consequence except to pierce the lover, near the beginning of the poem, and to pull out the dart, just before the close. This proceeding on the part of the god is, as Bech aptly remarks, "eine höchst überflussige manipulation, da ja Gower vorher bereits vor liebesweh seufzt." [1]

Though the prevailing idea is ecclesiastical, no one metaphor is consistently sustained in the setting of the story. It changes from the feudal to the ecclesiastical and back again without any reason. When the lover, overcome by his pain and grief, prayed, he

> caste up many a pitous lok
> Unto the hevene, and seide thus:
> O thou Cupide, O thou Venus,
> Thou god of love and thou goddesse,
> Wher is pite? (i, 122–126.)

He has no sooner finished his prayer than the divinities appear to him as the

> king of love and qweene bothe (i, 139).

The classical conception of the god appears in Cupid with his fiery dart, with which he pierces the heart of the lover. The

[1] *Anglia*, V, 367.

figure becomes the feudal one again, when Venus bids the despairing lover tell her who he is, and he replies :

> Ma dame, I am a man of thyne,
> That in thi Court have longe served,
> And aske that I have deserved
> Some wele after my longe wo " (i, 168–171).

Yet, when she bids him confess his sins to her priest Genius, the ecclesiastical figure is again employed. And all these changes occur in less than one hundred lines. This confusion, which is seen throughout the early part of the poem, appears again toward the close, where Venus excuses the lover from attendance on her court, immediately after which the priest grants the absolution demanded.

In the main part of the poem, that is, in the confession and the incidental stories, the use of the ecclesiastical figure is limited. The feudal convention, on the other hand, is employed largely, and allusions to it are frequent. The lover, acknowledging his jealousy of more fortunate wooers, says :

> Whan I the Court se of Cupide
> Aproche unto my lady side,
> Of hem that lusti ben and freisshe,—
> Thogh it availe hem noght a reisshe,
> Bot only that thei ben in speche, —
> My sorwe is thanne noght to seche (ii, 39–44).

Later he speaks of

> these lovers that —
> Ben poursuiantz fro yeer to yere
> In loves Court (ii, 237–240).

The confessor warns the lover against Detraction :

> In loves Court a man mai hiere . . .
> That many envious tale is stered. . . .
> If thou have mad such janglerie
> In loves Court, mi Sone, er this,
> Schrif thee therof (ii, 443–454).

Referring to the patience of Socrates, the confessor humorously remarks :

> If it falle in eny stede
> A man to lese so his galle,
> Him oghte among the women alle
> In loves Court be juggement
> The name bere of Pacient (iii, 702–706).

Speaking of talebearers, he says :

> And suche adaies be now fele
> In loves Court, as it is seid,
> That lete here tunges gon unteid (iii, 828–830).

He advises the lover not to be " foolhasty" :

> Thogh thou to loves Court poursuie,
> Yit sit it wel that thou eschuie
> That thou the Court noght overhaste,
> For so miht thou thi time waste (iii, 1673–1676).

Venus is referred to as

> the goddesse
> Which loves Court hath forto reule (iv, 1262–1263).

Prowess of knighthood is exalted as,

> to love sufficant
> Aboven al the remenant
> That unto loves court poursuie (iv, 2017–2019).

Love lays down his law with regard to largess :

> What man wol noght be felawe
> To yive and spende, . . .
> He is noght worthi forto duelle
> In loves Court to be relieved (v, 4864–4867).

In his discussion of " gentilesse," the confessor remarks :

> Bot for al that, yit now aday
> In loves Court to taken hiede,
> The povere vertu schal noght spede,
> Wher that the riche vice woweth (iv, 2278–2281).

Describing the man addicted to somnolence, the confessor warns the lover :

> and in such wise
> He doth to love all his service;
> I not what thonk he schal deserve;
> Bot, Sone, if thou wolt love serve,
> I rede that thou do noght so (iv, 2741–2745).

It should be noted that, except in the setting, no attempt is made to use either Venus or Cupid consistently as the love deity. The personality changes from one to the other without any reason. Either or both may be used in any story, or in any single part of the confession. In attributing characteristic traits to the divinity, Gower hardly discriminates between the two. Thus Love is described as a being of irresistible power:

> For love is lord in every place,
> Ther mai no lawe him justifie
> Be reddour ne be compaignie,
> That he ne wole after his wille
> Whom that he liketh, spede or spille (v, 4556–4560).

Of Pyramus and Thisbe it is said:

> Cupide hath so the thinges schape
> That thei ne mihte his hand escape,
> That he his fyr on hem ne caste (iii, 1351–1353).

The god is represented as punishing those who attempt to resist. Gower heads that part of his treatment of Pride devoted to Surquidry with the lines:

> Qui magis astutus reputat se vincere bellum
> In laqueos Veneris forcius ipse cadit.
> Sepe Cupido virum sibi qui presumit amantem
> Fallit, et in vacuas spes redit ipsa vias.

The priest warns the lover:

> If thou refuse
> To love, thou miht so percas
> Ben ydel, as sometime was
> A kinges daughter unavised
> Til that Cupido hire hath chastised (iv, 1238–1242).

The king's daughter was Rosiphelee, who refused to be affected by the tender passion,

> Til whanne Venus the goddesse, . . .
> Hath broght hire into betre reule
> Forth with Cupide and with his miht, . . .
> For he that hihe hertes loweth, . . .
> Cupide, which of love is godd,
> In chastisinge hath made a rodd
> To dryve awei hir wantonesse (iv, 1262–1278).

We may observe that Gower's " Rosiphelee " is a version of the story told in Andreas's work by the knight to the lady who would not be persuaded to love.

Lovers pray to the divinity for grace in their love affairs, or for help in their troubles. The lover made angry by those who by their lies hinder him in his suit for his lady's favor, can wish them nothing worse than that they may fare in love as he does ; he declares :

> For that schal I alway beseche
> Unto the mihti Cupido
> That he so muchel wolde do . . .
> To smyte hem with the same rodd
> Withe which I am of love smite (iii, 906–911).

Progne, overcome by her own sorrows and those of her sister, makes a vow that the treachery of Tereus shall be avenged :

> And with that word sche kneleth doun
> Weping in gret devocioun:
> Unto Cupide and to Venus
> Sche preide . . . (v, 5817–5820).

In the hands of this deity is the weal or woe of all lovers. The lover recognizes this when he denies that he is guilty of avarice in love

> If I that tresor [his lady's favor] mihte gete,
> It scholde nevere be foryete
> That I ne wolde it faste holde
> Til god of love himselve wolde
> That deth ous scholde parte atuo (v, 69–73).

According to the whim of the god, weal or woe is dealt out. Sometimes he is a beneficent god. Venus is gracious to Pygmaleon ; for

> of his penance
> He made such continuance
> Fro dai to night, and preith so longe
> That his preiere is underfonge,
> Which Venus of hire grace herde (iv, 415–419).

Speaking generally, the confessor remarks :

> The god of love is favorable
> To hem that ben of love stable (iv, 442–444).

This deity is capable of feeling pity. Touched by the devotion of Iphis and Iante, he

> Tok pite for the grete love,
> And let do sette kinde above,
> So that hir lawe mai ben used (iv, 489–491).

Both Cupid and Venus showed favor to Viola, who was cursed with an avaricious husband :

> This yonge lusty wyht . . .
> . . . was wo bego withal,
> Til that Cupide and Venus eke
> A medicine for the seke
> Ordeigne wolden in this cas (v, 4823–4829).

With their help, the generous Croceus supplanted the niggardly Babio, and

> the bowe bende
> Which Venus tok him forto holde
> And schotte als ofte as evere he wolde (v, 4858–4862).

Oftener, however, the god or goddess is unfavorable to lovers. At the very beginning of his work, Gower says :

> He [i.e. Love] yifth his graces undeserved,
> And fro that man which hath him served
> Fulofte he takth aweye his fees,
> As he that pleieth ate Dees (i, 51–54).

The idea occurs over and over again throughout the *Confessio Amantis ;* and it is often embodied in the representation of

Love as a personality who is unjust, neglectful, or deceitful. Thisbe, seeing the dead body of Pyramus, reproaches Venus and Cupid for their injustice:

> O thou which cleped art Venus
> Goddesse of love, and thou Cupide, . . .
> This Piramus, which hiere I se
> Bledende, what hath he deserved?
> For he youre heste hath kept and served. . . .
> Helas, why do ye with ous so? (iii, 1462–1470).

Similarly, the lover, commenting on his own lack of success, complains of Cupid's injustice:

> Bot this I se, on daies nou
> The blinde god, I wot noght hou,
> Cupido, which of love is lord,
> He set the thinges in discord,
> That thei that lest to love entende
> Fulofte he wole hem yive and sende
> Most of his grace; and thus I finde
> That he that scholde go behinde,
> Goth many a time ferr tofore (iv, 1731–1739).

Sometimes the god is neglectful of his votaries. The confessor warns the lover not to give way to despair:

> Mi Sone, of that thin herte siketh
> With sorwe, miht thou noght amende,
> Til love his grace wol thee sende (iv, 3502–3504).

Iphis, brought to despair because he did not speed in his love for Araxarathen, bewails his case:

> O thou Cupide, o thou Venus, . . .
> On you is ever that I crie,
> And yit you deigneth noght to plie,
> Ne toward me youre ere encline (iv, 3558–3565).

But it is the deceitfulness of Love that Gower remarks upon more than any other quality. Speaking of the part Venus played in the case of Albinus and Rosemund, he identifies her with Fortune:

> Bot sche which kepeth the blinde whel,
> Venus, whan thei be most above,
> In al the hoteste of here love,
> Hire whiel sche torneth, and thei felle
> In the manere as I schal telle (i, 2490–2495).

She is represented as playing a similar rôle when the lover speaks of his own fortunes :

> The trewe man fulofte aweie
> Sche [Venus] put, which hath hir grace bede,
> And set an untrewe in his stede (viii, 2377–2384).

Cupid too is a deceiver. Through him Geta was supplanted in Almeene's affections by his friend Amphitrion.

> Whan he [Geta] best wende have ben above
> And sikerest of that he hadde,
> Cupido so the cause ladde
> That whil he was out of the weie,
> Amphitrion hire love aweie
> Hath take (ii, 2468–2473).

The power of Venus, acting as the goddess of carnal passion, is shown in the story of the violation of Leucothea:

> Venus which hath this lawe in honde
> Of thing which mai noght be withstonde,
> As sche which the tresor to warde,
> Phebum to love hath so constreigned
> That he withoute reste is peined . . .
> To coveite a maiden [Leucothea] (v, 6715–6722).

She appears in the same rôle in the " Marriage of Perithous," where she joins forces with Bacchus, and together they make the Centaurs drunk with wine and lust, until the fair Hipotace is carried off from her husband.[1]

In giving expression to these conventional ideas, Gower does not confine himself to the use of personifications. The attributes of the all-powerful god or goddess are even more often expressed

---

[1] vi, 506–510.

abstractly; and the idea of the absolute dominion of love over the lives of men and women occurs on almost every page. The following passage, out of a great number, will suffice as an illustration :

> And though a man be resonable,
> Yit after kinde he is menable
> To love, wher he wole or non [1] (iii, 389–391).

The doctrine of secrecy, which ordinarily occupies so prominent a place in mediaeval love-poetry, is found also in the *Confessio Amantis*. But it is not set forth with nearly so great insistence as we might expect in so long a poem. This is partly due to the fact that the hero and his lady are decent people in whose affairs there is no real need for secrecy. But it is due largely to the plan of the work itself. For Gower is treating of the seven deadly sins conceived with respect to love, and in such a scheme he seldom has occasion to mention secrecy at all. The most pronounced expressions of the doctrine occur in the section on Advantance or Boasting. Here Gower begins with the statement :

> Estque viri culpa iactancia, que rubefactas
> In muliere reas causat habere genas.[2]

Upon the lover's protesting that he is innocent of the sin of boasting, the confessor replies :

> Mi Sone, I am wel paid withal;
> For wite it wel in special
> That love of his verrai justice
> Above alle othre ayein this vice
> At alle times most debateth,
> With al his herte and most it hateth (i, 2449–2455).

In telling of Jason and Medea's precautions against detection, the confessor remarks :

> For love is evermore in doute
> If that it be wisly governed
> Of hem that ben of love lerned (v, 3850–3852).

---

[1] Cf. iii, 344–346, 1194–1195; vi, 317–318; viii, 153–158, 1761–1764.
[2] Latin lines preceding i, 2399.

A curious enlargement of the conventional idea of secrecy is found in the confessor's treatment of the sins of the eye. Many an evil man uses his eyes to find means of harming other people, by seeing what he ought not to see.

> And thus ful many a worthi knyht,
> And many a lusti lady bothe,
> Have be fulofte sythe wrothe,
> So that an yhe is as a thief
> To love, and doth ful gret mischief (i, 310–320).

The implication is, that love's observances demand secrecy, and that whoever sees what he ought not in such affairs sins against Love in so doing. It was this offense for which Laar was punished :

> Hire tunge he kutte, into helle
> For evere he [Jupiter] sende hir forto duelle,
> As sche that was noght worthi hiere
> To ben of love a Chamberere,
> For sche no conseil cowthe hele (iii, 823–827).

The last two examples not only set forth the doctrine of secrecy, but they reveal an abhorrence of spies and talebearers, the fear of whom we have found associated with the desire for secrecy as far back as the troubadours. These pests were evidently at work in the time of the confessor, for immediately after his remarks upon the punishment of Laar, he says :

> And suche adaies be now fele,
> In loves Court, as it is seid,
> That lete here tunges gon unteid (iii, 828–830).

A very interesting figure in the poem is that of the lady. She is conventionally presented, in the main. Her position in the background, her beauty, her superiority, her attitude toward the lover — these are all in accord with long-established precedents.

It is noteworthy that the physical charms of the lady are but little dwelt upon by a lover who is so much in earnest in his love as is Gower's hero. He seems to be much more interested in her qualities of mind and heart. The sole description of her person is appropriately connected with the delicacies upon which the lover's heart feeds through the sight. When he comes where the lady is, his eye

> taketh a fode of such delit,
> That him non other deynte needeth.
> Of sondrie sihtes he him fedeth:
> He [the eye] seth hire *face of such colour*
> That *freisshere* is *than eny flour;*
> He seth hire *front* is *large and plein*
> Withoute fronce of eny grein,
> He seth hire *yhen lich an hevene,*
> He seth hire *nose strauhgt and evene,*
> He seth hire *rode upon the cheke,*
> He seth hire *rede lippes* eke,
> Hire *chyn acordeth to the face,* . . .
> He seth hire *necke round and clene,*
> *Therinne mai no bon be sene,*
> He seth hire *handes faire and whyte,*
> He seth hire schapthe forth withal,
> Hire *bodi round,* hire *middel smal,*
> So wel begon with good array,
> Which passeth al the lust of Maii (vi, 765 ff.).

The italicized words show without further comment the conventional plan of enumerating the lady's features one by one, and also the usual mediaeval ideas of feminine beauty.

Macaulay remarks apropos of this description of the lady's person[1] that it "is not offensive, as such descriptions almost always are." This is doubtless true; details which might be regarded as offensive are not mentioned, or if mentioned, not dwelt upon. But Gower's description is not without sensual suggestiveness; note, for example, the lines:

> For al this thing withoute wyte
> He [the eye] mai se naked ate leste,
> So is it wel the more feste
> And wel the mor Delicacie (vi, 780–783).

[1] Macaulay, II, xvi.

And elsewhere the author is not averse to dwelling on the sensual in his consideration of the lady's physical charms :

> Somdiel I mai the betre fare
> When I, that mai noght fiele hir bare,
> Mai lede hire clothed in my arm :
> Bot afterward it doth me harm
> Of pure ymaginaccion ;
> For than this collacion
> I make unto miselven ofte
> And seie, " Ha lord, hou sche is softe,
> How sche is round, hou sche is smal !
> Now wolde god I hadde hire al
> Withoute danger at mi wille ! "

To the beauty of the lady's character, no great amount of space, comparatively speaking, is devoted by the author. The plan of the work gives first importance to the lover's confession as to his fortune in love ; anything which bears directly on this element of the story is given prominence. For example, the lady's coldness, as we shall see, is mentioned repeatedly. Her good qualities of mind and heart, on the other hand, though they appear in the course of the work, are not much dwelt upon by the lover himself. Yet he gladly recognizes his lady's· excellences of character. The one quality which he most fondly brings into prominence in speaking of her, is her discretion.

> For fame, that can nothing hide,
> Alday wol bring unto myn Ere . . .
> How sche is fair, how sche is wis
> How sche is womanlich of chiere.

" Governaunce," or a discreet and dignified self-control, was a quality highly valued in ladies by their lovers.[1] The beauty of discretion in this case is enhanced by the fact that the lady is very popular with the opposite sex. She is beset by wooers ; and, if the lover's opinion may be accepted as trustworthy,

---

[1] Cf. Chaucer's *Complaint to Pity*, ll. 40–41.

they are not all actuated by the highest motives. Yet she knows well how to fashion her conduct towards them. The lover says :

> Bot, Sire, as of my ladi selve,
> Thogh sche have wowers ten or twelve,
> For no mistrust I have of hire,
> Me grieveth noght, for certes, Sire,
> I trowe, in al the world to seche
> Nis woman that in dede and speche
> Woll betre avise hire what sche doth,
> Ne betre, for to seie a soth,
> Kepe hire honour ate alle tide,
> And yit get hire a thonk beside (ii, 50–60).

And again :

> And for men sein unknowe, unkest,
> Hire thombe sche holt in hire fest
> So close withinne hire oghne hond,
> That there winneth noman lond.
> Sche lieveth noght al that sche hiereth,
> And thus fulofte hirself sche skiereth,
> And is al war of " hadde I wist " (ii, 467–473).

As is usual in the love literature, the position of the lady with regard to the lover is one of superiority. The figure employed most frequently is the feudal one. The lover is her vassal and her obedient servant. He shows his relation to her in the couplet :

> With al that evere I may and can,
> Sche hath me wonne to hire man (v, 4495–4496).

The service which such a relation entailed is constantly brought out :

> And evere I love and evere I *serve*,
> And evere I am aliche nerr (iii, 1146–1147).

> Nouther yive ne behote
> In rewarding of mi *servise*
> It list hire in no manner wise (v, 5193–5195).

Attendant upon this service of his lady is a constant fear of her :

> Men sein that every love hath drede;
> So folweth it that I hire drede
> For I hire love (v, 6059–6062).

Before her, his humility is absolute. Though he knows that love lurks in the heart of man, and every man is free to love, he does not consider himself worthy to be loved, except in his lady's mercy.

> I trowe ther be noman lesse
> Of eny maner worthinesse
> That halt him lasse worth thanne I
> To be beloved (i, 1925–1928).

As a servant to his lord, so he remembers obedience to his lady. No trained dog is so ready to " go lowe " at his master's command as he is to do her will.

> What thing sche bit me don, I do
> And wher sche bit me gon, I go
> And whanne hir liste to clepe, I come. . . .
> I serve, I bowe, I loke, I loute,
> Myn yhe folweth hire aboute;
> What so sche wole, so wole I (iv, 1157–1171).

The subject upon which the lover speaks most feelingly, because it concerns him most closely, is the attitude of the lady toward him, and the treatment he receives from her. She is cold, neglectful, and indifferent. She bids him not to speak to her of love, but to choose another for his *amie*, averring that he stands far from her grace. She will not even receive a gift from him, lest he might have some small cause to hope. Yet she takes gifts from others by way of friendliness, so that all speak well of her. Everything the lover does to please her is fruitless. He essays rondeaus, ballades, virelays, carols, but all in vain. She has never yet given him a " goodlie word " as a recompense for his love. She has his love " by large weight and great measure," and he has nothing of that for which he has paid so dearly with his heart. She has never even said to him " grant mercy " to lighten his pain.

> Sche wolde noght hire yhe swerve
> Min herte with o goodly lok
> To fede (vi, 715–717).

His condition he sums up in the words :

> Min herte stant evere in o stede
> And axeth besiliche grace
> The which I mai noght yit embrace (iv, 57–59).

It will be needless to go through the numerous reiterations of the idea of the lady's indifference to her lover's feelings. Ingenious as some of the expressions are, the idea does not change, but is always the conventional one.[1]

Before leaving this feature, however, we should note Gower's use of the allegorical figure of Danger. He follows the example of the French writers in making a generous use of this figure to set forth the coldness of the lady. Danger is the lover's mortal enemy, and may well be called " sanz pité." He hinders the lover in all things, and will not let the lady receive his suit. He is always with her and gives an evil answer to all the lover's prayers. So between the two there is deadly war. If he can overcome Danger, his joy will then begin. But no man can daunt this enemy with sword or weapon, nor enchant him with any charm. One might not even steal the least look of one's lady's eye if Danger saw it.

Of such cruel treatment the lover naturally complains, as every lover was expected to do. When he sees and hears the " hevy chiere " and the " hevy word " of his lady, he is " disesed " in his heart. Yet his complaint is not to her. He keeps it all to

---

[1] The idea is expressed, among others, in the following places : i, 2373–2375; iii, 55, 63–70, 871–877 ; iv, 279–291, 2788–2813; v, 5190–5195.

himself; for he dares not displease her by speaking of his sorrow. He calls her to witness that he has never chidden her. On the contrary,

> if it mihte her like,
> The beste wordes wolde I pike
> Whiche I cowthe in myn herte chese (iii, 499–501).

Yet in his heart he cries out against Fortune, because he does not speed in his love.

The figure of first interest in the *Confessio Amantis* is the lover himself. The lady interests and attracts ; but she remains in the background. The confessor, one may say, is a piece of the machinery of the poem. As the central figure, the lover is intended by the poet to engage our sympathies in the recital of his experiences, and in the confession of his shortcomings in the religion of love.

Much is found in mediaeval love-literature, by way of reference, allusion, and injunction, regarding the qualities which go to make up the model lover ; but the plan of a confession to a priest of love affords an opportunity of presenting an array of qualities that might daunt even a Gawain with his " olde curtesye." In general, the lover must avoid each of the seven deadly sins, with the various divisions and subdivisions, and embrace the opposite virtues. We may call to mind the passage in the *Troilus* in which Chaucer is describing the ennobling effect of love upon his hero :

> Thus wolde Love, y-heried be his grace
> That Pryde, Envy, Ire, and Avaryce
> He gan to flee, and every other vyce.[1]

An interesting example of the use of this idea is to be found in the story of the little Jehan de Saintré.[2] The Lady of the Fair Cousins takes the little Jehan, then thirteen years old, whom she has chosen as worthy of her favor, and whom she expects to

---

[1] *Troilus*, iii, st. 258.
[2] A. de la Salle, *Histoire et Cronicque du Petit Jehan de Saintré et de la Jeune Dame des Belles Cousines*, Paris, 1830, chap. v, pp. 20 ff.

model into a courtly lover and knight, and gives him detailed instructions how to conduct himself. She puts before him the nature of each of the deadly sins, and shows him why, as a lover and a knight, he must avoid them all.

In considering the confessor's use of these sins and his application of them to love matters, we must take into account the fact that all, considered as sins against the Christian God, were to be shunned by the courtly lover. But we must also keep in mind that what would be a sin in the Christian religion, might in some cases be a virtue in the religion of Love. In examining the lover's confession, then, the following questions naturally arise :

1. How far are the sins, considered as such from the Christian standpoint, sinful in the religion of Love ?

2. How far is the confessor consistently a priest of Venus, and how much does he let Christian teaching obtrude ?

3. How does his teaching accord with the courtly love ideas ?

4. What is the character of the lover, which would result from following the priest's counsel ?

The first sin which the confessor takes up is Pride, and he discusses it under five heads : Hypocrisy, Inobedience, Surquidry or Presumption, Boasting, and Vainglory. The virtue corresponding to Pride is Humility. Considered as a sin in a Christian sense, Pride is to be shunned by all courtly lovers ; Humility, on the contrary, is to be practised. Modesty is enjoined upon lovers in Rule 8 of Andreas's shorter code.[1] The branches of Pride in Love's religion have particular meanings. Hypocrisy, as the confessor here applies it, is the deception of women in order to gain their love. This is a sin against the god of Love, and it is frequently denounced. A good example occurs in the *Romance of the Rose*, where the god exacts hostages from the lover as an evidence of his good faith.[2] In treating this topic, therefore, Gower's confessor is a consistent priest of Venus.

[1] Andreas, p. 106.   [2] English Translation, ll. 2043–2060.

The most obvious sense in which Inobedience could be considered as a sin from the Christian point of view would be with reference to God. The parallel in the religion of Love would be Inobedience to the god of Love. This application, however, the confessor does not make until he reaches the discussion of Surquidry. The other sense in which Inobedience might be viewed as a sin in the Christian religion is with reference to human beings in authority. This application the priest does make in considering the sin from the standpoint of love, the person in authority being the lady. Here, then, we have good courtly love doctrine. Perfect and unfaltering obedience to his lady was incumbent upon every lover. The confessor is, therefore, consistent with his office as a priest of Venus in enjoining obedience upon his penitent, and his illustrative tale of Florent is pertinent.

Presumption, as the confessor applies it to love affairs, consists in deeming oneself more worthy than one is. He is right, therefore, in condemning it; for though the courtly lover was expected to be worthy of his lady's favor, yet his humility should keep him from thinking himself to be so. The presumption which would lead a lover to think he was loved when he was not would likewise be a sin against Love. Disdain of Love, inspired by presumption, the priest is right in saying, is the worst sin of all against the god. It thus appears that Presumption and Inobedience with reference to the god are practically identical. The tale of Narcissus aptly illustrates them both. So far, then, the confessor is consistent in his condemnation.

The two forms of the sin of Advantance, or Boasting, are rightly condemned by a priest of Venus. For a lover to proclaim his own merit in other than love affairs would be a violation of the injunction relating to modesty given by the god.[1] To proclaim his merit in love would be an act of presumption. As

---

[1] Andreas, Short Code, Rule 8, p. 106.

for boasting of favors received, this would be a violation of the law of secrecy, which is everywhere enjoined. The confessor is right in saying that Love hates Advantance above every other vice.

In the application of the sin of Vainglory to love, the priest seems to strain things a little. The vainglorious man sets his thought on the world and delights in new things, without ever thinking that death is coming. So, the priest says, the lover makes his songs and carols and does not think of death. But why death ? The obvious parallel would be, seemingly, that the vainglorious lover is flippant and forgets that at any moment the god of Love may turn his joy to sorrow. As for the lover's being light-hearted and merry, he had the god's own command for this.[1] It looks here as if the poet were letting a little of his own seriousness intrude in the counsel of the confessor. With the exception of this slight inconsistency, however, it is clear that all the prohibitions of the priest, with his concluding in-junction to practise humility, fit well with the ideas of the courtly system. And his advice so far, if followed, would make a good courtly lover.

Envy, the second sin, manifests itself in five forms : Sorrow for another's joy, Joy for another's sorrow, Detraction, False-Semblant, and Supplanting. Like Pride, Envy, judged from the Christian point of view, is to be shunned by the lover. The con-fessor's statement gives a sufficiently good reason for this : " The envious lover is not ' shapely ' to marry, for there is in him no ' matiere wherof he mihte do plesaunce,' because he always seems ' unglad.' The fire within him dries up the blood which should flow kindly through his veins. ' Toward love, Envy is noght,' for he is moved by malice in all he does."

According to the religious convention, love is the gift of the god. He inspires in a lover's heart affection for some particular woman ; if she grants the lover her favor, it is because the god

[1] *Romance of the Rose*, l. 2275.

puts it into her heart to do so. This being true, for a lover to
envy the joy of a man who has been favored when he himself
has not, would be a sin against the god. The confessor is right,
therefore, in condemning envy in love which manifests itself in
sorrow for another's happiness. For the same reason, joy for
another's sorrow is properly condemned.

The other three points of Envy, — Detraction, Supplanting,
and False-Semblant, — as the confessor applies them, are closely
related. Supplanting was expressly forbidden in Rule 3 of
Andreas's shorter code.[1] As a corollary, False-Semblant and
Detraction as means of supplanting are violations of the same
law. Moreover, Slander is especially forbidden in Rule 9 of
the same code. We may note, in passing, the common sense of
the priest's remarks concerning Detraction. "A lover who finds
fault with his rival and detracts from his good qualities," says
the confessor, " only injures his own cause. The lady needs no
one to tell her of the faults of her wooers ; she probably knows
them. Furthermore, she will only think the less of the detractor
for his envy." The observation is true to human nature ; and
in matters of love the priest's advice with regard to speaking
unfavorably of one's rivals is good, whether for mediaeval or for
modern lovers. He is, therefore, consistent as a priest of Venus
in forbidding Envy with its five divisions and in commending
Charity as the " vertu sovereine."

The five ministers of Wrath, the next sin to be considered,
are Melancholy, Cheste or Chiding, Hate, Contek (which has
Foolhaste for chamberlain), and Homicide. In his application of
some of these sins to matters of love, the confessor is evidently
forcing things. As far as the general injunction to eschew wrath
and to practise patience is concerned, he is in accord with the
ideas of the courtly system. One of its fundamental principles
was that love easily obtained is not greatly appreciated ; and that

[1] Andreas, p. 106.

the lover should, therefore, suffer, if not in patience at least in submission, the ups and downs of his fortune. Patience would be a measure of common sense, and it is upon this basis that the confessor makes his injunction. Upon the same basis, the vice of Cheste, or Chiding, in love is condemned; for it would indeed be a foolish lover who chid the lady whose favor he sought.

The tale of Canace, which the priest uses to illustrate the evils of Melancholy, although it does this admirably in a general way, illustrates much more forcibly another doctrine. Gower, through the confessor, here voices one of his favorite ideas: that by nature every man is amenable to love, whether he will or not; and that whoever works against nature is apt to come to woe. Now Canace and her brother are only following the dictates of nature when they are guilty of incest. The important lesson the priest draws from the story is that

> it sit every man to have
> Reward to love and to his miht,
> Ayein whos strengthe mai no wiht (iii, 344–346).

and

> What nature hath set in her lawe,
> Ther mai no mannes miht withdrawe (iii, 355–356).

The lesson which the priest professes to teach by the tale, namely, the evil of Melancholy, follows as a corollary from this proposition. In venting his wrath upon his children, the father is guilty of a sin against the god of Love, — a perfectly just conclusion for a priest of Love to arrive at. The logic of such a conclusion, coming, as it does, from Gower the moralist, will be discussed later in this study.[1]

As for the other divisions of Wrath — Hate, Contek, and Homicide — the author seems to be put to it to make them fit into his scheme. Whom may a lover hate? The confessor

[1] See p. 85, below.

says : " It would be better to hate no man, even though he had hindered the lover. The lover should beware, however, of those who hate him, for such hate is often disguised under a false appearance " — all of which is an admonition to caution on the one hand, and to the exercise of Christian charity on the other. As for romantic love, like Envy, " it is noght."

Contek and Homicide are closely related. What have these sins to do with love ? The confessor's argument is : " Reason often tells the lover that he ought to cease from his love ; but Will urges him on to it. But Will should always be ruled by Reason. For when Contek is in the heart, Will, overpowering Reason, may lead to Homicide." Coming from a priest of Venus, this is strange doctrine. The confessor is clearly confusing erotic with Christian philosophy. To subject Will or Desire to the control of Reason is the part of practical wisdom, but it is not in the spirit of the religion of Love ; love, as the confessor teaches elsewhere, stops at no bounds to attain its ends. Homicide, as the result of unrestrained passion, is a manifestation of the power of the god of Love ; when it becomes suicide, as it does in the illustrative story of Pyramus and Thisbe, it exalts the victim of his own madness to the rank of martyrdom in the service of the god.

Sloth is the next sin taken up ; it has seven points : Lachesse, Pusillanimity, Forgetfulness, Negligence, Idleness, Somnolence, Despondency. The poet is on safe ground in his application of the sin of Sloth and its divisions. This vice is bad in the pursuit of anything valuable, and certainly in the pursuit of love. It is largely on the basis of common sense that the priest condemns the sin with its subdivisions. He has opportunity, in considering these, to give some very sensible and practical counsel, which does not always accord with courtly love ideas ; and also to give some which is not so sensible, but none the less thoroughly in the spirit of the courtly system.

Lachesse, which in the Christian sense means slackness in the service of God,[1] the priest interprets as meaning, in a lover's case, postponing his pursuit of the lady's favor. This he condemns, and his condemnation is in accord with courtly ideas. The lover was supposed to be in constant service of his lady, and to beseech her favor in and out of season; as Pandarus says, he must

> ever in oon be fresh and grene
> To serve and love his dere hertes quene,
> And thinke it is a guerdon hir to serve
> A thousand-fold more than he can deserve.[2]

"Unknowe, unkist, and lost that is unsought."[3] This implies that the lover must not be pusillanimous.

When, however, the confessor's strong practical sense leads him to condemn a lover's fear to tell his love, his teaching is contrary to the conventional ideas. Under the courtly system, the proper humility of the lover always made him fearful in his lady's presence, especially in the matter of declaring his passion. Similarly, in his condemnation of Forgetfulness, the priest departs from courtly conceptions. The lover's confusion in his lady's presence was supposed to make him forget half of what he had to say. The god in the *Romance of the Rose* remarks to the lover :

> Il n'iert ja si apenses
> Qui en ce point n'oblit asses
> S'il n'est tiex que de guile serve.[4]

Again the confessor's common sense makes him vary from the accepted doctrine.

Of course, Negligence, as the priest explains the term, would be a sin against Love. Every lover was supposed to know the art of love. Such manuals as the *Romance of the Rose* were designed to teach this very thing.

---

[1] Chaucer, *Persones Tale*, sect. 59.   [3] Ibid., st. 116.

[2] *Troilus*, i, st. 117.   [4] *Romance of the Rose*, ll. 2491–2493.

In his observations on Idleness, the confessor is in full agreement with conventional ideas. The principle that love is the
duty of all young people has a prominent place in the book of
Andreas. The injunctions with regard to the lover's going on
expeditions into foreign lands, in order that his fame may reach
the ears of his lady, are in line with courtly love principles.
Andreas teaches that love is to be the reward of noble deeds;
and his teaching is reflected constantly in the other erotic literature. The confessor's remarks on Courage and Manhood lead
him to the "inevitable discussion of the nature of 'Gentilesse'
and how far it depends upon birth, riches, or personal merit." [1]
Gower's conception of *Gentilesse*, as voiced by the confessor,
differs much from that of such poets as confine themselves
strictly to the courtly view; but all agree that the lover
must possess the quality in question.

As to Somnolence, the confessor's remark,

Love and slep acorden noght (iv, 3186)

is good courtly love philosophy, and merely expresses the
conventional idea long present in the love literature.

Despair, in the Christian sense, was one of the worst of sins;
for in despairing of God's mercy the sinner put himself beyond
the power of God to save him.[2] In much the same sense the
confessor applies the sin to love, and he is right in condemning
it. For, to quote his own words,

I not what other thing availeth
Of hope whan the herte faileth (iv, 3507–3508).

Of Avarice, the next sin, the confessor says, in effect: Avarice
renders a man a slave to his gold. It makes him strive to get
more and more, and to let nothing go. This vice must be shunned
by every lover who hopes for his lady's favor; and he must use

---

[1] Macaulay, II, 508.   [2] Chaucer, *Persones Tale*, sect. 56.

largess and give for his love's sake. It is natural that a lover should be a slave to Love; but there is a form of avarice in love that is a great evil. This is Jealousy. As the avaricious man is in constant fear that his gold will be stolen, so the jealous man is never at peace for fear of having his treasure taken from him. Thus he makes both himself and his lady miserable. Love hates nothing more than the sin of Jealousy.

Avarice has eight servants:

1. Covetousness. The evils of Covetousness are illustrated by the stories of *Virgil's Mirror, The Two Coffers*, and *The Two Pasties and the Beggars*. The moral of the last two is that though a man covet love, yet shall he not obtain more than Fortune has allotted him. Some there are, however, who covet every woman they see, because something in her pleases them. Other lovers covet women, not because of their beauty or virtue, but for their riches. Such love must be condemned; only pure love shall last. Marriages made for money are a great evil; but riches may sometimes be a help in love affairs. Perjury and False-witness often work in the service of Covetousness. Treacherous lovers frequently beguile women by swearing faithful service to them. Such men are worthy neither to love nor to be loved.

2. Usury. The usurer in love gives as little as possible, and takes all he can get.

3. Parsimony or Scarceness. Stinginess never accords with love, and the stingy lover often changes the coat for the hood. Judicious giving accomplishes much, and meed keeps love in the house.

4. Ingratitude. The ungrateful lover is he, who, when he has had what he will of love, begrudges giving anything in return.

5. Ravine. As some take other men's goods without payment, so some lovers force women to their desires. Such conduct is against Love's law.

6. Robbery. The robber forces women to his will when he meets them in lonely places.

7. Stealth. Lovers sometimes take kisses or other things by stealth.

8. Sacrilege. Lovers are guilty of sacrilege when they use occasions of worship to whisper, sigh, and ogle.

All these servants of Avarice the lover must avoid ; he must cultivate the virtue of Largess, which is a mean between Prodigality and Avarice. The prodigal lover spends and wastes his love by bestowing it on many women.

The remarks of the confessor with regard to Avarice are such as might be expected from any exponent of the principles of the courtly system. Avarice was unalterably opposed to love. Andreas has a law to the effect that love and avarice cannot dwell together,[1] and many allusions to the incompatibility of the two occur in his work. A positive statement of the principle is repeatedly found in the literature of love, in the insistence upon generosity as a qualification of the true lover. The three qualities most commonly demanded of lovers are Prowess, Courtesy, and Largess. The vice of Avarice, to which all men may be addicted, is the one especially to be shunned by lovers.

In making the special application of Avarice to love, the confessor departs a little from the courtly ideas. His assertion that Love hates nothing more than jealousy is not quite in accord with the courtly tradition, one of the principles of which was that he who does not become jealous does not love.[2] The confessor's description of the jealous man, however, applies rather to the husband than to the lover ; and if he means to restrict his assertion to the relation between man and wife, it is directly in

---

[1] Andreas, p. 310.

[2] " Ex vera zelotypea affectus semper crescit amandi." — Andreas, Longer Code, No. 21, p. 310.

line with the courtly doctrine, which held that jealousy could not, or at least should not, exist in marriage.[1]

The application of the different points of Avarice to love accords on the whole with the courtly system; but the priest sometimes finds it necessary to force things. For example, in the consideration of Covetousness, the conclusion to which he comes, that though a person covet love, yet he shall obtain only what has been allotted to him by Fortune, is obviously far-fetched. On the other hand, the observations with regard to a lover's coveting more than one woman are good courtly doctrine. Constancy or Steadfastness was a virtue always insisted on, and the light and easy transference of affection from one person to another was abhorrent to the votaries of courtly love.

The confessor's strictures on marriages made for money probably express Gower's personal views. In the courtly system, marriage was deemed of little consequence, so far as love itself was concerned; and it is certain that many a marriage was contracted for no other object than to obtain riches.

The condemnation of treacherous lovers is, of course, a commonplace in all courtly love literature. What has already been said regarding Avarice in general, applies equally well to

---

[1] Although jealousy is made a necessary condition of love in Andreas's philosophy, the love poets are not at all agreed on this point. The character Esperance, in Froissart's *Paradys d'Amours*, remarks that, although some who know much about loving hold that without jealousy there can be no love, yet in her opinion it is neither fair nor good, and ought to be shunned by all lovers. We may compare with this Criseyde's pathetic remarks:

> Eek al my wo is this, that folk now usen
> To seyn right thus, "ye, Jalousye is Love!"
> And wolde a busshel venim al excusen
> For that o greyn of love is on it shove!
> But that wot heighe god that sit above,
> If it be lyker love, or hate or grame;
> And after that, it oughte bere his name (*Troilus*, iii, st. 147).

Many similar expressions could be cited to show that not all writers agreed with Andreas on this point.

Parsimony. Ravine and Robbery, as the confessor uses the terms, are practically identical, and are contrary to the law of love in any system.[1] Of the remarks on the other four points, those on Usury and Ingratitude are forced, while those on Stealth and Sacrilege are not only forced but childish. Just why stealing kisses should be a sin against Love is hard to see. One fears the poet's austerity is speaking here. Certainly this is true with regard to what he says about Sacrilege. The confessor of Venus has again become the Christian priest, and the observations would be far more fitting in the *Mirour de l'Omme* than in a work dealing with romantic love.

In considering the sin of Gluttony, the confessor wisely limits himself to two points, Drunkenness and Delicacy. His discussion of even these two is not particularly happy. Why should Love's priest condemn love-drunkenness? The more intoxicated with love one is, the greater is the manifestation of the god's power. Here the confessor returns to the relation between reason and love, which was discussed under Wrath. As in that connection, so here he is overstepping the bounds which a priest of Venus should observe. And though on the basis of wisdom his condemnation of intoxication is appropriate, yet it is quite out of place on the lips of Love's confessor.

The remarks on love-delicacy, too, are more those of a Christian priest than we should expect, coming as they do from a priest of Love. Considered from the standpoint of courtly love, the condemnation of a man's forsaking his wife for other

[1] Under the latter of these two sins, the poet's teaching reaches the height of absurdity. He takes occasion to commend virginity and to preach the beauty of this virtue both in men and women. As illustration, he tells the tale of Phirinus, who put out his own eyes to enable him to keep himself chaste. In only one other place is the confessor so absurd; that is, in his survey of the different religions of the world (v, 747–1970), where he " occupies himself in demolishing the claim of Venus to be accounted a goddess, and that too without even the excuse of having forgotten for the moment that he is supposed to be her priest" (Macaulay, II, xx).

pleasures is all wrong. The same is true with regard to the lover's demanding the ultimate favors.

Two sins remain to be treated by the confessor, Unchastity and Incest. The former does not receive a separate consideration in the *Confessio Amantis ;* but Chastity is treated as the fifth point of that Policy which teaches kings how to govern their kingdoms. Chastity is, therefore, according to the priest, one of the virtues which should be found especially in kings. Chastity, according to the teaching of the Church, was of three kinds : chastity in marriage, by which the wife was true to her husband ; chastity in widowhood, by which a widow, or a woman who had been guilty of illicit love, kept herself clean ; and chastity of virginity.[1] It is the first of the three which the priest discusses. His remarks have nothing to do with the confession of the lover ; the author, speaking through the confessor, is giving his ideas on the duties of sovereigns and intends, perhaps, to deliver a lecture through the medium of his book to the young King Richard. In treating Incest, he adopts the teaching of the Church. Hence he denounces marriage within the third degree, as well as guilty love of women " of religion," which the Church regarded as incest.[2] All this has nothing to do with the lover's shrift. The confessor has already treated the subject of Incest as a priest of Venus, in the story of Canace (under the head of Melancholy) ; he here considers it from the point of view of a Christian moralist.

We may briefly summarize the confessor's teaching in the following terms. He is in accord with the courtly love ideas in condemning six of the deadly sins — Pride, Envy, Wrath, Sloth, Avarice, and Gluttony. Incest, which he also condemns, comes under the head of Lechery, but this latter sin as a whole he does not treat. Of the divisions of these several sins, as

---

[1] Chaucer, *Persones Tale*, sect. 77–84.
[2] See *Mirour de l'Omme*, ll. 9085 ff.

applied especially to love, those belonging to Pride and Envy
are rightly denounced by a priest of Venus. Of the divisions of
Wrath, none have any direct connection with the courtly ideas.
Chiding is censured on grounds of common sense. The condemnation of Melancholy proceeds rather from the particular
view of love held by the author ; while Hate, Contek, and
Homicide are looked at from the Christian point of view.
Under the head of Sloth, — Lachesse, Pusillanimity, Negligence,
Idleness, Somnolence, and Despondency are all contrary to the
spirit of courtly love, and the confessor rightly speaks against
them. He departs from that spirit, however, in his treatment of
Forgetfulness, and of one phase of Fear as he defines it, condemning both on grounds of common sense. Five of the phases
of Avarice he is right in reprehending as a love priest. His
remarks on two of them, Usury and Ingratitude, are so trivial
that they mean nothing, judge them from whatever standpoint
we will. Stealth and Sacrilege are prohibited, the former because of the austerity of the poet, the latter because of his
Christian zeal. Under Gluttony, Drunkenness and Delicacy
are both considered from the Christian point of view, as are
also the last two sins, Unchastity and Incest.

What, now, would be the character of the lover who should
follow the priest's counsel ? Before answering this question, we
must disregard all the offenses which the confessor judges by
the Christian standard (except, of course, the seven principal
sins themselves). Thus we exclude Hate, Contek, Homicide,
Stealth, Sacrilege, Love-Drunkenness, Love-Delicacy, Unchastity, and Incest. Omitting these absurdities, we find that
the confessor's counsels, if followed, would result as follows :
The lover would be humble, charitable, patient, courageous, and
generous. His humility would keep him from presumption, and
make him obedient to his lady. He would be innocent of be-
guiling other women ; and he would not be guilty of boasting or

of frivolity. He would not resort to detraction or "false-semblant" in order to supplant another lover; indeed, he would not be guilty of the sin of "supplanting" at all. He would keep his love engagements with promptness. He would not fear to speak his love to his lady, nor would he forget what he had to say when he attempted to speak. He would know all the art of love. He would show his love by his deeds of prowess and would seek fame in distant wars. He would not sleep while others were merry; indeed, his love would allow him little sleep at any time; but he would never grow despondent nor despair. He would shun jealousy. He would not force favors from any woman; and his constancy to his own lady would prevent him from even desiring such favors except from her. But for his attitude toward his lady in the matter of Fear and Forgetfulness, he would be a genuine courtly lover, and all his conduct would bear the stamp of "gentilesse."

From this description of the courtly lover we may pass to other related conventions which appear frequently in the *Confessio Amantis*.

The favorite idea that love ennobles a man's character is well expressed by Genius:

> For evere yit, it hath be so
> That love honeste in sondri weie
> Profiteth, for it doth aweie
> The vice, . . .
> It makth curteis of the vilein,
> And to the couard hardiesce
> It yifth, so that verrai prouesce
> Is caused upon loves reule
> To him that can manhode reule; . . .
> I trowe that ther is no beste
> If he with love scholde aqueinte,
> That he ne wolde make it queinte
> As for the while that it laste (iv, 2296–2315).[1]

[1] Compare also the story of the False Bachelor, ii, 2586 ff.

The conventional notions as to the effect of love upon the feelings occur frequently. Love is a malady so grievous that it " might make a wise man mad if it should long endure."[1] Very often it is described in general terms of pain and woe.[2] In his lady's presence the lover is confused and timorous ; he loses his memory and even his power of speech.[3] In shriving himself of forgetfulness, he remarks that, when he is about to see his lady, he rehearses in his mind many things to say, but when he comes where she is he forgets them all, — because he is so afraid of her.[4] Sleeplessness from love is mentioned again and again : the confessor even tells a tale to illustrate the doctrine that "love and slep acorden nought."[5] A good summary of the lover's symptoms may be found in the lines which describe the passion of the maiden of Pentapolim for Apollonius :

> Thenkende upon this man of Tyr,
> Hire hert is hot as eny fyr,
> And otherwhile it is acale ;
> Now is sche red, nou is sche pale,
> Right after the condicion
> Of hire ymaginacion.
> Sche stant for love in such a plit,
> That sche hath lost al appetit
> Of mete, of drinke, of nyhtes reste,
> As sche that not what is the beste (viii, 845–860).

There remain to be noted a few conventional ideas in Gower's work which do not admit of particular classification. A conceit which was a favorite with Chrétien, that love attacks the heart through the eyes, occurs in the *Confessio Amantis*. Genius advises the lover to guard the eyes, for through them, as through gates, such " sotie " comes to a man as may make his love exceed measure.

---

[1] *Confessio Amantis*, i, 130–131.   [2] Ibid., vi, 718 ff.
[3] Ibid., i, 559–567 ; iv, 355–362.
[4] Ibid., iv, 557–587.   [5] Ibid., iv, 3186.

> Fulofte thilke firy Dart
> Of love, which that evere brenneth
> Thurh him [the eye] unto the herte renneth (i, 322–324).

Chrétien's idea of the enmity of one's own eyes appears in the lines :

> And thus a mannes yhe ferst
> Himselve grieveth alther werst (i, 325–326).

Another doctrine of Chrétien, that lovers' hearts remain together, though their bodies are separated, is reflected in the words of the lover :

> Thus ate laste I go to bedde,
> And yit min herte lith to wedde
> With hire, wher as I came fro ;
> Thogh I departe, he wol noght so,
> Ther is no lock mai schette him oute,
> Him nedeth noght to gon aboute,
> That perce mai the harde wall ;
> Thus is he with hire overall (iv, 2875–2882).

Gower is fond of describing love in terms of contradictions, after the manner of the well-known eighty-eighth sonnet of Petrarch. The following are a few of the many examples :

> Est amor egra salus, vexata quies, pius error,
> Bellica pax, vulnus dulce, suave malum.[1]

> Love is the unsely jolif wo (i, 88).

> And thus soffre I the hote chele
> Which passeth othre peines fele ;
> In cold I brenne, and frese in hete,
> And than I drinke a bitter swete (vi, 247–250).

Gower's most elaborate use of the conceit is found in the Latin verses entitled *Carmen de variis in amore passionibus breviter compilatum :*

> Est amor in glosa pax bellica, lis pietosa,
> Accio famosa, vaga sors, vis imperiosa,
> Pugna quietosa, victoria perniciosa,

---

[1] Macaulay, II, 35.

> Regula viscosa, scola devia, lex capitosa,
> Cura molestosa, gravis ars, virtus viciosa,
> Gloria dampnosa, flens risus et ira iocosa,
> Esca venenosa, fel dulce, fames animosa,
> Vitis acetosa, sitis ebria, mens furiosa,
> Flamma pruinosa, nox clara, dies tenebrosa,
> Res dedignosa, socialis et ambiciosa,
> Garrula, verbosa, secreta, silens, studiosa,
> Fabula formosa, sapiencia prestigiosa,
> Causa ruinosa, rota versa, quies operosa,
> Urticata rosa, spes stulta, fidesque dolosa.[1]

Some features which perhaps may not be properly classed under the head of conventions, but which, nevertheless, were not original with Gower, may here be mentioned. The use of Genius as the confessor has already been referred to as taken from the *Romance of the Rose*. The contest in which Wit and Reason are pitted against Will and Hope (iii, 1157–1192) is, as Macaulay remarks, "quite in the style of the *Roman de la Rose*, where Reason and the lover have an endless dispute." [2] A variation of the idea is found in the controversy between the priest and the lover, the result of which is told in the lines :

> Mi resoun understod him wel,
> And knew it was soth every del
> That he hath seid, but noght forthi
> Mi will hath nothing set thereby (viii, 2191–2194).

The representation of love as an insatiable thirst was common.[3] The story of the two tuns of Jupiter appears in the *Romance of the Rose*, but Gower has modified the original, making Cupid, instead of Fortune, the butler, and using the whole to express

---

[1] Macaulay, I, 392.   [2] Ibid., II, 496.
[3] Note, for instance, the following from Watriquet de Couvin :

> M'est vis que pis m'en soit,
> Et que plus bui et plus oi soit,
> Si qu'en bevant fui touz ravis.

> *La Fontaine d'Amours*, ll. 175–177.

the thought, frequently employed by him, that love is a matter of chance. The three cooks, Sight, Hearing, and Thinking, who cater to the lover's appetite for delicacies, remind one of the Dous-Penser, Dous-Parler, and Dous-Regard of the *Romance of the Rose*.

The large array of conventional ideas and sentiments pointed out in the foregoing pages is only indicative of a much larger mass, which comprises practically all that part of the *Confessio Amantis* that is devoted to the treatment of love. Is there anything in the work, we are naturally led to ask, which lifts it above mere conventionality? Does it show any of that vital quality which we might expect to find in a story of love? Deep, earnest passion, to be sure, it does not express; the plan and object of the work forbid. What made the book attractive to its readers, apart from its moralizing elements, was the large number of well-told tales which it contains. The story of the lover's fortunes, while interesting, was no doubt secondary in importance, both for the author and for his contemporaries. Still, in the two main characters, the lover and his lady, there is both human quality and charm.

In the lady, as Macaulay remarks, " we recognize a creature of flesh and blood, no goddess indeed, as her lover himself observes, but a charming embodiment of womanly grace and refinement. She is surrounded by lovers, but she is wise and wary. She is courteous and gentle, but at the same time firm ; she will not gladly swear, and therefore says nay without an oath, but it is a decisive nay to any who are disposed to presume. She does not neglect her household duties, merely because a lover insists upon hanging about her, but leaves him to amuse himself how he may, while she busies herself elsewhere. If she has leisure and can sit down to her embroidery, he may read to her, if he will, but it must be some sound romance, and not his own roundels, balades, and virelays in praise of her. Custom allows him to kiss her when he takes his leave, but if he comes back on any pretext and takes his leave again, there is not often a second kiss permitted. She lets him lead her up to the offering in church, and ride by her side when she drives out, but she will take no present from him, though with some of her younger admirers, whose passion she knows is a less serious matter, she is not so strict but takes and gives freely. Her lover suspects that her soul may be in a perilous state, seeing that she has the power of saving a man's life and yet suffers him to die, but he admits there is no more violence in her than in a child of three years old, and her words are as pleasant to him as the winds of the South."[1] The attractiveness of the picture cannot be denied. There is no extravagance here, no idealization ; only the portrait of an everyday woman, who is sensible as well as fair :

> A creature not too bright or good
> For human nature's daily food.

The general tendency of Gower to keep his feet on the ground appears also in his portrayal of the lover. The practical common sense of the answers which the lover gives to the confessor's questions pleases us ; their perfect sincerity and frankness awaken our sympathy. In the story of his love, as he tells it, there is no deep passion which stirs us. Yet he retains our interest, because we see in him a man who, in the pursuit of his love, feels the same hopes and joys, and suffers the same disappointments which a lover of to-day might experience. Thus in spite of conventions, from which the author could not have escaped had he desired, he has managed to depict in the lover and the lady two figures which are thoroughly human.

It is with a distinct shock that we learn, having followed the perfectly natural story of the lover's fortunes, that, after all, he is only an old man whose "lockes hore" do not accord with

---

[1] Macaulay, II, xvi.

"loves lust." We wish that the poet might have chosen a less bungling way of ending his poem. Of course, it is necessary in a love-vision, which Gower's poem practically is, to have the hero dismissed in some manner from his interview with the god or goddess. But he is usually dismissed with some word of approval or with an injunction appropriate, in either case, to the part that he has played throughout the story. Thus the lover in the *Dit dou Vergier* is advised by the god who is departing :

> Mais je t'apenray au partir,
> Se tu vues aus dous biens partir,
> Et estre garis de tes maus,
> Que secrez soies et loiaus.[1]

Similarly, the god of Love in the *Romance of the Rose* leaves the hero with the injunction :

> Good-Hope alway kepe by thy syde
> And Swete-Thought make eek abyde,
> Swete-Lokyng and Swete-Speche.[2]

It is not unusual, too, for the author to appear in a love-vision, and to be dismissed with a command. For example, in the Prologue to the *Legend of Good Women*, the poet is ordered at the close to write his *Legend*. Machaut likewise appears by name in the *Jugement dou Roy de Navarre*,[3] and is dismissed by the king with the command to write certain poems in certain metres. In the first two instances, the hero is left a lover as he has been throughout ; in the last two, the heroes are poets at the end as they have been from the beginning. In the *Confessio*, on the other hand, after being led to think of the hero as a young man,

> A lovyere and a lusty bachelere,

we are confronted with the statement that it is only John Gower, the gray-haired old poet. The spectacle of "olde Grisel" growing

---

[1] Ll. 1191–1194.   [2] English Translation, ll. 2941–2943.

[3] This is not a love-vision; but is modelled on such love-poems as the *Phyllis and Flora*. It will therefore serve well enough for illustration.

cold about the heart and lying there in a swoon for love, is in-congruous, to say the least. A poet with more imagination and with less desire to make clear the fact that his chief interest was in moral affairs,[1] would certainly have devised a. more attractive conclusion for a poem which, in its main features, is not without attractive qualities.

We must now inquire into the nature of the love which is treated in the *Confessio Amantis*. Being familiar with Gower's aversion to all moral obliquity, we should not expect to find the sensual element prominent in his work. The end of the lover's passion, we may infer from the general tone of the story (though nothing is said on this point), is possession of the lady in mar-riage. We have already noted, however, some passages which are suggestive of the more earthy nature of his love. In the illustrative stories, love is repeatedly identified with physical passion. Thus :

> Anon the wylde loves rage,
> In which no man him can governe,
> Hath mad him [Helmege] that he can naght werne
> Bot fell al hol to hire assent (i, 2620–2623).

> Be daie bothe and ek be nyhte,
> Whil thei be yonge, of comun wone
> In chambre thei togedre wone,
> And as thei scholden pleide hem ofte,
> Til thei be growen up alofte
> Into the youthe of lusti age,
> Whan kinde assaileth the corage
> With love and doth him forto bowe,
> That he no reson can allowe,
> Bot halt the lawes of nature (iii, 148–157).

---

[1] Cf. the injunction of Venus :

> Mi sone, be wel war therfore,
> And kep the sentence of my lore
> And tarie thou mi Court nomore,
> But go ther vertu moral dwelleth,
> Wher ben thi bokes, as men telleth (viii, 2922–2927).

Anything approaching Platonic love, however remotely, is not to be found in the *Confessio Amantis*. The author's own view probably was, that love, if not identical with physical passion, is based upon it and largely influenced by it. This view, together with his decided leaning towards fatalism,[1] leads him over and over again to emphasize the irresistible character of love. For example :

> Love is maister, wher he wile (i, 35).

> For loves lawe is out of reule
> And though a man be reasonable
> Yet after kinde he is menable
> To love wher he wol or non (iii, 389–391).

> Bot love is of so gret a main
> That where he taketh an herte on honde
> Ther mai nothing his might withstonde (vi, 90–92).

Such expressions are apt to occur whenever love is mentioned.

Taken in connection with these facts, Gower's repeated use of the conventional idea that love is entirely under the dominion of chance, has more than conventional significance. At the beginning the author, speaking in his own person, says :

> For if ther evere was balance
> Which of fortune stant governed,
> I may well lieve as I am lerned
> That love hath that balance on honde,
> Which wol no reson understonde (i, 41–45).

Passages like this strengthen the impression which the poet manifestly endeavors to make, that in the hands of his physical passions man is utterly helpless.

We may, perhaps, now see some reason for Gower's leniency toward certain faults which otherwise his moral austerity would lead him unequivocally to condemn. Critics generally have

---

[1] The frequency with which phrases like " as it scholde " and " as it scholde be " occur in the work, leaves no doubt as to the poet's belief in the doctrine of fate. See iii, 1222, 1348, 1677 ; iv, 92, 1542 ; vi, 995, 1026, 1613, 1702.

wondered at his condoning the sin of the brother and sister in the tale of Canace. "We are completely at a loss," writes ten Brink, "to know what to think of the 'moral' Gower's logic, when, in the story of Canace, he blames indeed the rage of the father, but excuses the incest of the children on the ground of strong natural impulse."[1] From what has been said, it will appear, I think, that the poet's excuse of the children's sin is not at all illogical, even on the part of a moralist. If it be true, as the author seems to believe, that human beings under certain circumstances are powerless to resist the impulses of their natures, and if at the same time human actions are largely determined by fate (as Gower also believed), for the poet to condone the sin of incest under the circumstances is not only logical, but just.

But apart from any personal views which Gower may have held on such questions, he would no doubt have had a ready answer for those who might accuse him of inconsistency. He could have replied that he was here setting forth the doctrines and ideas of romantic love (with which, as we shall see, Gower felt but scant sympathy). If these doctrines lead to such a situation as is seen in the tale of Canace, and the priest of Venus condones the sin of incest, it is, Gower might say, speaking as a moralist, all the worse for romantic love. He could rightly shift the responsibility for any immoral teachings in the tale from his own shoulders to those of the confessor of Venus. However, Gower's belief on the question is a sufficient explanation of his treatment of the sin ; and it was doubtless sufficient justification to him for including in his great collection of stories, not only the *Canace*, but also the *Apollonius*, against both of which the Man of Lawe remonstrated.[2]

---

[1] Ten Brink, *History of English Literature*, translated by Kennedy, New York, 1893, Vol. II, pt. i, p. 135.

[2] Prologue to *Man of Lawe's Tale*, ll. 77–89.

Interesting to note in this connection is another view of Gower's, quite at variance with the teachings of the Church, of which the poet was a stanch supporter. The Church, while it glorified marriage,[1] and commended the part that woman took in the lawful relations between the sexes, yet regarded her generally with suspicion, since she tempted man by her beauty, and caused him to sin. The woman, according to the Church's teaching, was strictly responsible for any evil effects her beauty might have. A good expression of this teaching is found in the *Ancren Riwle:* " Vorþi was ihoten a Godes half iþen olden law þet put were ever iwreien, & ȝif eni unwreie put were, & best feolle þer inne, he hit schulde ȝelden þet þene put unwreih. Þis is a swuþe dredlich word to wummen þet scheaweþ hire to weopmones eien. Heo is bitocned by þe þet unwrieþ þene put." And the writer goes on to say that the woman's face, her white neck, her trivial eye, her hand, and anything belonging to her, whatsoever it be, " þurh hwat muhte sonre ful luve aquiken " is the pit. And whenever her beauty awakens guilty love in a man, even though she does not know it, she thereby uncovers the pit, and she shall be responsible for the man's sin. " Hund wule in bliþeliche hwar se he ivint hit open." [2] Now Gower comes out flatfooted against this doctrine.

> For in the woman is no guile
> Of that a man himself bewhapeth;
> Whan he his oghne wit bejapeth,
> I can the wommen wel excuse:
> But what man wole upon hem muse
> After the fool impression
> Of his ymaginacioun
> Withinne himself the fyr he bloweth,
> Wherof the womman nothing knoweth,
> So mai sche nothing be to wyte (vii, 4266–4275).

---

[1] Cf. *Persones Tale*, sect. 77.
[2] *Ancren Riwle*, ed. Morton, pp. 58–60.

And he goes on to say that if a man drown himself, it is not the fault of the water ; if men covet gold, the gold is not to blame. It is natural for a man to love ; but it is not natural for a man to lose his wits.

Another question of interest remains to be considered : What was the poet's attitude toward the courtly love ideas ? He leaves us in very little doubt as to the answer to this question. In the first place Gower, in one or two places, makes his views perfectly clear on certain important doctrines of the courtly system. The confessor speaks :

> For thou miht understonde and wite
> Among the gentil nacion
> Love is an occupacion
> Which for to kepe hise lustes save
> Scholde every gentil herte have (iv, 1450–1454).

The poet's marginal note shows his own position on this point. It reads :

> Non quia sic se habet veritas, set opinio amantum.

Speaking of the effects of love, the confessor says :

> For evere yit it hath be so,
> That love honeste in sondri weie
> Profiteth, for it doth aweie
> The vice, *and as the bokes sein*,
> It maketh curteis of the vilein
> And to the coward hardiesce
> It yifth — (iv, 2296–2301).

The words *and as the bokes sein* are doubly significant as indicating the conventionality of the idea, and as intimating Gower's desire to dissociate himself from the sentiments expressed.

We have already observed that the confessor's good sense sometimes led him to make suggestions in regard to certain points of love, which run counter to the courtly theories. For example, the conventional idea that a lover should be struck

with fear in the presence of his lady, and should forget everything he had to say in his own behalf, the confessor meets
with the practical argument : " He who fails to speak, loses all.
As a man pursues love, so fortune follows. As for forgetfulness,
no grace is to be obtained unless it be asked." And he advises
the lover, who confesses that he has sinned in this matter, to
" pull up a busy heart " and not to let any chance to speak
escape him.[1]

Another courtly notion which the poet opposes is that lovers
must approve themselves in arms. The lover argues that little
or no good can come from passing over the seas and slaying
the heathen. It would be better to spend time in converting
them in harmony with Christ's command than in slaying them
for the sake of glory. As for himself in particular, it would be
very foolish of him to cross the seas to fight Saracens, if in the
meantime he lost his lady at home.

The good sense which the lover manifests in this argument
is characteristic of him throughout the work. In portraying him
the author evinces his own sentiments toward courtly love.
Gower utilizes the conventions freely. Yet there emerges a
figure which is very different from the usual courtly lover. The
confessor sets before him, as we have seen, the qualities which
the courtly lover should have ; the hero falls short of the ideal
in many points. The confessor recites in detail the sins which
a lover should avoid ; the penitent admits that he is in many
respects a grievous offender. Throughout he is far less romantic
than the traditional lover, but he is far more human. A similar
departure from the courtly type appears in the lady. She is a
creature to be loved, but she is not the perfect being who is set
upon a pedestal and worshipped. She is indifferent to the
lover's passion, but her coldness is a matter of principle and
not of caprice. She is far from being " the abstract divinity of

[1] See bk. iv, l. 723.

the old lyric convention." [1] The homely quality in these two
pictures is highly significant. Obviously Gower found little to
his taste the extravagances of his predecessors in their delineation of the ideal lover and his *amie*.

Adulterous love, which was inherent in the courtly system,
Gower frankly condemns.

> The Madle is mad for the female,
> Bot where as on desireth fele,
> That nedeth noght be weis of kinde. . . .
> Forthi scholde every good mon knowe
> And thenke how that in mariage
> His trouthe plight lith in morgage,
> Which if he breke, it is falshode,
> And that discordeth to manhode (vii, 4215–4229).

Here the moralist speaks with no uncertain voice. This is
the doctrine he teaches in his *Traitié*, which he wrote, as he says,
"touchant lestat de matremoine dont les amantz marietz se
pourront essampler a tenir la foi de lour seintes espousailes." [2]
The examples he uses as warnings are such stock lovers as
Hercules, Jason, Helen, and others who took delight in wanton
love. Contrary to the old courtly idea that love and marriage
are incompatible, he exalts marriage and speaks rather slight-
ingly of love *par amours:* " Men see that the love *par amours*
is seldom without troubles arising from false envy and jangling.
But love leading to marriage dares show its face openly in all
places. It is a great wonder that maidens do not hasten to
that feste," Whereof the love is al honeste (iv, 1473–1484).

Elsewhere he is even more outspoken. The heading of the
Traitié reads : " Puisqu'il ad dit ci devant en Englois par voie
d'essample *la sotie de cellui qui par amours aime par especial*,
dirra ora apres en François a tout le monde en general un traitié

---

[1] W. P. Ker, *Essays on Medieval Literature*, p. 123.
[2] Macaulay, I, 379.

selonc les auctors pour essampler les amantz marietz, au fin q'ils la foi de lour seintes espousailes pourront par fine loialté guarder, . . ." [1] As the poet, at the end of the *Confessio*, declares that his Muse bids him to write no more of love which turns the heart from reason, and that he will therefore take his final leave of such love, so in this statement, which can refer only to the *Confessio*, he condemns completely the ideas put forth in that work. This is nothing more than we should expect of a man in whom the practical was so prominent, a man who decided to treat the subject of love only after having concluded that it was a task greater than he could compass to stretch his hand up to the heaven and set the world in order. [2]

[1] Macaulay, I, 379.   [2] *Confessio Amantis*, i, 1-5.

CHAPTER IV

THE ELEMENT OF LOVE IN CHAUCER'S WORKS

In examining the element of love in Chaucer's works,[1] we shall, for the sake of convenience, make a division of the poems which is purely arbitrary.

In the first group will be included those poems which are entirely lyric in quality, and which were composed on French models. This group falls into two parts : (1) those pieces which contain little or nothing but ideas common in the conventional love poems of contemporary French writers; and (2) those poems which, though in form following French models, are infused with the personality of the poet, and are written in the racy style characteristic of Chaucer at his best.

The second group consists of the *Complaint of Mars* and the *Anelida and Arcite*. They are classed together because of a certain similarity of structure, each of them containing a narrative portion followed by a lyric in the French style.

The third group comprises *The Book of the Duchess*, *The House of Fame*, and *The Parliament of Fowls*. These all have the form of the love-vision, common in Old French poetry.

The fourth group consists of the *Troilus* and the *Legend of Good Women*.[2]

The fifth and last group contains such parts of the *Canterbury Tales* as we may have to consider.

[1] The references are to the Oxford Chaucer, ed. by Skeat, Oxford, 1894–1897.

[2] The form of the Prologue to the *Legend* would justify us in classing it with the third group ; but the arrangement here adopted seems better on account of the close connection between the *Legend* and the *Troilus*.

In this arrangement, no account has been taken of chronology, and yet the order of the poems mentioned is roughly chronological. With the exception of the second subdivision of the first group, — poems which must have been written towards the end of Chaucer's life, — the order of the pieces is not far from the order in which they were composed.

Conventional Lyric Poems

The Complaint to Pity

The *Complaint to Pity* belongs to the large class of pieces in which the poet-lover laments the rigor of his lady. By translating the allegory into its underlying meaning, we shall make the conventional elements clearer:

The poet is unfortunate in his love. Although he is true and constant, the lady does not look with favor on his suit. This lady is the possessor of all the good qualities of the perfect being:

> Bountee parfit, wel armed and richely,
> And freshe Beautee, Lust and Jolitee,
> Assured Maner, Youthe and Honestee,
> Wisdom, Estat, and Dreed, and Governaunce.

One of her attributes, too, is pity, which however has not been spent on the unhappy lover (ll. 29–32). It is the conventional situation: a lady beautiful in person and character is cold and cruel to her devoted servant, and he utters his complaint. The " bille " itself, reduced to a single statement, is the lover's appeal for mercy and for relief from his woes. Other conventionalities may be seen in the idea of the malevolence of Love, conceived as a personality (ll. 4–6); in the lover's woes and pains, his service, and his declaration of its continuance (ll. 113–116).

The allegory is well sustained; briefly stated, it is: The poet, driven by pain of love, composes a bill of complaint against

Cruelty, which he intends to present to Pity, the "coroune of vertues alle." The charge is, that Cruelty, strengthening herself by an alliance with Bountee, Gentilesse, and Courtesy, and disguising herself in the shape of Womanly Beauty, has usurped the place of Pity in the realm of Feminine Virtues. Because of her being deposed, Manner and Gentilesse are of no avail, and Truth (representing the lover) can receive no help in his adversity. Wherefore, he begs Pity to break this "perilous alliaunce" and reassert her rights. Else shall lovers who have sought her grace be in despair.

This "bille" he intended to present to Pity; but after seeking her for many years, he at length found her dead and "buried in a heart." About the hearse stood Beauty, Lust, Jolitee, Assured Manner, Youth, Honesty, Wisdom, Estaat, Dread, and Governance. But none of them showed any sorrow for the death of Pity, for all were

Confedered bothe by bonde and alliaunce

with Cruelty, who had plotted to slay all lovers, and particularly the poet. Realizing that it would avail him nothing to complain to his foes, he puts up his "bille" and continues to suffer, feeling that for him the world is lost.

The poem is thoroughly in the style of the love lyrics of Deschamps and Machaut. There is some ingenuity displayed in the allegory; but it is no greater than we have seen in the French poems noticed earlier in this study. The language and ideas are all conventional, and the piece is very probably a translation or an adaptation of some Old French poem now lost.

A Complaint to His Lady

The story of the *Complaint to Pity* might serve equally well for the *Complaint to His Lady*. The situation is the same. Both belong to the class of poems in which the lover laments his hard

fate in love, caused by the coldness of the lady. A mention of
the well-known conventions of love-poetry which appear in the
Complaint will make clear the spirit of the piece.

Love is a personality; he is the deceptive god, who has brought
the lover into his present trouble. As in the *Romance of the
Rose*, the god has used his darts on the unfortunate lover, and
after thus subduing him, has taught him his art:

> Thus am I sleyn with Loves fyry dart,
> I can but love hir best, my swete fo;
> Love hath me taught no more of his art
> But serve alwey, and stinte for no wo.

The lady is endowed with all excellent qualities, but her sur-
name " Faire Rewthelees " indicates that she is lacking in the
gentle virtue of pity. She recks not whether her lover floats or
sinks; nor does she deign to think on his woe, or in any wise
to take heed of the heavy life he leads for her sake. The more
he loves her, the less (he finds) she cares for him, the more she
makes him " smerte "; wherefore, he sees that he may in no
wise escape death.

Until death relieves him, however, the lover determines to
serve his lady; and whatsoever woe he suffers, she shall not drive
him from her service. He is the least worthy of all the servants,
good or bad, that such a fair being must have; all he asks is to
be allowed to serve her as best he can, for he is not so rash nor
so mad as to desire that she, who is so good, love him, who is so
little worthy. He is obedient to her as a servant to his master.
No one living would more gladly fulfil her heart's wish than he,
and had he power equal to his will, she should see how fain he
is to add to her pleasure.

He undergoes the sufferings incident to such a passion : his
sorrow keeps him awake; the long night, when every creature
should have its rest, he spends in lamenting that nothing but
death may relieve him from his sorrow.

Here again, as in the *Complaint to Pity*, none but conventional ideas are found ; and the language is equally conventional with the ideas. The piece is devoid of any mark of the poet's personality, — either of that tone of sincerity which is felt in his best lyrics, or of that humor which he often employs in so charming a manner in his later work.

The Complaint of Venus

In utilizing the *balades* of the French poet Granson, Chaucer has made an interesting change. Instead of putting the words in the mouth of a lover, he has made the lady the speaker. In so doing, he has not employed any idea or language that was not conventional ; but it is interesting to note what changes were necessary. These appear in the following summaries of the two poems.[1]

CHAUCER	GRANSON
I	I
1. No comfort is so great when I am in sorrow, as to think of the manhood, worthiness, truth and steadfastness of him, whose I am entirely, and always shall be. No one ought to blame me, for every one praises his " gentilesse."	1. No comfort is so great when I cannot speak to my lady, as to think of her worth and her sweet womanly deeds. She is my life ; no one can blame me, for every one praises her.
2. In him, more than any one can guess, dwells beauty, wisdom, good conduct ; he is the flower of knighthood, the soul of honor and of nobility.	2. In her, more than any one can guess, is bounty, beauty, and grace. It is a great blessing that the gods have assembled all good in so small a place. Honor wishes to honor her above all. Never have I seen so sweet, so pleasing, so noble a woman.

[1] In these, the language of the summary of Chaucer's poem is used in that of the French poem, as far as is possible in a faithful rendering of the ideas of the latter.

3. Notwithstanding all his worthiness, he is humble and gentle before me, and is attentive to serve and honor me in all things. I ought to bless my good fortune; for everybody praises his "gentilesse."

3. Wherever she is, she does good, and effaces evil. She knows well how to laugh and to play. She brings delight and "solace" to all. None can refrain from looking at her; and her look is worth all the wealth of a kingdom.

II

1. It is fitting, Love, that men should pay dearly for what you give; they must wake when they should sleep, fast when they should eat, weep instead of laugh, complain instead of sing; they must cast down their visages, and often change their color; they must complain while they sleep, and dream when they should dance.

2. Jealousy spies upon everything, and turns all however reasonable, to harm. Love is dearly bought; he gives inordinately; but he gives little pleasure, and much sorrow.

3. Love's gift is pleasing for a while; but "ful encomberous is the using"; for jealousy disturbs lovers, and causes them fear, and suffering, and uncertainty.

II

(Chaucer's version is here a sufficiently close translation of Granson's verses to render it unnecessary to epitomize the latter.)

III

1. But I do not say this, Love, as though I wished to escape from your power. I have been in your service so long that I will never leave it, no matter how jealousy torments me. It is sufficient for me to see him when I may; I will always be true to him.

III

But be certain, Love, that I do not say this as wishing to escape from your power. I have borne my martyrdom so long, that, while I live, I will endure it. It suffices me to have so much of "solace" as comes from seeing my fair and gracious one. Although she be "dangerous," I will never cease to serve her.

2. And certainly, Love, when I consider the "estate" of men, I see that you, through your generosity, have made me choose the best on earth. Therefore, my heart, love on; let jealousy do its worst; for I shall never cease to love him.

3. My heart, it ought to be sufficient for you, that Love has shown such grace to you, that he has led you to choose the worthiest in every way. He is my sufficiency, and I will not seek for any other.

2. And certainly, Love, when I consider the "estate" of men, I see that you have made me choose the best possible love. Therefore, my heart, love on; for you will never have pain so grievous on account of my lady, that I shall not be joyous; and I shall never cease to serve her.

3. My heart, it ought to be sufficient for you that you have chosen her whom you have. Seek now neither kingdom nor empire; for so good a one you will never find, nor so fair a one will you ever see.

" C'est jeunesce sachant et savoureuse."

Though she be disdainful of my love, I will never cease to serve her.

Chaucer's poem is interesting as an example of the comparatively small number of pieces in which the lady tells of her lover. We note that he here has the usual characteristics expected of the courtly lover; namely, manhood, worthiness, "truth," steadfastness, "gentilesse," bounty, wisdom, good conduct, honor, nobility — in short, all virtues are his. Notwithstanding this, his behavior toward her is that of a humble servant, and this behavior he consistently maintains.

If we turn to the French poem, we find the lover singing of the good qualities of his mistress; these are the conventional ones of bounty, beauty, grace, worth (valour) — all shown in her womanly deeds. She is accomplished and brings happiness to all with whom she comes in contact.

In the second *balade*, both poems enumerate the conventional effects of love: sleeplessness, loss of appetite, weeping, sadness, solitariness, and loss of color. Jealousy is execrated, and the sad fact that the course of true love never did run smooth is lamented.

In the third *balade*, the English again differs from the French. The lovers of both poems congratulate themselves that Love has made them bestow their affections in the best possible place. But both are disturbed in their happiness; the lady is bothered by jealousy; the man meets his usual enemy in the "daunger" of his lady. Yet both alike vow to be true — the lady will continue to love her lover, and the man to serve his mistress.

The conventionality of the two productions is alike, and neither has the advantage over the other as regards cleverness. Indeed, with the exception of the alterations made necessary by the change of the speaker, Chaucer's poem, as he says, rather faithfully follows

> word by word the curiositee,
> Of Graunson, flour of hem that make in Fraunce.

Against Women Unconstant

In the French erotic poetry, especially in that of Deschamps, there are a considerable number of pieces in which a lover, man or woman, takes his or her love to task for some fault. One or two examples we have seen in the *Cinkante Balades* of Gower; the ballade *Against Women Inconstant* is one of Chaucer's contributions to this class.

Madam, on account of your " newe-fanglenesse," you have destroyed many a lover's happiness. I am through with your fickleness; for I know that you cannot bestow your love in one place half a year at a time.

Your love is like an image in a mirror, which comes and goes. You are like a weather-cock that turns his face with every wind. You deserve to be canonized better than Dalilah, Cressida, or Candace.

> For ever in chaunging stant your sikernesse;
> To newe thing your lust is ever kene;
> In stede of blew, thus may ye were al grene.

Compleint d'Amours

In the case of the *Compleint d'Amours* no analysis is necessary. The piece does not contain an idea or a sentiment that was not thoroughly conventional. The lofty position of the lady ; her power over the lover's life and death ; her disdain of his passion ; his feeling of unworthiness ; his protestation of service till death ; his unwillingness to blame the lady for his woes ; the conceit that the eyes are the lover's enemies ; the idea of sending a complaint to the cruel one on Saint Valentine's Day, — all were the stock ideas of mediaeval love-poetry.

A Balade of Complaint · Womanly Noblesse

Unlike the other lyrics so far considered, the *Balade of Complaint* and *Womanly Noblesse* have a ring of sincerity that surprises us, even though these poems come from the pen of Chaucer. It is true that the sentiments expressed are conventional, and that they are somewhat piled up besides. Still, both poems produce an impression of genuine feeling. The second piece in particular shows well the ability of the poet to stamp his own individuality upon his work. There is a charm in the delight with which the lover exalts his lady's worth by addressing her in the envoy in four different complimentary phrases, as well as in the simple humility with which he recommends himself. The beauty of the expression, the music of the language, the feeling of completeness which is left on the reader's mind, are all delightful and admirable.

> Auctor of norture, lady of plesaunce,
> Soveraine of beaute, flour of wommanhede,
> Take ye non hede unto myn ignoraunce,
> But this receyveth of your goodlihede,
> Thinking that I have caught in remembraunce
> Your beaute hool, your stedfast governaunce.

The observations thus far made on Chaucer's early lyrics have a further significance which it may be worth while to point out before dismissing them from consideration. Some of these poems have been taken to furnish evidence of a " long, early, and hopeless " love-affair of the poet's own.[1] This view, although revived of late by Mr. Coulton,[2] is now pretty thoroughly discredited, and arguments against it are hardly necessary.[3] But we may observe that the utterly conventional character of the pieces in question would go far to destroy any confidence we might have in their autobiographical value. If occasionally they ring true, this is accounted for by the genius of Chaucer. The same dramatic power which he manifests everywhere in his narrative writing produces the conviction of truth when he writes in the first person. But the fiction is none the less to be recognized as such. Poets of the period were always writing in the first person and complaining of the misfortunes of love.[4] Yet very few of their poems are held to express personal feeling. The *Confessio Amantis*, which we have already considered, is an instructive case in point. For here we appear to have an elaborate story which we should accept as genuine if we accepted Chaucer's. But Gower has prefixed a Latin note which forbids such an interpretation : *Hic quasi in persona aliorum, quos amor alligat, fingens se auctor esse Amantem, varias eorum passiones variis hujus libri distinccionibus per singula scribere proponit.*[5]

---

[1] See particularly Furnivall's *Trial Forewards* to the *Parallel Text Edition of Chaucer's Minor Poems*, 1871, pp. 12, 15, 31, 32, 34, 57, 58, 89–90, 92, and Notes, pp. 112, 114, 119, 120; also Koch, *The Chronology of Chaucer's Writings*, 1890, pp. 7, 23, 25.   [2] G. G. Coulton, *Chaucer and his England*, London, 1908, p. 23.

[3] An effective argument against Dr. Furnivall's theory was made by Professor Lounsbury in his *Studies in Chaucer*, New York, 1892, I, 210 ff.

[4] Citations are hardly necessary, but reference may be made to the numerous ballades, roundels, and complaints of Machaut, Deschamps, and Froissart. With regard to the *Cinkante Balades* of Gower see Macaulay's ed., I, Introduction, p. lxxii. Another striking example is the *Livre du Voir-Dit* of Machaut. Cf. the references given above on p. 34.

[5] Macaulay's ed., II, 37, marginal note.

Lyrics showing the Poet's Personality

Merciles Beaute — *a Triple Roundel*

None but conventional ideas appear in the *Merciles Beaute*. The conceit of beauty striking the lover's eyes and wounding his heart, was a favorite one with the troubadours and Chrétien de Troies. To pass from the abstract to the concrete, and to make a specific part of the lady's beauty, the eyes, the agent of the lover's undoing, is but a step, which had been taken long before Chaucer wrote.[1] The lady's ability to heal the wound, her power over the life of the lover, and his certain death if she does not intervene, are all familiar traits in Chaucer's predecessors.

In the second and third roundels, conventional allegory is employed to express conventional ideas. In the second, the theme is the common one of the lady's coldness. Danger has bound Mercy in his chain, and Beauty has driven Pity out of the heart. In the third, Love is a malevolent personality. Lovers become lean from languishing in his prison. But the poet, thanks to the lady's rejection of him, has escaped from his custody, and has retained his flesh too. The contrast between the apparent seriousness of the first two parts and the playfulness of the third gives the poem its charm. It is a good example of Chaucer's ability to work with materials and ideas which are thoroughly

---

[1] For instance, in the roundel of William d'Amiens :

> Jamais ne serai saous
> d'esguarder les vairs ieus dous
> qui m'ont ocis.

Bartsch, *Chrestomathie de l'ancien Français* Leipsic, 1866, p. 315.

See also the lyric of the Provençal Peirol (1189–1225):

> Be m trahiron siey belh huelh
> Cum a fals messatge
> E m'an mes ins el coratge
> S'amor don mi duelh.

Mahn, *Die Werke der Troubadours*, II, 23.

conventional, and yet to vitalize them with his own individuality. Only Chaucer could have written :

> Love hath my name y-strike out of his sclat,
> And he is strike out of. my bokes clene
> Forevermo; ther is non other mene.
> Sin I fro Love escaped am so fat,
> I never thenke to ben in his prison lene;
> Sin I am free, I counte him not a bene.

Balade to Rosemounde

The subject of the graceful *Balade to Rosemounde* is the lover's protestations of devotion and service to the lady, even though he receives no encouragement in his suit. The situation is humorously pictured in the third stanza :

> Nas never pyk walwed in galauntyne
> As I in love am walwed and y-wounde;
> For which ful ofte I of my-self divyne
> That I am trewe Tristam the secounde;
> I brenne ay in an amorous plesaunce.
> Do what you list, I wil your thral be founde,
> Thogh ye to me ne do no daliaunce.

He has his woes, and weeps, as a lover should ; yet the sight of his lady's perfect beauty, her merry joyous bearing, and the sound of her " seemly voys " heal his wounds, and it suffices him merely to love her.

The attribution of perfect qualities of body and heart to the lady is, of course, conventional. The idea of the lover's pain being eased by a sight of her laughter and smiles ; the protestation of perfect truth and continued service; the sufficiency of love though unrewarded, — all these ideas are as old as the troubadours.

Though the sentiments are all conventional, the spirit of Chaucer's treatment of them is his own. We catch a glimpse of his individuality in the blending of the serious with the humorous, which is so characteristic of him. In the ballade, whether he intends to burlesque the extravagance of contemporary love-poetry, or his natural humor gets the better of the seriousness with which he wishes to treat his subject, the effect is equally pleasing. The idea of the poet's weeping " of teres ful a tyne " and of his being " walwed and y-wounde" in love as a "pyk walwed in galauntyne " is delightful ; and the humor lifts this little poem far above the insipid amorous ballades on which it is modeled.

The Complaint to his Purse and The Envoy to Scogan

Chaucer has left to the world two delightful pieces in which he has utilized for the central ideas, to be treated humorously, a feature or features of courtly love. The first of these pieces, we need only mention ; it is *The Complaint to his Empty Purse.* As the courtly lover complains to his lady of her coldness and disdain, so Chaucer complains to his purse that it is light, and beseeches it to be heavy again, and thus save his life :

> Be hevy agayn, or elles mot I dye!

Chaucer, at this time, was an old man (it was the year before his death),[1] and this was his appeal for help to King Henry IV, whom in the Envoy he calls " conquerour of Brutes Albioun." Charming as the humor is, pathos is not wanting when we remember the circumstances. We recognize again the individuality of the poet, who, though in misfortune, kept a cheerful face to the world and brightened an appeal for help with that gaiety which no adversity could destroy.

Another poem of undoubted autobiographical interest is the *Envoy to Scogan.* The theme is the blasphemy of Chaucer's friend Scogan against the divinities of love, and the result of his sin. Scogan had spoken

> Swich thing as in the lawe of love forbode is.

[1] If the Envoy was written at the same time as the *balade.*

This mention of the law of love is interesting as showing that the conception, which was as old as the troubadours, was still alive. The reference is, of course, to the principle of the courtly system, that lovers must not expect to obtain the object of their desire too easily, but that the service of love is sufficient reward in itself. This principle is nowhere better expressed than in the words of Pandarus :

> What ! many a man hath love ful dere y-bought
> Twenty winter that his lady wiste,
> That never yet his lady mouth he kiste.
> What ! shulde he therfor fallen in despeyr,
> Or be recreaunt for his owne tene,
> Or sleen himself, al be his lady fayr ?
> Nay, nay, but ever in oon be fresh and grene
> To serve and love his dere hertes quene,
> And thenke it is a guerdon hir to serve
> A thousand-fold more than he can deserve.[1]

It was this law that Scogan had been guilty of breaking when he declared that he gave up his lady at Michaelmas, because she heeded not his distress. He had been guilty further of calling Cupid to witness that he had spoken this blasphemy. The result was that Venus was in tears, and Cupid was angry. The tears of the goddess are deluging all the region of Greenwich, and the poet is afraid that equally dire consequences will follow from the wrath of Cupid. For although both Scogan and the poet have nothing to fear from the god's arrows, yet on account of the former's blasphemy, there is danger

> Lest . . . the wreche of Love procede
> On alle hem that ben hore and rounde of shape,
> That ben so lykly folk in love to spede.

This is a clever use to which to put the old conventions ; and as in the *Complaint to his Purse*, the humor is heightened by the serious personal element. After bantering his friend in his

---

[1] *Troilus and Criseyde*, bk. i, st. 116–117.

delightful way, quickly as the cloud follows the sunshine on a summer day the tone changes. The poet thinks of the instability of impressions made by human effort, and makes the melancholy observation:

> But al shal passen that men prose or ryme;
> Take every man his turn, as for his tyme.

POEMS PART NARRATIVE AND PART LYRIC

The Complaint of Mars

In the *Complaint of Mars* the interest is rather astronomical than human. With the astronomy, however, we are not at present concerned.

The poet hears a bird singing before sunrise on Saint Valentine's day. After a short preliminary exhortation to lovers, the bird tells the Ovidian story of Mars and Venus, and concludes by repeating at full length the complaint of Mars for the loss of his lady. The god tells of his devotion to Venus, of her beauty, and of her other excellences. The mention of his distress leads him to speak of the woes which lovers suffer, and of the instability of their happiness. He ends with an appeal for sympathy addressed to the brave knights of renown who are of his "division," to all true ladies, and to all lovers who have received the aid of Venus.

Ideas commonly used in love-poetry are seen in the allusion to the fear of slanderers, in the lines which speak of "the god that sit so hye" as constraining us to love against our will, and in all the remarks on the woes and sorrows of lovers; but the conventional features relate, for the most part, to the figure of the lady.

> My lady is the verrey sours and welle
> Of beaute, lust, fredom, and gentilnesse,
> Of riche aray, . . .
> Of al disport in which men frendly dwelle,

> Of love and pley, and of benigne humblesse,
> Of soun of instruments of al swetnesse;
> And therto so wel fortuned and thewed,
> That through the world hir goodnesse is yshewed.

Her beauty is the cause of Mars's passion, though not of his present sorrow. It is like the famous brooch of Thebes, which was fashioned with such art that no one could resist its charm, but whoever laid eyes on it must either possess it or go mad. Yet the possessor was in constant fear; and after he had parted with it, he had double the woe for having given it up. The blame for all this sorrow was not his who desired the brooch, but his who fashioned it so cunningly. So is it with the beauty of Venus:

> For thogh my lady have so gret beaute,
> That I was mad til I had gete her grace,
> She was not cause of myn adversite,
> But he that wroghte hir, also mot I thee,
> That putte such a beaute in hir face,
> That made me to covete and purchace
> Myn owne deth.

This paragon of excellence occupies the usual position of superiority. The lover is her servant, humble, docile, and patient. He binds himself to perpetual obedience, and after he has lost her, he still vows lasting service.

"This worthy Mars, that is of knighthod welle," has, like other lovers, his woes and sorrows. Since the story deals with the intrigue after the lady has been won, we miss the troubles with which the lover is usually burdened. His own particular woe in loving his lady leads him to remark:

> Alas! that ever lovers mot endure
> For love, so many a perilous aventure!

Among the sorrows of lovers, Mars mentions coldness of ladies, the slanderous tongues of envious people, and in general,

> he that hath with love to done
> Hath ofter wo then changed is the mone.

Our summary of the conventional elements of the poem shows that it is, as Mr. Manly calls it, " a mere exercise of ingenuity in describing a supposed astronomical event in terms of human action and emotion " ; [1] and that, of human emotion, it sounds no great depths. The narrative is conducted with Chaucer's usual skill. There is cleverness, too, in the *Complaint* proper, in the use of the two very apt illustrations of the fish hook and the brooch of Thebes. Such illustrations are exceptional in this kind of poetry ; but the ideas which they illuminate are wholly conventional.

Anelida and Arcite

The *Anelida and Arcite*, like the *Complaint of Mars*, consists of two parts : a narrative portion and a lyric in the form of a complaint. Of the latter, little need be said. The varieties of metre indicate that the poet is exercising his ingenuity. It is written on French models and contains little that is new. For the most part, it exhibits no great spontaneity. The elaborate stanzaic devices produce an effect of artificiality, which the sentiments, ideas, and language serve only to strengthen.[2] In the narrative, on the other hand, there is abundant vitality and spirit. Though the stock ideas are used, their conventionality is not conspicuous. In the description of the " newe lady," who was all of another kind from the trusting Anelida, the commonplace of

[1] Harvard *Studies and Notes*, 1907, p. 124. Shirley's statement (Furnivall, *Trial Forewords*, p. 80) that the poem has reference to the intrigue of the Duchess of York and the Earl of Huntingdon lacks evidence, and in view of the conventionality pointed out above it seems unlikely.

[2] In one or two passages of the *Complaint*, however, pathos is unmistakable. Take, for instance, the lines :

> And if I slepe a furlong wey or tweye,
> Than thinketh me that your figure
> Before me stant, clad in asure,
> To profren eft a newe asure
> For to be trewe and mercy me to preye.

the lady's coldness appears; but the freshness of the language makes us forget the triteness of the sentiments. The new lady gives Arcite his fill of " daunger " and

> holdeth him so narowe
> Up by the brydel, at the staves ende,
> That every word, he dradde hit as an arowe;
> Hir daunger made him bothe bowe and bende,
> And, as hir liste, made him turne or wende.

There are allusions, too, to the lover's humility, and to his sorrows; but here again is seen the same refreshing manner of expressing such ideas. The new lady, the poet tells us,

> ne graunted him in hir livinge
> No grace, why that he hath lust to singe.

Most of the conventions of the love literature find their root in real life. In Chaucer's better work, such ideas take on their original naturalness; and this is true in the narrative portion of *Anelida and Arcite*. On the whole, students and critics have underrated the merit of this remarkable poem.

The Earlier Love-Vision Poems

The general relation of *The Book of the Duchess, The House of Fame, The Parliament of Fowls*, and the Prologue to the *Legend of Good Women* to the Old French love-visions has been made clear by Professor Sypherd,[1] who has proved conclusively that Chaucer was writing under the immediate influence of French models. The form, the setting, and the devices employed for heightening the interest in the English poems are all " determined by the literary *genre* of the love-vision." [2] Disregarding the form and setting, therefore, we may proceed to examine the element of love.

[1] Sypherd, *Studies in Chaucer's "Hous of Fame,"* Chaucer Society Publications, 1907.   [2] Ibid., p. 10.

The Book of the Duchess

In the *Book of the Duchess* the poet relates a dream. One morning in May he was awakened by the singing of birds. As he lay there listening, the sun's rays streamed through the windows, in the stained glass of which were wrought the stories of famous lovers, and lighted up the chamber walls, which were painted " bothe text and glose " with all the story of the *Romance of the Rose*. At the sound of a hunter's horn he quickly left his bed, joined the hunting party, and rode away. The chase was soon abandoned. As he walked from the tree where he had been stationed, a whelp came by him and fawned on him. He tried to catch it, but it fled. Following it, he was led through a flowery path into a beautiful green wood. As he gazed at the many wonders about him, he was aware of a man dressed in black sitting near him, and lamenting in a pitiful manner the death of his lady. Out of pure sympathy, the poet accosted him and offered to relieve him of his woe, as far as he was able. The man in black tells how he has lost his queen in a game of chess which he played with Fortune. At the poet's request, he then tells the story of how he wooed and won the fair lady, and how they lived together in happiness till death took her from him. This courtship and marriage is the real subject of the poem, and this is the part in which we are here especially interested.

The *Book of the Duchess* is among the earliest of Chaucer's works. Naturally, therefore, we find in it abundant use of conventional ideas and language. The knight in black relates his courtship and marriage in the general style of the contemporary love story. The love deity appears as a feudal lord. The knight says :

> Sir . . . sith first I couthe
> Have any maner wit fro youthe, —
> . . . I have ever yit
> Be tributary, and yiven rente
> To Love hooly with god entente,

> And through plesaunce become his thral,
> With good wil, body, herte, and al.
> Al this I putte in his servage,
> As to my lord, and dide homage.

This conception of the deity is not consistently maintained; immediately, Love becomes a god to whom the lover prays:

> And ful devoutly prayde him to,
> He shulde besette myn herte so,
> That it plesaunce to him were,
> And worship to my lady dere.

This prayer was answered after many years.[1]

The perfections of the lady, both physical and spiritual, her position of superiority, her indifference to the lover, are all told in the conventional way. Her physical beauty is described in minute detail in lines which, like much of the rest of the poem, are taken from Machaut's *Jugement dou Roy de Behaigne*.[2]

It is to the credit of Chaucer's delicacy that he has left out some of the suggestiveness of his original. A common method in the mediaeval descriptions of womanly beauty was to enumerate such charms as were visible, and conclude with a hint of what was concealed. For example, in Chrétien's *Cligès*, Alexander tells how he has been struck by the dart of Love. The dart is the beauty of Soredamours. The golden tresses are the feather; the forehead, eyes, nose, cheeks, mouth, teeth, chin, ears, throat, bosom, — all go to make up the dart. Having described all these, he adds:

> Ne m'an mostra Amor adons
> Fors que la coche et les penons;
> Car la fleche iert el coivre mise:
> C'est li bliauz et la chemise,
> Don la pucele estoit vestue.[3]

[1] See ll. 835 ff.   [2] See Kittredge, *Modern Philology*, VIII, 465 ff.
[3] Chrétien de Troies, *Cligès*, ll. 853–857.

Alain de Lille, in *De Planctu Naturae,* after a similar list of the beautiful features of Nature, says : " Caetera vero quae thalamus secretior absentabat, meliora fides esse loquebatur." [1] So, Boccaccio, with reference to Emilia :

> quale poi fosse
> La parte agli occhi del corpo celata,
> Colui sel seppe per cui ella cosse
> Avanti con amor lunga fiäta:
> Immagino che a dirlo le mie posse
> Non basterieno avendola io veduta ;
> Tal d'ogni ben doveva esser compiuta.[2]

We have already noted that Gower's lover adopts the same method ; [3] and in the poem of Machaut which, as we have observed, was Chaucer's model in this part of the *Book of the Duchess,* the usual procedure is followed.

> Dou remenant
> Que pas ne vi, dame, vous di je tout
> Qu'a nature tout estoit respondant,
> Bien fassoné et de taille excellent.[4]

These lines, however, do not recur in Chaucer.

Every good quality of mind and heart is attributed by the knight in black to his lady : moderation, " goodly speche," goodness, " trouthe," lack of coquetry, and chastity. These, like her physical beauties, are dwelt upon at length, as is appropriate in such a eulogy. The significance of Chaucer's elaborate treatment of the lady's character will be mentioned later. Here, we merely note the conventional idea of the lover's depicting his lady as a being perfect in all her attributes of mind and heart.

[1] Alain de Lille, *De Planctu Naturae,* ed. Thomas Wright in *The Anglo-Latin Satirical Poets of the Twelfth Century,* London, 1872, II, 432.

[2] Boccaccio, *Teseide,* xii, st. 63 ; in *Opere Volgari,* ed. I. Moutier, 1827–1831, Vol. X.   [3] *Confessio Amantis,* vi, 780–781. See p. 56, above.

[4] *Le Jugement dou Roy de Behaigne,* ll. 380–383.

The position of the lady with regard to the lover is the conventional one of superiority. The feudal figure is employed. The lover is a vassal and makes his vows to be a true and devoted servant. Describing his first sight of the Duchess, he expresses the very old sentiment :

> . . . purely tho myn owne thoght
> Seyde hit were bet serve hir for noght
> Than with another to be wel.[1]

The idea is reiterated in the lines :

> But as my wit coude best suffyse,
> After my yonge childly wit,
> Withoute drede, I besette hit
> To love hir in my beste wyse,
> To do hir worship and servyse
> That I tho coude, by my trouthe,
> Withoute feyning outher slouthe.

After the usual fortunes of the lover, the lady came to understand that he

> . . . ne wilned thing but good,
> And worship, and to kepe hir name
> Over al thing, and drede hir shame,
> And was so besy hir to serve,

and so she gave him " al hooly the noble yift of hir mercy " ; and, as he says of himself,

> In alle my youthe, in alle chaunce,
> She took me in hir governaunce.

In the attitude of the lady toward the lover, conventional ideas appear, partly in allusions and partly in actual description. In his raptures over her eyes, the lover remarks :

> Her eyen semed anoon she wolde
> Have mercy ; fooles wenden so ;
> But hit was never the rather do ;

---

[1] We may compare this statement with the following words of the Provençal Rambaud d'Orange :

> E platz mi mais viure desesperatz,
> Que si ieu fos altra domn' amatz (Raynouard, III, 17).

and again:

> But ever, me thoghte, hir eyen seyde,
> " By god, my wrathe is al foryive ! "

The same idea of the lady's wrath is alluded to in the poet's question to the lover, regarding his loss:

> " What los is that, sir ? " quod I tho;
> " Nil she not love yow ? is it so ?
> Or have ye oght y-doon amis,
> That she hath left yow ? is hit this ? "

The lover, telling of his fear to speak his passion, explains:

> . . . I durste noght
> For al this worlde telle hir my thoght,
> Ne I wolde have wratthed hir trewely,

and again, he tells how he debated within himself:

> And, but I telle hir, I nam but deed;
> And if I telle hir, to seye sooth,
> I am adred she wol be wrooth.

All these allusions indicate the conventional attitude of indifference on the lady's part.

The effects of the lover's passion are set forth in the usual way : he suffers sorrow and woe ; yet he is silent because he fears to tell his love. When he finally speaks, only to be refused, his woe is greater than ever.

> Allas ! that day
> The sorwe I suffred, and the wo !
> That trewly Cassandra, that so
> Bewayled the destruccioun
> Of Troye and of Ilioun,
> Had never swich sorwe as I tho.
> I durste no more say therto
> For pure fere, but stal away ;
> And thus I lived ful many a day:
> That trewely, I hadde no need
> Further than my beddes heed
> Never a day to seche sorwe ;
> I fond it redy every morwe.

The lover finds, however, the conventional relief from his sorrows. The sight of his lady is a sovereign remedy:

> wonder fayn I wolde hir see.
> So mochel hit amended me,
> That, whan I saw hir first amorwe,
> I was warished of al my sorwe
> Of al day after, til hit were eve;
> Me thoughte nothing mighte me greve,
> Were my sorowes never so smerte.

In this the lover shows that he is availing himself of the comforts promised by the god of Love to his followers: Dous-Penser, Dous-Parler, and Dous-Regard.[1] It was the last of these which came to the relief of the lover. Another solace he found, too, like the unhappy Aurelius, in making "songs, compleintes, roundels, virelayes."[2]

> Trewely I did my besinesse
> To make songes, as I best coude,
> And ofte tyme I song hem loude;
> And made songes a gret del . . .
> . . . songes thus I made
> Of my feling, myn herte to glade.

Here again, he did what all lovers were expected to do, and what was commanded by the god of Love in the *Romance of the Rose*. It was a part of the god's directions to the lover,

> . . . for thy lady sake
> Songes and complayntes that thou make.[3]

Another conventional effect of the lover's passion is seen in the usual experience of confusion and loss of speech, fear and loss of color, when attempting to declare his love:

---

[1]   ge te doing
> Trois autres biens, qui grans solas
> Font à ceus qui en mes las.
>
> *Roman de la Rose*, ll. 2728-2730.

[2] *Franklin's Tale*, l. 948.   [3] *Romance of the Rose*, ll. 2325-2326.

> I not wel how that I began,
> Ful evel rehersen hit I can ;
> And eek, as helpe me god withal,
> I trowe hit was in the dismal,
> That was the ten woundes of Egipte,
> For many a word I over-skipte
> In my tale, for pure fere
> Lest my wordes mis-set were.
> With sorweful herte, and woundes dede,
> Softe and quaking for pure drede,
> And shame, and stinting in my tale
> For ferde, and myn hewe al pale,
> Ful ofte I wex bothe pale and reed ;
> Bowing to hir, I heng the heed ;
> I durste not ones loke hir on,
> For wit, manere, and al was gon.
> I seyde " mercy ! " and no more ;
> Hit was no game, hit sat me sore.

The favorite conceit of Chrétien de Troies, that love enters the heart through the eyes, also appears.

There remain to be noted two ideas, which are not merely literary conventions, but which perhaps reflect views held by contemporary lovers. The first is one which we have already met, that it is the paramount duty of young people to engage in the service of love. As far back as Andreas, the god of Love is represented as meting out punishment to those who do not serve him. Gower uses the idea in connection with his tale of Rosiphelee.[1] Pandarus refuses to believe that Criseyde will not, in time, bestow her favor upon Troilus, since

> Was never man ne woman yet bigete
> That was unapt to suffren loves hete
> Celestial, or elles love of kinde,

[1] Among the gentil nacion
Love is an occupacion
Which forto kepe his lustes save
Scholde every gentil herte have.

Confessio Amantis, iv, **1451-1454.**

and Criseyde, as he says, was never " celestial." When Troilus,
too, came to experience the tender passion, which, although he
had reached the years of maturity, he had never felt, this same
priest of Love, Pandarus, welcomed him into the fold as a repent-
ant sinner, one whom

> Love of his goodnesse
> Hath . . . converted out of wikkednesse.[1]

And so the sorrowing knight of our poem tells how from his
youth, since he had had any comprehension or understanding,
he had been tributary to Love and had become his thrall, with
good will, body, heart, and all. This childish love remained for
a long time purely ideal, unbestowed upon anyone, but ready to
be transformed into a real passion for his lady, when he should
meet her :

> And this was longe, and many a yeer
> Or that myn herte was set o-wher,
> That I did thus, and niste why.

This feature Chaucer took from Machaut.[2]

The other idea to be noted is that lovers must go on expeditions in order to win favor with their ladies. The knight, in
speaking of the sincerity of the Duchess, says that she did *not*

> . . . sende men into Walakye,
> To Pruyse and into Tartarye,
> To Alisaundre, ne into Turkye,
> And bidde him faste anoon that he
> Go hoodles to the drye see,

---

[1] *Troilus and Criseyde*, i, st. 143.

[2] Coulton (*Chaucer and his England*, pp. 223 ff.) mentions, as an excellent
comment on the passage, the conversation between the little Saintré and the
lady of the Fair Cousins. Calling the little Jehan, who was then only thirteen
years old, before her, she makes him miserable by demanding of him the
name of the lady whom he loves best *par amours*, and how long it is since he
had seen her. Unable to answer her, because he did not understand the
mystery of *love par amours*, he is dismissed in disgrace. But he is called up
another day, and another, and yet another, until, in order to escape her badger-
ing, the little fellow confesses to her in tears that she herself is his love
(*Jehan de Saintré*, chap. iii, pp. 8 ff.).

> And come hoom by the Carrenar;
> And seye, " Sir, be now right war
> That I may of yow here seyn
> Worship, or that ye come ageyn ! "
> She ne used no suche knakkes smale.

Machaut, in his *Dit du Lion,* describes different kinds of lovers. One kind, he says, are the " dous, humble, courtois," who go beyond the seas into forays, battles, and upon various adventures, in order that they may stand high in their ladies' favor. When they return, their stay with their ladies is but short, " for if there should be an expedition into Austria or Bohemia, into Hungary or Denmark, or into any foreign land, . . . into France or into England, they would go there to seek honor."[1] Gower also, as we have seen, refers to the same custom. It is note-worthy that neither Chaucer nor Gower treats it sympathetically. Gower devotes one hundred and twenty-two lines to arguments against the notion that lovers must approve themselves in arms; and the knight, in Chaucer's poem, names the sending of lovers on such expeditions as one of the things his perfect lady did not do, with the significant comment,

> She ne used no suche knakkes smale.

Enough has been said to prove that the conventions of courtly love are abundantly represented in the *Book of the Duchess;* indeed, they make up most of the six hundred lines with which we are especially concerned. Here, as elsewhere in Chaucer's love-poetry, the originality consists not in the invention of new material, but in the vitality he infuses into what is old and out-worn. How, then, does this vitalization appear in the *Book of the Duchess?* First of all, in the setting. The spring morning with the songs of birds, blue skies, green fields and woods and beautiful flowers, had been used as setting for love-poems for hundreds of years. Yet, when Chaucer employs it, we at once

---

[1] *Les Œuvres de Guillaume de Machault*, ed. P. Tarbé, Paris, 1849, pp. 40 ff.

feel that freshness which is characteristic of so much of his work. When he describes the singing of birds, the bright sunlight streaming through his windows, the clear sky, old ideas take on new life under his touch, and we feel in them a charm that defies analysis. We forget the triteness of the matter in the vividness of its presentation.

Something more than mere convention appears, too, in the character of the lover-knight. In describing his passion for the fair duchess, he repeats ideas that have been in use since the time of the troubadours. Yet we are persuaded that his passion is genuine. His account of his lady's perfections is hyperbolical; yet we attribute the exaggeration to love and grief.

Most of all does Chaucer's originality appear in the treatment of the lady. For, though the details are not original, they are so skilfully combined that there emerges what Lowell has called "one of the most beautiful portraits of a woman that were ever drawn."[1] Even after the parallels in Machaut are noted, extending even to identity of phrase, one remains persuaded that the character is that of the Duchess Blanche and no other. In his description of her Chaucer reveals for the first time that sympathetic insight into woman's nature which has given us the pictures of Criseyde, the Prioress, Constance, and, we are all glad to add, the Wife of Bath. His imagination, too, was surely quickened by personal attachment. Mere desire to compliment a patron will not account for the impression conveyed. We feel certain that Chaucer knew the Duchess well, that he loved her and honored her, and came under the sway of her beauty and "womanly noblesse."

The House of Fame

Something with regard to love and lovers was intended to be the culmination of the *House of Fame*. This, I think, Professor

[1] *Conversations on Some of the Old Poets*, p. 89.

Sypherd has shown conclusively.[1] But Chaucer left the poem unfinished, and what we have of it is, in a way, an introduction, just as the *Ceyx and Alcyone* and the other parts of the *Book of the Duchess* are introductory to the interview with the knight in black ; and just as, in the *Parliament of Fowls*, the account of the dream and the description of the Temple of Venus lead up to the love story of the birds. Except for the general plan and structure of the poem, which Chaucer found in the old French love-visions, the actual love element in the *House of Fame* is very slight. It is practically confined to two passages : (1) that part of Book I which tells the story of Æneas and Dido and of the other women of antiquity who were betrayed by false lovers ;[2] and (2) the lines in Book II in which the eagle explains the purpose of the poet's aërial journey.[3] We may take up the second of these passages first.

The poet professes to be, not a lover himself, but one who is interested in the subject as an outsider. Jupiter has observed how he has for a long time served Cupid and Venus without any reward ; but his service, we learn, had not been that of a lover. It had consisted in writing praises of the Art of Love, and in composing " bokes, songes, dytees " in honor of the deity and his servants. Love had neglected or refused to advance his interests ; yet he had persevered in humble devotion. This attitude of mind on Chaucer's part is here expressed for the first time. It is maintained, however, in the *Parliament of Fowls*, in the *Troilus and Criseyde*, and in the Prologue to the *Legend of Good Women*.[4] Jupiter is now about to reward the poet by

---

[1] Sypherd, *Studies in Chaucer's " Hous of Fame*," p. 15.
[2] Bk. i, ll. 238–432.   [3] Bk. ii, ll. 606–698.
[4] Cf. also the lines :

> What shulde I speke more queynte,
> Or peyne me my wordes peynte
> To speak of love ? hit wol not be.
> I can not of that facultee (i, 245–248).

letting the eagle conduct him to a place where he shall have some "disport and game" in return for his unselfish devotion to Love. There he shall hear wonderful things of "Loves folk," some of which the eagle mentions in detail. This passage, as Dr. Sypherd has shown,[1] clearly announces the ultimate purpose of the poem ; and the announcement is confirmed later, when Chaucer, in reply to the question of the man who stood at his back in the House of Fame, says that he had come there,

> Some newe tydings for to lere . . .
> Tydings, other this or that,
> Of love, or swiche thinges glade.

The story of Dido the poet tells as part of the picture he saw painted on the walls of the Temple of Venus. In less than fifty lines (if we disregard his digressions) he summarizes the fourth book of the *Æneid*, along with certain incidents from the earlier books. It is Chaucer's digressions, however, which concern us here. These consist of Dido's lament and of reflections in the poet's own person on the perfidy of men.

The lament has only the slightest similarity to anything in Virgil. It is tender rather than wrathful, and the poet's sympathies are altogether with the forsaken queen.[2] True, he mentions Virgil's apology for Æneas, but his tone in repeating it is cool and almost perfunctory.[3]

The observations on the perfidy of men are in keeping with the modifications just noted. After telling of the treachery of Æneas, Chaucer exclaims :

> Lo, how a woman doth amis,
> To love him that unknowen is, . . .
> For this shal every woman finde
> That som man, of his pure kinde,
> Wol shewen outward the faireste,
> Til he have caught that what him leste ;

---

[1] P. 15.   [2] Compare i, 315 ff., with *Æneid*, iv, 305–306.   [3] i, 427–432.

> And thanne wol he causes finde,
> And swere how that she is unkinde,
> Or fals, or prevy, or double was.[1]

Again, after speaking of Dido's suicide as the result of her be-
trayal, he denounces the faithlessness of lovers :

> But, welaway ! the harm, the routhe,
> That hath betid for swich untrouthe,
> As men may ofte in bokes rede,
> And al day seen hit yet in dede,
> That for to thenken hit, a tene is.

And he cites the famous stories of Demophoön, Achilles, Paris,
Jason, Hercules, and Theseus.

The most noteworthy feature of these passages is their sympathy for women whose lovers have proved untrue. We need
not hesitate to accept such utterances as sincerely expressive of
Chaucer's own feelings. Indeed, that sense of the sadness of
human life which so often manifests itself in his writings could
find no more compelling cause for expression than man's faithlessness and woman's sorrow.

Parliament of Fowls

The *Parliament of Fowls* is a tale of love. The first two
stanzas of the Proem, and the last (the invocation to Venus),
announce the author's intention in the clearest terms. The
intervening stanzas prepare us for the vision, which makes up
the body of the poem.

The first lines of the Proem involve the same attitude of
detachment toward love which we have already seen in the *House*

---

[1] With the last seven lines, we may compare Chaucer's statement of the
conduct of Arcite in *Anelida and Arcite :*

> For he bar hir on honde of trecherye,
> And swoor he coude hir doublenesse espye,
> And al was falsnes that she to him mente.

Anel. and Ar., ll. 157–159.

of Fame,[1] and which will appear later in the *Troilus*[2] and the *Legend of Good Women*.[3] The poet is amazed at the "wonderful working" of Love on men's lives.

> Whan I on him thinke,
> Nat wot I wel wher that I wake or winke.[4]

Not that he knows anything about love at first hand; but he often reads of the god's miracles and of his cruelty, and how he *will* be lord and master. All he can say is " God save swich a lord! "[5] He then tells how he once had a dream after reading the *Somnium Scipionis*, and the poem closes with an invocation to Cytherea, who, as he says, caused him to have this dream.

The vision begins with Scipio's conducting the poet to the gate of a beautiful park. Over the gate are inscriptions proclaiming the joys and the griefs of loving. He hesitates to enter, but "African" leads him in. Then comes a description of the park and of the wonders to be seen there. In a garden of Love there is of course an abundance of flowers, fountains, singing birds, and the music of instruments. Here also is " lord Cupid " with his arrows. The qualities and characteristics of lovers appear as Cupid's courtiers,[6] personified under the names Plaisance, Aray, Lust, Curtesye, Craft, Delyt, Gentilnesse, Beautee, Youthe, Fool-hardinesse, Flaterye, Desyr, Messagerye, Mede, and so on. Here is also the brazen Temple of Venus, in which the poet hears the " hot sighs," and sees Priapus, Venus and her porter Richesse, Ceres and Bacchus, and the paintings of ancient lovers. Having dwelt upon the glories of the garden (as Boccaccio gives them in the *Teseide*[7]), the poet is ready for

---

[1] Ll. 621–640. [2] i, st. 3; ii, st. 2, 3; iii, st. 6, 190–191.

[3] B Prologue, ll. 58–59, 81–83, 412–413, 490–491.

[4] Ll. 6–7. Cf. Deschamps, *Balade* 475.

[5] This attitude of detachment he maintains in the vision itself. Cf. ll. 155 ff.

[6] Neilson, *Origins &c.*, p. 142. Cf. p. 116.

[7] Bk. vii, st. 51 ff. See Furnivall, *Trial Forewords*, pp. 59 ff., and Skeat, *Minor Poems*, pp. lxii ff. and Oxford Chaucer, I, 68–73.

his story, — the account of St. Valentine's day and of the rivalry of the three tercelets for the love of the "formel" eagle. This is the tale of love which was promised in the Proem.

Each of the tercelets urges his claim, and representatives of the various classes of birds give their opinions on the question. Finally Nature, the presiding goddess, leaves the choice to the "formel" herself, who postpones her decision for a year. The story, we perceive, is very simple indeed; but it is elaborated by Chaucer with extraordinary skill.

The most interesting feature of the *Parliament*, for the purposes of this investigation, is the manner in which the author brings the conventions of courtly love into sharp contrast with the ideals of the *bourgeoisie* and the "vileins." Well-nigh every conceivable variety of opinion is expressed, from the "dunghill" babblings of the duck to the refined sentiments of the royal tercelet.

The lady in this love-story is the formel eagle. She is portrayed in the usual fashion. Her position of superiority comes out in the pleading of the tercelets; she is the sovereign whom each serves, and whom each asks for favor and mercy. She is "of shap the gentileste," "the most benigne and the goodlieste," and is endowed with every virtue. Nevertheless, she is kept in the background, as convention requires. Her part in the action is confined to deferring her choice of suitor for a year.

The qualities of the royal tercel are also those of the conventional lover. He is "wys and worthy, secree, trewe as stel." He is humble, as his manner of pleading shows:

> With hed enclyned and ful humble chere
> This royal tercel spak.

His plea is also the conventional plea of lovers. Not as his mate, but as his lady sovereign, he chooses the formel eagle. He is all hers and will serve her ever. He cannot live long in his present pain; therefore he begs her for mercy and grace, and beseeches her to consider his loyalty and have pity on his woe. If he is ever found unfaithful, disobedient, wilfully negligent, a boaster, or inconstant, he hopes he may be torn to pieces by the other fowls. None loves her so well as he, although she has made him no promises; therefore she ought to have mercy on him. This is the only plea he can make. But he will serve her always, no matter where she may be.

The skill which the poet displays in the contrast between this appeal and that of the next tercel is noteworthy. The fact that the latter is " of lower kinde " is made very clear by the absence from his speech of the extreme courtliness seen in the first tercel's pleading. And yet it is not entirely without courtly sentiment. He loves her better than the first tercel, he says, and he has served her longer; if the period of devotion is to be the basis of reward, her love and favor belong to him. He can say as well as his rival, that he will gladly submit to hanging if she ever finds him " fals, unkinde, jangler, rebel any wyse, or jalous," or if he does not conduct himself so as to keep her honor, at least so far as he has wit. His argument, though it makes some use of courtly terms, has much the sound of a business arrangement. We miss the perfect humility of the royal tercel, as well as his polish and refinement.

The same business-like tone pervades the plea of the third tercel. " I do not boast of long service," he says, "but for all that it is as possible for me to die to-day of my woe, as it is for him who has been languishing for twenty years. Furthermore, one man's service of six months may be more satisfactory than that of another who has served for a long time." But he quickly tempers the boldness of the assertion by adding, " I do not say this with regard to myself; for I can do no service that will please my lady. But I dare say, I am her truest liegeman, in short, until I die. I will be all hers and true to her in every way." By this courtly speech he avoids the sin of boasting.

Having thus set forth the question in the elegant and graceful plea of the royal tercel and the mingled courtly and practical observations of his two rivals, the poet proceeds to give the views of the lower orders of society. The other birds murmur at the long debate, and Nature decides to let each class of fowls choose a spokesman. The tercelet of the falcon speaks for the " foules of ravyne." His verdict is what we should expect : " Let the formel choose the worthiest in his knighthood, the greatest in dignity, the gentlest of blood ! " The water fowls are represented by the goose, who gives as her judgment : " If she will not love him, let him love another." Nothing more opposed to courtly doctrine could be imagined. A lover was required to be true to his lady till death, even if she showed him no favor. This principle, indeed, is immediately asserted by the turtle-dove, speaking for seed-fowl :

> Nay, god forbede a lover shulde chaunge !
> Thogh that his lady evermore be straunge,
> Yet let him serve hir ever, til he be deed.[1]

And the sparrowhawk, taking up the cudgels for the courtly group, shows a fine contempt for the " parfit reson of a goos ! " Nobody but a churl would ever have thought of such a sentiment. Indeed, as the sparrowhawk says of a courtly lover,

> Hit lyth not in his wit nor in his wille

to love another lady.

It is of interest to note that the poet has ascribed to the " turtel " the courtly sentiment of constancy, although this bird

---

[1] Cf. Pandarus's question, " Shall a lover cease to serve his lady because she is indifferent ? " and his own reply :

> Nay, nay, but ever in oon be fresh and grene
> To serve and love his dere hertes quene,
> And thenke it is a guerdon hir to serve
> A thousand-fold more than he can deserve. — *Troilus*, i, st. 117.

represents the next to the lowest class in his social scale of fowls.[1] The reason is obvious.[2]

The duck, however, thinks it a great joke that anybody should continue to love a woman who cares nothing for him. As he says : " Who can find any reason or sense in that ?

> Ye, quek," yit quod the doke, ful wel and faire,
> " Ther been mo sterres, god wot, than a paire ! "

This churlish prating is too much for the tercelet :

> " Now fy, cherl ! " quod the gentil tercelet,
> " Out of the dunghil com that word ful right,
> Thou canst noght see which thing is wel beset;
> Thou farest by love as oules doon by light,
> The day hem blent, ful wel they see by night;
> Thy kind is of so lowe a wrechednesse,
> That what love is, thou canst not see ne gesse."

Here the tercelet merely gives expression to the feelings entertained by the courtly classes for the " vilains " from early times.

---

[1] In lines 323–329, Chaucer arranges the birds thus : " the foules of ravyne were hyest set; and *than* the foules smale that eten as hem Nature wolde enclyne, as worm." The " water-fowl " are lowest. This leaves the third place for the seed-fowl ; and strange to say, he puts the turtle in a lower class than the " lewed " cuckoo. This is Chaucer's own arrangement; at least, it is not in the description of Alain (*De Planctu Naturae*, pp. 437–439), which seems to have influenced the poet here. But then, we need not hold the poet down to a scientific accuracy in the play of his humor. Besides, the real dispute is between the courtly set and the " vileins " represented by the goose and the duck.

[2] Courtly love did not demand such devotion as this. Andreas's dictum on this was that two years of widowhood was long enough to elapse before taking a new love. " Biennalis viduitas pro amante defuncto superstiti prescribitur amanti " (Longer Code, Rule 7, p. 316). The constancy of the turtle in its love was proverbial. For example : " Illic turtur, suo viduata consorte, amorem epilogare dedignans, in altero bigamiae refutabat solatia " (Alain de Lille, *De Planctu Naturae*, p. 439). Also :

> Turtre çeo est oisel simple, caste, e bel,
> E sun malle aime tant, que jà à sun vivant
> Altre malle nen averat, ne puis que il murrat
> Jà altre ne prendrat, tut tens puis le plaindrat,
> Ne sur vert ne serad. — *Bestiary* of Philip de Thaun.

Compare the opening lines of Jean de Condé's *Des Vilains et des Courtois :* [1]

> Vilain et courtois sont contraire ;
> De l'un ne puet on bien retraire,
> Et en l'autre n'a fors que bien.

The " vilain " was regarded as contemptible in every way. But especially despicable, it was thought, were his views of love. For love in any true sense was absolutely unknown to him. Literature abounds in statements of this idea.[2] It is clear, then, that with the scoffing of the duck at the idea of constancy in love, and the contemptuous retort of the tercelet, the debate reaches its climax.

But there is yet one report to be heard. The cuckoo crowds to the front to give the verdict for worm-fowl. " So I get my mate," he says, " I do not care how long this debate lasts." I fear the cuckoo does not really represent his party. Although he belongs to the second rank of fowls, he is, according to the mediaeval standard, " vilain," [3] because his characteristics are those of a " vilain," [4] just as the turtle would be judged " cortois." Nothing could be more " vilainish " than the sentiments of the cuckoo, not even those of the duck and the goose. And the merlin, again one of the " fouls of ravyne," proceeds to anni-hilate him ; there is a splendid finality in the merlin's closing thrust :

> Go, lewed be thou whyl the world may dure !

This ends the debate, and, as Nature says,

> In effect yet be we never the nere.

The poet now returns to the main theme of the story, and quickly brings it to an end by having Nature submit the ques-tion to the " formel " herself, with the result already mentioned.

---

[1] *Dits et Contes*, ed. Scheler, Brussels, 1866, III, 189 ff.

[2] See on this whole subject G. Paris, *Romania*, XXIV, 142 ff. Particu-lar reference may be made to the *Roman de la Rose*, ll. 2163–2170; *Le Clef d'Amours* (in Suchier's *Bibliotheca Normannica*, Vol. V, Halle, 1890), ll. 173–180; *Florance et Blancheflor*, ll. 9–11 ; *Li Fablel dou Dieu d'Amours*, p. 17.

[3] Adjectival use.   [4] Galpin, *Cortois and Vilain*, p. 10.

The *Parliament of Fowls* is certainly a love-vision, as Dr. Sypherd has shown.[1] It is also a love-debate, and as such has been well compared by Koeppel with the Old French *Florance et Blancheflor.*[2] In this the birds are the barons of the god of Love, and take part in discussing a question submitted by Florance and Blancheflor to him. No doubt Chaucer was writing under the general influence of this *genre*. But he has cleverly complicated the usual scheme, for the *Parliament* is in fact a double debate.

The primary question at issue is, which of the three tercelets shall win the formel? This might have been decided by Nature on the basis of their several pleas, in which case the simplest form of love-debate would have been followed. But the intervention of the goose precipitates a general discussion, which quickly introduces a new question, — whether a lover should be loyal to his lady under all circumstances. This second problem had been treated by Machaut in two poems, *Le Jugement dou Roy de Behaigne* and *Le Jugement dou Roy de Navarre;* and it was elaborately discussed by the authors of *Les Cent Balades*[3] not so very long after the date of the *Parliament of Fowls*. In the *Parliament*, however, the contest is not between two classes of courtly lovers, as in the French poems, but between " cortois " and " vilain." Here the birds line up on two sides : the seed fowls, holding with the courtly group represented by the " foules of ravyne," and the worm-eating birds with the " vilains," represented by the waterfowl.

[1] *Studies in the "Hous of Fame,"* pp. 20 ff.

[2] In Herrig's *Archiv*, XC, 149–150. Courthope (*History of English Poetry*, I, 270) says the idea of a council of birds is taken from the Old French *Hueline and Eglantine*.   [3] Cf. pp. 34 ff., above.

TROILUS AND CRISEYDE AND THE LEGEND OF GOOD WOMEN

Troilus and Criseyde

For a correct appreciation of Chaucer's genius, as exhibited in his great love-poem, the *Troilus and Criseyde*, a knowledge of the nature of the love therein treated and of the limitations within which the poet, voluntarily or involuntarily, worked, is particularly necessary. Only with such a knowledge can the characters and actions of the personages of the poem be understood. It is perfectly obvious that neither Chaucer nor Boccaccio was attempting to reproduce the life of the Trojans in the heroic age. It is equally obvious, although perhaps it is not always so regarded, that our opinion of the lovers should not be formed entirely on the basis of present-day ideas. To both Boccaccio and Chaucer, Troilus and his lady were contemporary young people, and their love affair is related in terms of contemporary life. Since they belong to the appropriate rank in society, they are treated as courtly lovers. The most casual reading of the poem shows this. Yet the fact is often forgotten by critics and commentators, and it is worth while to examine, somewhat in detail, the courtly elements which appear in the *Troilus*, and which agree with the principles of the system as they have been already expounded.

One of the commonest sentiments in the love-poetry of the troubadours, in that of Chrétien, and in the book of Andreas, was that love is not only good in itself, but is the cause and origin of all good. This idea appears in Pandarus's words to the love-stricken Troilus :

> And for-thy loke of good comfort thou be;
> . . . for nought but good it is
> To loven wel, and in a worthy place;
> Thee oughte not to clepe it hap, but grace (i, 128).[1]

[1] The references are to the Books and Stanzas of the *Troilus*.

The ennobling nature of love finds many expressions in the
Troilus; the most important are perhaps the following. Chaucer
himself speaks in the lines :

> And ofte it [Love] hath the cruel herte apesed
> And worthy folk maad worthier of name
> And causeth most to dreden vyce and shame (i, 36).

Elsewhere, in the proem to Book III, he imputes this power of
abstract love to Venus, the goddess of Love :

> Algates hem that ye wol sette afyre,
> They dreden shame, and vices they resigne,
> Ye do hem corteys be, fresshe and benigne (iii, 4).

Antigone, to the same effect, sings in praise of the lover's life :

> This is the righte lyf that I am inne,
> To flemen alle manere vyce and sinne :
> This doth me so to vertu for to entende,
> That day by day I in my wil amende (ii, 122).

And the hero of the poem himself furnishes a concrete example
of the ennoblement of one's nature by love :

> Thus wolde Love, yheried be his grace,
> That pryde, envye, ire, and avaryce
> He gan to flee, and every other vyce (iii, 258).

Another principle which seems to have been commonly accepted, was that to be in love is the normal condition for suitable
young people. We have seen this idea expressed in the *Book
of the Duchess*,[1] and also in the *Confessio Amantis*.[2] Pandarus
teaches the same doctrine in the lines :

> Was never man ne woman yet bigete
> That was unapt to suffren loves hete
> Celestial, or elles love of kinde (i, 140).

It is a natural inference that love ought not to be resisted.
The god of Love is often represented as punishing those who

[1] Ll. 775-777.   [2] iv, 1451-1454.

attempt to stand out against his power. This sentiment is voiced by Criseyde, speaking to Troilus :

> Lo herte myn, as wolde the excellence
> Of love, ayeins the which that no man may
> Ne oughte eek goodly maken resistence . . .
> This droof me for to rewe upon your peyne (iii, 142).

A doctrine prominent in Andreas's work is that a woman is responsible for the love her beauty arouses, and she cannot therefore justifiably refuse to grant her favor. This, in Andreas, has a sensual connotation. It got to be a convention in later times, with the sensual element minimized or absent altogether. Pandarus expresses the idea when endeavoring to comfort Troilus. Since everybody, he says, is apt (in the old sense of the word) to experience love,

> Celestial or elles love of kinde,

and since Criseyde is far too young and beautiful to go into a monastery,

> . . . it sete hir wel right nouthe
> A worthy knight to loven and cheryce,
> *And but she do, I holde it for a vyce* (i, 141).

Later he argues the point at length with Criseyde herself, when he tries to prove her responsibility in the matter of granting Troilus her love (ii, 46–50). The dialectic skill of this passage is Pandarus's own ; but the basic principle of his argument was well established, and Criseyde seems to have recognized it.

Another familiar principle of the courtly system was that love obtained too easily is not prized. Pandarus advances this argument to reassure Troilus, when he despairs of gaining the favor of Criseyde. " Think," he says, " of the oak ; under the repeated stroke of the woodman's axe, it must eventually fall. Remember also that a slender reed, when the wind blows on it, will bend to the ground and then become erect. Not so the oak. When it is blown to the ground, it is down for good and all.

> It nedeth me nought thee longe to forbyse.
> Men shal rejoysen of a greet empryse
> Acheved wel, and stant with-outen doute,
> Al han men been the lenger ther-aboute " (ii, 199).

Most of these doctrines are put into the mouth of Pandarus. The same authority on love matters also reminds Criseyde of the importance of constancy, which was another cardinal principle. He says : " If a woman pretend to love a man and calls him ' leef ' and ' dere herte,' and at the same time loves another,

> She doth hirself a shame, and him a gyle " (iii, 111).

We have seen that according to the conventional teaching, jealousy in husbands was to be deprecated ; but in lovers *par-amours*, it was natural and even requisite. The former idea Criseyde expresses in the lines :

> Shal noon housbonde seyn to me " chekmat ! "
> For either they ben ful of jalousye,
> Or maisterful, or loven novelrye (ii, 108).

She refers to the latter in that tender, pathetic scene where she speaks to Troilus of his jealousy :

> Eek al my wo is this, that folk now usen
> To seyn right thus, " ye, Jalousye is Love ! "
> And wolde a busshel venim al excusen,
> For that o greyn of love is on it shove ! (iii, 147).

Here she has in mind the courtly doctrine, and it is noteworthy that she shows little patience with such ideas. She calls Troilus's jealousy " swich folye," though she attributes it to his love for her. And she takes Jove to task for allowing such an evil spirit to exist.

> But that wot heighe god that sit above,
> If it be lyker love, or hate, or grame ;
> And after that, it oughte bere his name (iii, 147).

Once more, the courtly love ideas appear in the numerous passages dealing with the relation of the lover to his lady.

Pandarus, in his endeavor to arouse his lovesick friend to some action, well expresses the general doctrine of service. He argues that, even though Troilus has no prospects of being taken into the lady's favor, he should not for that reason fall into despair.

> Nay, nay, but ever in oon be fresh and grene
> To serve and love his dere hertes quene,
> And thenke it is a guerdoun hir to serve
> A thousand-fold more than he can deserve (i, 117).

The attitude of humility which Pandarus here advises is actually assumed by Troilus in the story, and in describing it Chaucer shows his peculiar skill in the language of love. Noticeable in this respect is the use of the feudal figure in Troilus's speech to the god of Love, soon after he has been smitten by the beauty of Criseyde in the temple :

> But whether goddesse or womman, y-wis,
> She be, I noot, which that ye do me serve;
> But as hir man I wole ay live and sterve.
> Ye stonden in hire eyen mightily,
> As in a place un-to your vertu digne;
> Wherfore, lord, if my servyse or I
> May lyke yow, so beth to me benigne;
> For myn estat royal here I resigne
> In-to hir hond, and with ful humble chere
> Bicome hir man, as to my lady dere (i, 61–62).

And the poet goes on to tell how all the hero's desire was directed to "this conclusion" —

> That she on him wolde have compassion,
> And he to be hir man, whyle he may dure (i, 67).

Similarly, Diomed professes to take Criseyde for his sovereign lady :

> But herte myn, sin that I am your man,

grant me permission to come to-morrow, and

> At better leyser, telle yow my sorwe (v, 135).

It is not necessary to call attention to the many passages where the idea of the lover's service is brought out. But one variation which Chaucer's poem shows from Boccaccio's may be cited as a striking example of the use of courtly love-ideas in describing the relations between the two lovers. In Boccaccio's story, just before Griseida's departure for the Grecian camp, Troilo says to her:

> Non mi sospinse ad amarti bellezza
> La quale spesso altrui suole irretire;
> Non mi trasse ad amarti gentilezza
> Che suol pigliar de' nobili il desire;
> Non ornamento ancora, non ricchezza
> Mi fe' per te amor nel cor sentire:
> Delle qua' tutte se' più copiosa,
> Che altra fosse mai donna amorosa.

> Ma gli atti tuoi altieri e signorili,
> Il valore e 'l parlar cavalleresco,
> I tuoi costumi più ch' altra gentili,
> Ed il vezzoso tuo sdegno donnesco,
> Per lo quale apparien d'esserti vili
> Ogni appetito ed oprar popolesco,
> Qual tu mi se', o donna mia possente,
> Con Amor mi ti miser nella mente.

Now practically these same sentiments are put by Chaucer into the mouth of Criseyde. Thus the heroine is given an added dignity, which is in close conformity with the courtly conception. Perhaps the best description, on the whole, of the lover's attitude, and the clearest assertion of the lady's superiority, is found in Troilus's words in his interview with Criseyde at the house of Deiphebus:

> And than agreën that I may ben he,
> Withoute braunche of vyce in any wyse,
> In trouthe alway to doon yow my servyse,
> As to my lady right and chief resort,
> With al my wit and al my diligence,

> And I to han, right as yow list, comfort,
> Under your yerde, egal to myn offence,
> As deeth: if that I breke your defence;
> And that ye deigne me so muche honoure,
> Me to comaunden ought in any houre
> And I to been your verray humble trewe,
> Secret, and in my paynes pacient,
> And ever-mo desire freshly newe,
> To serven, and been y-lyke ay diligent,
> And, with good herte, al hooly your talent
> Receyven wel, how sore that me smerte,
> Lo, this mene I, myn owene swete herte (iii, 19–21).

Consequent upon the superiority of the lady, are not only the many perturbations of the lover, but also her own coldness and indifference.   Chaucer cannot tell whether Criseyde did not know of Troilus's sorrows, or whether she feigned she did not:

> But wele I rede that, by no maner weye,
> Ne semed it [as] that she of him roughte,
> Nor of his peyne, or what-so-ever he thoughte (i, 71).

Pandarus, after persuading Criseyde to write to Troilus, says:

> But ye have played tyraunt neigh to longe,
> And hard was it your herte for to grave;

and he tells her right out that it is time to make some show of mercy to Troilus.   Criseyde had been acting just as any lady would have done, as Pandarus's words show:

> But thus ye faren, wel neigh alle and some,
> That he that most desireth yow to serve,
> Of him ye recche leest wher he bicome,
> And whether that he live or elles sterve (ii, 165).

The courtly love doctrine most prominent in the *Troilus* is perhaps the doctrine of secrecy.   The importance attached to this idea is, of course, due to the nature of the love treated in the poem.   We have seen that, although the same conventions came to be employed in the treatment of the various kinds of

love, in that love which was in essence sensual the demand for
secrecy was a real one. It needs no argument, of course, to prove
the sensual element in the love of Troilus and Criseyde for each
other. Obviously Pandarus knew to what end all this affair
tended ; and if Pandarus understood, it follows that Troilus did.[1]
It is equally clear, I think, that Criseyde knew what was implied
in granting her love to Troilus. This question, as well as the
prominence given in the poem to the idea of secrecy, and its
bearing upon the personal character of the heroine, will be considered in our study of Criseyde. Here it is important to realize
that the nature of the love which Chaucer treats in his great
erotic work is that of the love *par amours* of the days of Marie
of Champagne and of her mother Eleanor.

In connection with the conventional doctrines in the *Troilus
and Criseyde*, it may be well to cite some of Chaucer's uses of
conceits common in love-poetry. The favorite conception of the
troubadours and Chrétien de Troies, that beauty was the cause
of love, making its attack through the eyes of the lover, appears
in Chaucer's poem in the lines :

> Yet with a look his herte wex a-fere
> That he, that now was most in pryde above,
> Wex sodeynly most subget unto love (i, 33).

The commonplace idea of the fatal potency of the beautiful
being's eyes Chaucer frequently expresses :

> Lo, he that leet himselven so konninge,
> And scorned hem that loves peynes dryen,
> Was ful unwar that love hadde his dwellinge
> Within the subtile stremes of hir yën ;
> That sodeynly him thoughte he felte dyen,
> Right with hir look, the spirit in his herte,
> Blessed be love, that thus can folk converte ! (i, 44);

---

[1] Mr. Root evidently misses the point entirely, when he remarks :   One
feels that Pandarus has seduced him [Troilus] quite as much as he has Criseyde." — Root, *The Poetry of Chaucer*, New York, 1906, p. 117.

and again,

> Whan he was fro the temple thus departed,
> He streyght anoon un-to his paleys torneth,
> Right with hir look thurgh-shoten and thurgh-darted (i, 47).

Troilus, making his confession to the god of Love, says :

> For certes, lord, so sore hath she me wounded
> That stod in black, with loking of hir yën,
> That to myn hertes botme it is ysounded,
> Thourgh which I woot that I mot nedes dyen (ii, 77).

Later the lover addresses his lady's eyes :

> It were ye that wroughte me swich wo,
> Ye humble nettes of my lady dere !
> Though ther be mercy writen in your chere,
> God wot, the text ful hard is sooth to finde (iii, 194).

The classification given above shows that no important doctrine of the courtly love of the early days is omitted in the *Troilus*. Chaucer is clearly working within the limits imposed by the principles and conventions of the system ; and only by recognizing this fact can we understand the spirit of the poem.[1] Bearing it in mind, we may now proceed to our study of the principal characters ; and we shall begin with the lover himself.

The sorrow of Troilus is the poet's primary theme :

> The double sorwe of Troilus to tellen,
> That was the king Priamus sone of Troye,
> In lovinge, how his aventures fellen
> Fro wo to wele, and after out of joye
> My purpos is . . . (i, 1).

However much besides this Chaucer tells, the idea of speaking of the ups and downs of lovers as woes and sorrows was

---

[1] Disregard of this fact by writers on Chaucer's poem is the only reason for the present analysis of the *Troilus*. Critics generally have formed the wrong conception of Chaucer's hero and heroine, the present writer believes, because they have failed to take into account the connection between the *Troilus* and the courtly love ideas. The latest instance of this is the recent work on Chaucer by Legouis (Paris, 1910) ; see the study of the *Troilus*, pp. 116–127.

conventional. It is unnecessary, therefore, to refer to the numerous places in which the author refers to his hero's pains, sighs, groans, and to his dying for love. Omitting these, we may note that Troilus exhibits the usual symptoms of courtly lovers :

1. Sleeplessness, loss of appetite, and paleness.

> And fro this forth tho refte him love his sleep,
> And made his mete his foo; and eek his sorwe
> Gan multiplye, that whoso toke keep,
> It shewed in his hewe, both eve and morwe (i, 70).

Chaucer again states, in his droll fashion, the same idea :

> Nil I nought swere, although he laye softe,
> That in his thought he nas sumwhat disesed
> Ne that he tornede on his pilwes ofte (iii, 64).

2. Sickness. In arranging for the first meeting of the lovers at the house of Deiphebus, Pandarus's plan is for Troilus to feign sickness.

> Quod Troilus, " y-wis, thou nedeless
> Counseylest me, that sykliche I me feyne!
> For I am syk in ernest, douteless,
> So that wel neigh I sterve for the peyne " (ii, 219).

3. Fear to tell his lady of his woe. Pandarus, anxious to help his friend, asks :

> But tel me, if I wiste what she were,
> For whom that thee al this misaunter ayleth,
> Dorstestow that I tolde hir in hir ere
> Thy wo, sith thou darst not thyself for fere,
> And hir bisoughte on thee to have som routhe? (i, 110.)

4. Confusion and forgetfulness in the lady's presence. Troilus rehearses in his mind what he will say to Criseyde at Deiphebus's house (iii, 8) ; but when she speaks to him (10–11), he becomes speechless and

> . . . his lesson, that he wende conne
> To preyen hir, is thurgh his wit y-ronne (iii, 12).

The rest of the interview is quite as difficult for Troilus. The poet describes him :

> In chaunged vois, right for his verrey drede,
> Which vois eek quook, and ther-to his manere
> Goodly abayst, and now his hewes rede,
> Now pale, unto Criseyde, his lady dere,
> With look doun cast and humble yolden chere,
> Lo, thalderfirste word that him asterte
> Was, twyes, " mercy, mercy, swete herte ! "

We may next see how far the hero possesses the character of the conventional lover. Pandarus deftly sounds the praises of his friend in answering Criseyde's inquiry about Hector :

> And eek his fresshe brother Troilus,
> The wyse worthy Ector the secounde,
> In whom that every vertu list abounde,
> As alle trouthe and alle gentillesse,
> Wysdom, honour, fredom, and worthinesse (ii, 23).

To which Criseyde replies that she hears how all those whose opinion is to be valued praise Troilus both for his noble conduct in the war and for his courtesy toward everybody while at home (ii, 27). Pandarus, taking advantage of the situation, gives a specific instance of Troilus's prowess, and adds that he is

> . . . the freendlieste man
> Of gret estat, that ever I saw my lyve (ii, 30).

The object of Pandarus in this interview is, of course, to paint his friend's virtues in as glowing colors as possible. It is to be noted, however, that his praise of Troilus is confirmed by the reports which have reached Criseyde's ears, and by her own testimony later in the poem.[1] By common consent, then, Troilus is known for " trouthe," " alle gentillesse," " wysdom," " honour," " fredom," " worthinesse," " prowesse in war " and " courtesye," — for such virtues, in short, as were conventionally required of a

---

[1] Cf. ii, 95, 106.

knight and a lover. The same qualities are attributed, in almost identical terms, to the model knight of the Prologue to the *Canterbury Tales*.

Chaucer's own testimony concerning Troilus, as near as we may arrive at it, is consistent with that of Pandarus and Criseyde. In speaking of the effect which Pandarus's comforting words have had upon the sighing Troilus, he says : " But Troilus lay there no longer, but he mounted at once on his bay steed and played the lion in the field. Woe to the Greek that met him that day ! And in the town, from that time forth, his goodly manner got for him the love and favor of all. For he became the friendliest creature, the gentlest, the most generous, the thriftiest (i.e. the most efficient in every way), and the very best knight that in his time was or might be. Gone were his jests and his cruelty, his supercilious bearing and his disdainful manner ; and each of these faults he exchanged for a virtue " (i, 155–156). This is Chaucer's own characterization of his hero, for no word of it is found in the *Filostrato*. But for a later description of the effect of love on Troilus, he is indebted to the Italian :

> In alle nedes for the tounes werre,
> He was, and ay the firste in armes dight ;
> And certeynly, but-if that bokes erre,
> Save Ector, most y-drad of any wight ;
> And this encrees of hardinesse and might
> Cam him of love, his ladies thank to winne,
> That altered his spirit so with-inne (iii, 254).

> And most of love and vertu was his speche,
> And in despyt hadde alle wrecchednesse ;
> And doutelees, no nede was him biseche
> To honouren hem that hadde worthinesse,
> And esen hem that weren in distresse (iii, 256).

> And though that he be come of blood royal,
> Him liste of pryde at no wight for to chase ;
> Benigne he was to ech in general,

> For which he gat him thank in every place.
> Thus wolde Love, y-heried be his grace.
> That Pryde, Envye, Ire, and Avaryce
> He gan to flee, and every other vyce (iii, 258).

This passage, in Chaucer and Boccaccio alike, simply states the conventional effects of love on the lover, under the courtly system.

It is clear that Chaucer intended his hero to be worthy of the spirited Criseyde and, as such, to have our sympathies. This is what we should expect a priori. Chaucer's primary interest in his mature productions is in characterization, and his method is distinctly dramatic. In none of his work is this truer than in the *Troilus*.[1] But however great his interest in character for itself, the *Troilus* still retains enough of the nature it had in the hands of Boccaccio to be called romance; and, in treating it as romance, is it likely that the poet would give to his heroine, who attracted him and whom he wished to portray sympathetically, a lover unworthy of her admiration or that of the reader? This could be done only on condition that she should not recognize his inferiority. Chaucer leaves no doubt as to Criseyde's opinion of Troilus; she does not, as we have seen, regard him as inferior, but as entirely worthy of her love; and the expressions with reference to him by Pandarus and by the author himself show the correctness of her estimate. To Chaucer, as to Criseyde, Troilus was a valiant warrior; in prowess, second only to Hector. But the prominence which is given in the poem to another side of his nature is likely to produce a wrong total impression of him. We have seen that under the system of courtly love a knight, though absolutely fearless elsewhere, must tremble before his lady. If his conduct in love only were to be considered, evidently our impression of him would be the wrong one. Both Dares, in his meagre account, and Benoit de Ste. Maure

---

[1] For a study of the dramatic features in the *Troilus*, see Price, *A Study in Chaucer's Method of Narrative Construction*, Publ. Modern Language Assoc., 1896, XI, 307–322.

describe Troilus as a valiant and thoroughly practical knight,[1] and in taking him for their hero neither Boccaccio nor Chaucer wished to undervalue this element of his character. But for the purpose of their story, the emphasis is put on another side. They are interested in him primarily as a lover. As Chaucer says :

> And if I hadde y-taken for to wryte
> The armes of this ilke worthy man,
> Than wolde I of his batailles endyte.
> But for that I to wryte first bigan
> Of his love, I have seyd as that I can (v, 253).

It seems to me, then, that one misses the spirit of the work if one regards Chaucer as having conceived his hero as an unpractical enthusiast, as a love-sick boy, who idealized not only his lady but also his passion for her.[2] The fact we should keep

---

[1] Chaucer, speaking of Troilus, tells us :

> His worthy dedes, whoso list hem here,
> Reed Dares, he can tell hem alle y-fere.

The direction to " reed Dares " is a bit misleading, since all that writer gives in regard to Troilus is the description : " Troilum magnum, pulcherrimum, pro aetate valentem, fortem, cupidum virtutis," and later the words :

> Troilus Diomedem sauciat.

(See Daretis Phrygii *De Excidio Troiae Historia*, ed. F. Meister, Leipzig, 1872, xii, 15; xxxi, 37.) Brief as this mention is, in describing him as " pro aetate valentem " and " cupidum virtutis " it gives the same idea that is seen in Benoit de Ste. Maure's lines :

> Poi est meins forz en son endreit
> Ne meins hardiz qu' Hector esteit ;
>
> > *Li Roman de Troie*, ed. Constans,
> > Paris, 1904–1908, ll. 3991–3992

and

> Tant come il ert en bon talent,
> Par esguardot si doucement,
> Que deliz ert de lui vesir ;
> Mais une rien vos di por veir,
> Qu' il ert envers ses enemies
> D'autre semblant e d'autre vis (ibid., ll. 5401–5406).

[2] Mr. R. K. Root's view. See Root, *The Poetry of Chaucer*, pp. 192–195 ff. Cf. " Bei Chaucer . . . ist er ein spröder Jungling " (Kissner, *Chaucer in seinen Beziehungen zur italienischen Litteratur*, Bonn, 1867, p. 44).

in mind is, that in presenting their hero, both Boccaccio and Chaucer portray him in accord with the established courtly convention as to what a lover should be ; and any seeming unpracticality of his can be satisfactorily explained by a consideration of him from this point of view. Certainly, we ought to estimate his conduct by such conventions, rather than by present-day ideas.

Chaucer, in the character of Troilus, does not seriously modify the Troilo of Boccaccio. It is true, however, that the interest of the respective authors in their hero is different in degree and in kind. It is generally held that Boccaccio's story had an autobiographical purpose ; that in setting forth the story of Troilo's utter subjugation by his love for Griseida, the Italian author had in mind his own *amour* with the daughter of King Robert of Naples.[1] For Boccaccio, therefore, the story centered in Troilo and his sorrows. Chaucer's interest in Troilus, on the other hand, not only lacked this personal element, but was secondary to that which he felt for Criseyde ; for there is no doubt that Chaucer's stronger personal sympathies were with her, although the story is professedly written to tell the sorrows of Troilus. The poet himself undoubtedly felt the charms of his heroine. It is perhaps from a desire to magnify her attractive qualities that he makes Troilus's affair with her the first love experience of the hero ; whereas, in Boccaccio, Troilo had often before felt the stings of love. To Troilo, the *amour* with Griseida was only one more in a series of love adventures ; [2] to Troilus, it is the first and last fatal passion. The victory of Love, working through the charms of Criseyde, was greater because he brought down one who felt himself superior to the

[1] Kissner, p. 42 ; Ebert, *Review of Sandras's "Etude sur Chaucer"* (translated), Chaucer Society Publications, 1868, p. 14.

[2] I have herd told, pardieux, of your livinge,
Ye lovers, and your lewede observaunces (i, 29).
Io provai già per la mia gran follia
Qual fosse questo maladetto fusco. — *Filostrato*, i, 23.

powers of the god. If such was the purpose of the poet in changing this detail, it follows that to Chaucer Troilus was no weakling. Chaucer knew well what we often observe, that the traits of character which make a man strong in one direction make him equally strong in the opposite, when once his interests and activities have been changed. Pandarus seems to have seen such a man in Troilus; for, in his ecclesiastical phraseology, he expresses this very idea:

> And, by my trouthe, I have right now of thee
> A good conceyt in my wit, as I gesse,
> And what it is, I wol now that thou see.
> I thenke, sith that love, of his goodnesse,
> Hath thee converted out of wikkednesse,
> That thou shalt be the beste post, I leve,
> Of al his lay, and most his foos to greve.
> Ensample why, see now these wyse clerkes,
> That erren aldermost ayein a lawe,
> And ben converted from hir wikked werkes
> Thorugh grace of god, that list hem to him drawe,
> Than arn they folk that han most god in awe,
> And strengest-feythed been, I understonde,
> And conne an errour alder-best withstonde (i, 143–144).

Such a person is apt to feel deeply and intensely. I see no objection to conceiving Troilus to be one who had strong convictions, together with a proud and supercilious manner of expressing them. After he was overcome by his passion for Criseyde, the softening effect of love was seen in his change of conduct. As the poet tells us, he became the friendliest person in the city, the gentlest and the most generous:

> Dede were his japes and his crueltee,
> His heighe port and his manere estraunge,
> And ech of tho gan for a vertu chaunge (i, 155).

But the very trait which before showed in the conviction that he was superior to love's charms, now shows in the constancy in love which he maintains to his death.

There is, so far as I can see, nothing in the hero's conduct after his subjugation by love which is inconsistent with this conception of him. Mr. Root, in his handbook, says : "His [Troilus's] . . . main attention is absorbed in the process of idealizing the new-found mistress. It never occurs to him, however, to take any active steps in his own behalf.

> ' She nil to noon swich wrecche as I be wonne,'

he thinks ; would God I were arrived in the port of death, to which my sorrow will lead me ! If Pandarus had not intervened, it is probable that Troilus would never have spoken a word to the lady of his heart. The love would have remained an ideal passion, like that of Petrarch for his Laura." [1] Nothing, it seems to me, could be more mistaken than the conclusion of this statement. It is true that Troilus, up to the time that he confided in Pandarus, did direct his attention to idealizing Criseyde ; that, however, was what every courtly lover was expected to do and did ; it is what most lovers do now-a-days. It is true, too, that as yet he had taken no active steps in his own behalf, and that he gave himself up to bewailing his misery. But here again Troilus was acting exactly like the conventional courtly lover. It was too early in the game for him to act for himself. " Love which is won too easily is not prized," was a dictum as old as the troubadours. Every lover was supposed to give himself up for a time to self-abasement, and to become the plaything of despair. When it occurred to him that he must die unless his lady knew of his sorrow, then it was time for him to act. We may not tell just how Chaucer would have made Troilus behave without Pandarus's intervention. But we may judge, perhaps, from what other lovers did in such circumstances. To say nothing of the many lovers in the Old French literature, take the case of the knight in the *Book of the Duchess.*

[1] Root, p. 116.

His lady knew nothing of his love for a long time, because he was afraid to tell her, lest he should make her angry. Only when he felt,

> But I telle hir, I nam but deed,[1]

did he muster up courage to speak his love. The unhappy Aurelius loved Dorigen

> Two yeer and more, as was his aventure,
> But never dorste he telle hir his grevaunce;
> Withouten coppe he drank al his penaunce.

But when he considered that he must die as did Echo for Narcissus, he found courage to tell Dorigen of the passion that was consuming him. The erotic literature of France and England of the twelfth to the fifteenth centuries indicates that platonic idealism was little known in these countries at that time. Troilus wanted Criseyde and wanted her badly; and it is highly improbable that his love would have remained an ideal passion like Petrarch's for Laura. On the contrary, it is safe to assume that it would have led him to seek his lady, as far as external circumstances permitted, and to beseech her favor, even had not Pandarus happened along at the proper moment.[2] In furnishing

---

[1] *B. of D.*, 1188.

[2] Mr. Root (p. 117) quotes Troilus's statement,

> But herke, Pandare, o word, for I nolde
> That thou in me wendest so greet folye,
> That to my lady I desiren sholde
> That toucheth harm or vilenye (i, 148),

to show the platonic nature of the lover's affection. This is in fact a conventional sentiment; Pandarus, far from considering it platonic, understands the conventionality of it, when he says:

> And I thy borw? fy! no wight dooth but so (i, 149).

The best proof of the conventionality of the phrase is seen in the fact that Boccaccio makes Troilo say the same thing:

> Ed oltre a questo, Pandar, non vorria
> Che tu credessi che io disiassi
> Di cotal donna alcuna villania. — *Filostrato*, ii, 31.

Surely, no one thinks of the love of Troilo and Griseide as platonic!

him the character Pandarus, Chaucer's "author Lollius" enabled him to manage the technique of his poem in accord with the conventional ideas ; for the intermediary between the lover and his lady was a recognized figure in mediaeval love affairs. The scope of the works of Boccaccio and Chaucer, however, allowed these authors highly to elaborate this feature ; and fortunately for those who love Chaucer, the exercise of his genius has resulted in the magnificent portrayal of Pandarus. In handing the management of his love affair over to Pandarus, Troilus does not, therefore, necessarily reveal his unpractical nature. Does his lack of action at the Parliament make such a revelation?

Chaucer gives as explanation of his hero's silence during the negotiations for the exchange of Criseyde, the fear that men might see his affection for her (iv, 22). Feeling thus, Troilus decides to await developments, having in mind two things : first, how to save her reputation ; second, how he might withstand the exchange in case the Parliament decreed it (iv, 23). This was a particularly hard problem for Troilus, since it was necessary to do both things at the same time. If he wished to defeat the purpose of the Parliament, he must do it in such a way as not to compromise Criseyde. Evidently, such a thing was impossible. But Chaucer assures us that his feelings were right in the matter :

> Love him made al prest to doon hir byde,
> And rather dye than she sholde go (iv, 24).

A twentieth-century lover, in free America, might, in these circumstances, have demanded his sweetheart in the face of all opposition, if he had the courage. Troilus had the inclination to do so. But what good would it have done ? What good did Hector's opposition to the proposed exchange do ? Yet Hector was more influential in Troy than was Troilus ; and he was not actuated by any motives of personal interest. Troilus saw all this ; and saw, furthermore, that any open action on his part

would not only be useless, but would destroy all hopes of future
happiness with Criseyde.

> But resoun seyde him, on that other syde,
> ' With-oute assent of hir ne do not so,
> Lest for thy werk she wolde be thy fo,
> And seyn, that through thy medling is y-blowe
> Your bother love, there it was erst unknowe ' (iv, 24).

This would have spoiled everything. It was the business of the
mediaeval lover to keep his *liaison* secret and to submit to the
will of his mistress. Had it been the affair of husband and wife,
the hero might have taken things into his own hands. But Troilus
and Criseyde were not married, and did not intend to be. Mere
prudence directed him to do just what he did do ; to speak out
at the Parliament would have been an action of unpractical
rashness.

> With mannes herte he gan his sorwes drye (iv, 22),

and it seems clear that the poet intended him, in his trying situation, to act like a man, reserving his indulgence in grief for the
privacy of his room, instead of fainting in the presence of the
Parliament like Boccaccio's hero, Troilo.[1]

In the interview with Pandarus which followed the decision
of Parliament, Troilus, it seems to me, shows himself of no
mean strength of character ; and it is equally clear, I think, that
Chaucer here intends to present him in the best light possible.
Pandarus finds him in the midst of lamentations over his cruel
fate, and, in his practical way, makes some suggestions,

> . . . for the nones alle,
> To helpe his freend, lest he for sorwe deyde.
> For doutelees, to doon his wo to falle,
> He roughte not what unthrift that he seyde (iv, 62).

His first suggestion is that Troilus take another mistress, since
it is unavoidable that Criseyde go to the Grecian camp ; and he

---

[1] *Filostrato*, iv, 18. See on this point Kissner, p. 43.

backs this up with his usual subtlety in argument. Troilus in his reply to this suggestion appears to good advantage, even if we measure his answer by present-day standards ; and certainly, if we judge it by those of mediaeval times. He says that Pandarus's suggestion would be very appropriate if he (Troilus) were a fiend. But since he has promised to be true to Criseyde, he will remain so, though he die. As for Pandarus's opinion that he may find a fairer mistress, such comparisons are useless ; he cannot agree. But above all, he has not the power to act on these suggestions ; and if he had, he would not do so.

> Thou most me first transmuwen in a stoon,
> And reve me my passiounes alle,
> Er thou so lightly do my wo to falle (iv, 67).

Defeated in this argument, the ever ready Pandarus suggests the alternative of forcibly abducting Criseyde. Troilus's answer is noteworthy. He says that he had thought of all this before, and of much more than Pandarus suggested. Abduction was out of the question if he cared anything for his own reputation ; everybody would blame him for opposing his father, since Criseyde was exchanged for the good of the town.[1] He had thought, he says, of asking Priam for Criseyde, provided she would consent (a very important proviso) ; but this would be sure to get her into trouble. The thing that he feared most of all was bringing slander upon his lady ; he would rather die than do this (iv, 81). His conclusion is that there is no way out of his difficulty.

> For certeyn is, sin that I am hir knight,
> I moste hir honour lever han than me
> In every cas, as lovere oughte of right.
> Thus am I with desyr and reson twight ;
> Desyr for to distourben hir me redeth,
> And reson nil not, so myn herte dredeth (iv, 82).

[1] iv, 78–79.

Only one alternative is left to be considered; that is, for Troilus to marry Criseyde. Why does not marriage occur to him and to her? Kissner, in considering why both Boccaccio and Chaucer have made their heroine a widow, explains: " Hätte er Chryseis als junges Mädchen dargestellt, so wäre die ganze Verwickelung der Knotenschurzung weggefallen." For, he explains, when Calchas asked for his daughter, all the hero would have had to do would have been to step forth and claim her as his wife. This would have left out the faithlessness of the heroine, and would have made necessary an entirely different treatment of the whole story.[1] Kissner's statement with regard to the dénouement of the story is evidently correct; but not for the reasons he gives. As a matter of fact, there would have been no more reason for the hero's claiming Criseyde as a maiden for his bride than Criseyde as a widow; certainly no objection attached to marrying a widow simply because she was a widow. Kissner forgets that Troilus was in exactly the same position as Hamlet:

> He may not, as unvalued persons do,
> Carve for himself.

As the son of the King of Troy, Troilus could not claim whom he wished as bride, regardless of the wishes of others and of the interest of the state. In Boccaccio's story difference of rank is definitely mentioned as an obstacle to marriage.[2] In Chaucer's

---

[1] Kissner, pp. 45–46.

[2] See *Filostrato*, ii, 76; iv, 69. Griseida in thinking the matter over, which Pandaro has proposed, says to herself:

> chi al presente t' ama,
> È di troppo più alta condizione
> Che tu non se'.

Troilo in giving an excuse for not asking Priam for Griseida, says:

> Nè spero ancora ch' el dovesse darla,
> Si per non romper le cose promesse,
> E perchè la direbbe diseguale
> A me, al qual' vuol dar donna reale.

poem, while Criseyde is evidently a lady of high station, and numbers among her friends members of the royal family, yet she is not of the blood royal. She herself says of Troilus :

> Eek wel wot I my kinges sone is he;
> And sith he hath to see me swich delyt,
> If I wolde utterly his sighte flee,
> Paraunter he mighte have me in dispyt,
> Thurgh which I mighte stonde in worse plyt (ii, 102).

These lines show that the heroine recognized the superior rank of her lover. The last line, too, recalls the " plyt " that she was really in. When Calchas forsook the Trojan party and went over to the Greeks, the Trojan populace, Chaucer tells us, were so enraged that they immediately took steps to be avenged on his family, threatening to burn them all. Criseyde was saved from a terrible fate by appealing to the generosity of Hector. The feeling which the people had against her is shown again in their actions at the Parliament which decreed her exchange for Antenor. Even the influence of Hector was not sufficient to withstand their demand for the proposed exchange. Clearly, had Troilus, or even Priam himself, been willing for the marriage of Troilus and Criseyde to take place, the turbulent populace of Troy and their hatred of everything and everybody connected with Calchas would have had to be reckoned with. Thus we see that difference of rank as well as questions of state would have been real barriers to the marriage. If Chaucer had been asked why he did not have the two marry, these reasons would have been natural ones to put forward. It is most likely, however, that the question was not considered by him at all. The poet found the plot of the story already made for him, and he chose to use it as it was. To bring about a marriage between the hero and heroine would have been to destroy the whole dénouement. He had his choice of telling the story without the marriage feature, or of making it a story different from the one he wished to tell, namely, one relating the faithlessness of Criseyde. Once more we must remember that Chaucer is narrating a tale of courtly love, with which marriage was incompatible. This was full and sufficient reason, to say nothing of those already mentioned, for adhering to his source.

The fact is, Troilus was face to face with a problem which was insoluble, if the conditions of the story are to be kept intact. These conditions render it necessary, first, that he, as a lover, make his will subservient to that of his lady ; and, second, that he shield her name at whatever cost. To violate either requirement is to come into conflict with his own sense of honor and self-respect. In refusing to free himself from his predicament at the expense of his honor, he shows himself a man of no small courage. The question as to whether the conditions which hedge the lover about are sensible or not, is irrelevant. We of this time may not think so ; what Chaucer thought, does not affect the case. He was working within the limitations of the conventional ideas of what a lover should be. His plot involved those ideas, and in following them out he brought his hero face to face with a difficulty which he could not surmount without compromise of honor.

Chaucer calls his poem a tragedy.[1] The force which brings about the tragical end of the story is Fate, and this element is brought into prominent relief throughout the poem. The author makes it very plain that it is Fate that forces the two lovers apart. But in effecting her purpose in this manner she works through the strength of the hero, and only because of his strength of character could she work as she did. Had Troilus followed Pandarus's suggestion and abducted Criseyde, Fate might still

---

[1] Bk. v, l. 256. For Chaucer's idea of what made a tragedy, see the first stanza of the *Monk's Tale*. See also Chaucer's gloss in Boëthius, Bk. ii, Pr. 2 : " Tragedie is to seyn, a ditee of a prosperitee for a tyme, that endeth in wrechednesse." Cf. ten Brink, *Studien*, Münster, 1870, p. 77.

have operated in separating the two, but the end would have
had to be achieved in some way different from that described
by Chaucer in the poem as we have it.

It seems clear, then, that Chaucer conceived the character of
Troilus, not as a vacillating, visionary, unpractical weakling ; but
as a man of strength, with the courage of his convictions, whether
such convictions led him to oppose love or, having been overcome by love, to be loyal till death. In addition to the quality
of physical courage, which every lover was expected to have, he
was endowed with sterling qualities of spirit. These it was which
the poet makes attract Criseyde. She says :

> For trusteth wel, that your estat royal
> Ne veyn delyt, nor only worthinesse
> Of yow in werre, or torney marcial,
> Ne pompe, array, nobley, or eek richesse,
> Ne made me to rewe on your distresse ;
> But moral vertu, grounded upon trouthe,
> That was the cause I first hadde on yow routhe !
>
> Eek gentil herte and manhod that ye hadde,
> And that ye hadde, as me thoughte, in despyt
> Every thing that souned into badde,
> As rudenesse and poeplish appetyt ;
> And that your reson brydled your delyt,
> This made, aboven every creature
> That I was your, and shal, whyl I may dure (iv, 239–240).

But how shall we explain some of the actions of Troilus which
seem strange to us, in a man of the strength of character he
appears to be ? To say nothing of his swooning at the bedside
of his beloved, what shall we say of the endless sighing and
weeping of the lover, and all the conduct which has led critics
to call him effeminate and unmanly ? Most of this can be explained by the conventions of love literature. Mediaeval lovers,
if we are to believe the literature, were an extraordinarily lachry-
mose lot. Lament was the principal article of their conduct, at

least up to the point when they gained the favor of their ladies, and swoons were certain to occur under any unusual stress of emotion. If these features are more noticeable in Troilus than in other lovers, the explanation from our point of view may be, perhaps, that his love opened up in him a vein of sentimentalism which he himself did not before know that he possessed. The question then is : Is sentimentality necessarily a sign of effeminacy ? and is it inconsistent with courage and strength of character ? That it was consistent with physical courage in the case of Troilus is perfectly clear; and it seems, too, from what has already been shown, that it was not inconsistent with strength of spirit.

The critics have expressed various opinions of the character of Criseyde. Ten Brink's, often quoted, is as follows : " The English Criseyde is more innocent, less experienced, less sensual, more modest than her Italian prototype. What a multitude of agencies were needed to inflame her love for Troilus ; what a concatenation of circumstances, what a display of trickery and intrigue, to bring her at last to his arms ! We see the threads of the web in which she is entangled drawing ever closer around her ; her fall appears to us excusable, indeed unavoidable ; and if afterwards, after the separation, she does not resist the temptation of Diomede, how is she accountable, if her mind is less true and deep than that of Troilus ? how is she accountable, when that first fall robbed her of her moral stay? . . . She only gives her heart to Diomede when touched with sympathy for the wounds he had received from Troilus ; and her infidelity is immediately followed by repentance." [1] Ten Brink here seems to picture the heroine as an innocent girl, who has been trapped into committing a grievous fault in yielding to Troilus ; who was involved in a chain of circumstances which was too powerful for her feminine weakness and inexperience to break. As such, she is to be pitied and her offence is to be condoned.

[1] Ten Brink, *Hist. Eng. Lit.*, Vol. II, pt. i, p. 92.

Much the same attitude appears in the expression of Furnivall, in which he speaks of Shakspere's conception of the character : " To have the beautiful Cressida hesitating, palpitating like the nightingale before her sin, driven by force of hard circumstances which she could not control, into unfaithfulness to her love ; — to have this Cressida whom Chaucer spared for very ruth, set before us as a mere shameless wanton, making eyes at all the men she sees, and showing her looseness in the movement of every limb, is a terrible blow." [1]

In the statement of Courthope,[2] another idea is made prominent. He says : " It is not till the fourth (sic) book that the *deterioration* (italics are mine) of Cressida's nature reveals itself incidentally in the facility with which she listens without displeasure though without response to the artful love making of Diomede." Mr. Courthope seems to consider that Criseyde after her departure from Troy is a different Criseyde from the one figuring in the story up to this exchange of prisoners.

In opposition to these estimates of the heroine — the unfortunate innocent of ten Brink, and the double Criseyde of Courthope and others — Professor Cook comes forward with a characterization [3] in which he considers the moral laxness of the various Briseidas, Criseides, or Griseidas from Homer to Boccaccio, as well as the despicable rôles played by the various prototypes of Pandarus and Calchas. After marshalling all the evidence possible to show that the mistress of Boccaccio was a shameless, sensual, self-indulgent, and heartless woman, he holds that "Criseyde virtually represents Boccaccio's mistress."[4]

---

[1] *Leopold Shakspere*, London, 1880, p. lxxx.

[2] *History of English Poetry*, i, 264.

[3] *Pub. Mod. Lang. Assoc.*, 1907, pp. 531 ff.

[4] Cook, p. 547. The general inference to be drawn from all this seems to be, that the society in which Criseyde had been moving for the preceding centuries was a bad lot, and that therefore little could be expected of her when she got into Chaucer's hands !

Substantially the same view of the heroine is taken by Mr. Root, in the characterization which he has elaborated from suggestions by Professor Cook.[1] The total impression given by the two characterizations is that Criseyde is a designing, calculating, sensual, "lightly-loving" adventuress, who plays "the rôle of betrayed innocence with just sufficient reluctance before the act, and reproach after it is accomplished, to carry out the illusion."[2]

None of these views of the heroine, I believe, shows us Criseyde as Chaucer conceived her. She is not, I think, innocent; at least in the sense that ten Brink seems to indicate. Certainly she is not, in Chaucer, calculating and designing, even if she is cool-headed. If we agree that she is amorous, it is not necessary to conclude that she is the worse for this element in her make-up. Finally the Criseyde who falls in love with Diomede is not, I believe, different in her essential character from the Criseyde who, until she met Diomede, was true to Troilus. It will be worth while to see how these beliefs are borne out by the poem itself.

In the first part of this study of the *Troilus* I have tried to show, with some detail, that the story is told in terms of the courtly love ideas, as embodied in the poetry of the troubadours and in the work of Andreas Capellanus. Of this proposition there can be no doubt; as corollaries to it, there follow two facts, a consideration of which underlies any correct estimate of the heroine of the poem.

The first of these has been already mentioned in the statement that Criseyde knew to what end her *amour* with Troilus tended. This comes out clearly in the poem. In that first interview of Pandarus with Criseyde, he argues that the worst that could come of her showing some favor to Troilus would be that

---

[1] See Cook, footnote to p. 531, and Root, footnote to p. 115.
[2] Root, p. 114.

people would wonder at Troilus's going and coming. But, he continues, every one, unless he were a fool, would deem this "love of friendship" (ii, 53); for, he says,

> Swich love of freendes regneth al this toun (ii, 55).

He follows this up by reminding her that she is growing older, and every hour wastes a part of her beauty. Criseyde understands the drift of his argument, as is clear from her answer, in which, weeping, she complains that he, whom she considered her best friend, advised her to a love that it was his duty to forbid (ii, 59). When Pandarus has effectually frightened her into thinking that not only Troilus's, but his own life depends on her relenting, she begins to look things in the face. She considers the possibility of saving both her uncle's life and her own good name (ii, 67–68); and she promises Pandarus that she will try to please Troilus, as far as is consistent with keeping her reputation unspotted (ii, 69). After Pandarus has gone, and she is arguing with herself the advisability of loving Troilus, she reckons in his favor the fact that he is no "boaster":

> To wys is he to do so gret a vyce (ii, 104).

"But," she adds significantly, "he will never get a chance to boast of my favors." The heroine is, however, not at all sure of her ground here; she is wavering between loving and not loving; she remembers how he is fit to have the love of the very best woman in Troy, "so she hir honour save." The necessity for guarding the reputation is clearly brought out. This is to be a love which demands very especial precautions in this respect. The first firm ground that she gets on in this self-examination seems to be the conclusion:

> And though that I myn herte sette at reste
> Upon this knight, that is the worthieste,
> And kepe alwey myn honour and my name,
> By alle right, it may do me no shame (ii, 109).

This is practically the same conclusion that Pandarus had tried to force on her mind in the interview; he held that as long as they could blind people and make them think that this was a case of "love of friendship" there could be no harm.

Taken in connection with Criseyde's anxiety to keep her fair name, the numerous references to secrecy have more than conventional significance. After the meeting at the house of Deiphebus, in which Criseyde promises Troilus her love, Pandarus is much concerned about its being kept strictly secret.

> But gode brother, do now as thee oughte,
> For goddes love, and keep hir out of blame,
> Sin thou art wys, and *save alwey hir name* (iii, 38),

for her name was as yet "halwed" among people, and no man could say that she had ever done amiss (iii, 39). And Pandarus goes on to preach a little sermon on the evils of boasting of favors received from women. Troilus, in his exaltation of spirit, not only promises to keep everything secret, but bids Pandarus choose for his *amie* whichever of his (Troilus's) sisters pleases him best. And he kept his promise faithfully, the poet assures us. No one could have told by word or deed of his, what were his intentions in this matter. In short, he was so discreet in everything and so secret that Criseyde laid aside her fears, and

> felte he was to hir a wal
> Of steel, and sheld from every displesaunce (iii, 69).

After the first night of the lovers together, Criseyde urges Troilus to haste away,

> Or elles I am lost for evermo! (iii, 204)

Pandarus's admonition, too, when Troilus tells him of his joys, is, in effect: "Keep it quiet; do and say nothing rash"; and Troilus's answer shows that he realizes that Criseyde's fair name is at stake (iii, 232–234). When the parliament, at which Troilus is present, decides to exchange Criseyde for Antenor, the lover can say nothing, lest men see his affection.   He decides to wait, casting in his mind,

> how to save hir honour (iv, 23).

Later, he rejects Pandarus's advice to abduct Criseyde, because

> It moste been disclaundre to hir name (iv, 81).

When Criseyde unfolds her plan of going to the Greek camp and returning in ten days, she comforts Troilus by telling him :

> I see that ofte, ther-as we ben now,
> That for the beste, our conseil for to hyde,
> Ye speke not with me, nor I with yow
> In fourtenight ; ne see yow go ne ryde (iv, 190).

When Troilus, in this same interview, urges her to flee with him, she objects :

> And also thenketh on myn honestee
> That floureth yet, how foule I sholde it shende,
> And with what filthe it spotted sholde be,
> If in this forme I sholde with yow wende (iv, 226).

This insistence on secrecy and the fear of slanderous tongues, this anxiety to keep her name unspotted, not only on the part of Pandarus and Troilus, but on that of Criseyde herself, can mean but one thing.   All seems to point to the fact that the heroine knew from the outset that this amour meant ultimately a full and complete yielding to the passion of Troilus.

The second fact following from the statement that the *Troilus* is told in terms of the courtly love is that Criseyde's crime does not consist in her yielding to Troilus, but in her unfaithfulness to him.   We have seen that at heart the courtly system of love was sensual ; that its basic principle was the ennobling power of a love which from the Christian point of view is illicit.   All the characters in the poem are believers in the religion of Love ; and Criseyde, as well as the rest, is not a Christian, even though she says it would be more becoming for her as a widow to be reading "holy seintes lives" than to be dancing a May dance (ii, 17). Clearly, she is not to be blamed for what is a part of the system. On the other hand, constancy was a cardinal principle of courtly love, and in giving her love to Diomede she was sinning against the religion of which she was an adherent.

One other important point in addition to those named is to be noted in connection with the heroine; this is the fact that Chaucer has carefully provided that she be a widow. In Benoit of Ste. Maure, she is unmarried; in Boccaccio's story, on the other hand, she is a widow, the Italian poet making the change, probably, to suit more nearly the circumstances of his own love affair.[1] Chaucer, in taking up the story, wisely retained this feature as he found it in Boccaccio; for the bearing of Criseyde's widowhood on her conduct in the *Troilus* is as clear as it is important. So far as Chaucer's story, or Boccaccio's either, is concerned, we have no reason to think that the heroine, up to the time of meeting Troilus, had been otherwise than discreet and circumspect in the highest degree. On the contrary, the impression is given strongly that she had been a true and faithful wife to her husband now dead. But as a wife she had lost the bloom of her virgin innocence; and in a perfectly legitimate way she knew things that as an unmarried woman she would not be expected to know, and, indeed, would have no business knowing. Clearly then Criseyde is not innocent in the sense that ten Brink's statement seems to indicate, if I have the correct impression of the meaning of his remarks.

If now we start with a heroine of whom the things just indicated are true: namely, that she is not innocent, and that she is fully conscious to what length she will be called to go, in case she decides to love Troilus; if we start with such a heroine,

---

[1] See Cook, p. 537; quoting from Della Torre, he shows that Maria of the *Fiammetta*, whom the critics take to be figured in Griseida, was already married.

remembering at the same time that, in case she does yield to Troilus, she is committing no fault from the point of view of the courtly system of love, in what light does her conduct in the story place her character? In the first place, may we say she is designing or calculating?[1] Let us see how her mind works in her interview with Pandarus, in which he has told her that Troilus loves her, adding at the same time that if the knight dies for her love, she will be responsible, not only for Troilus's death but for her uncle's. The reader cannot fail to notice with what skill Pandarus has managed his side of this conversation; how he has whetted her curiosity, how he has insinuated that her beauty is the cause of a passion in Troilus which may lead him to do violence to himself, and lastly how he has deftly hinted, and *only hinted*, at what he should like her to do for Troilus, and for him as the friend of Troilus and at the same time her uncle. Pandarus is sly; and who should realize this better than Criseyde, his own niece, who must have known him intimately for a long time? She grasps the situation, though vaguely, in a minute, and realizes that here is a design which concerns her closely. She thinks:

> I shal fele what he meneth, y-wis.

What could be more natural for a cool-headed person like Criseyde to think? For the heroine realizes that she must have herself well in hand in dealing with an adversary like her uncle; and she is quite able to take care of herself. And so she asks:

> Now eem . . . what wolde ye devyse,
> What is your reed, I sholde doon of this?

---

[1] See Cook, p. 547: "It is evident that Criseyde knew how to woo, under the guise of being wooed." Also Root: "There is an air of cool deliberation about this which strikes one as quite incongruous" (p. 108). "Once more — one discovers that curious tone of calculation" (p. 109). "Attention must be called again to the tone of calm calculation, not to say casuistry which characterizes it" (p. 109), — all referring to speeches by Criseyde.

This gives Pandarus the opportunity he wants ; and he presses Troilus's claims, and reminds her that age is wasting every hour a part of her beauty. But he goes too far. She tearfully reproaches him for persuading her to love, when his duty should lead him to forbid it. He falls back on a more telling argument, and works upon her pity through her sense of fear, holding before her constantly the probability of Troilus's death and of his own. The poet here assures us that Criseyde was naturally easily frightened :

> She was the ferfulleste wight
> That mighte be.

Are we to believe this ? Most certainly so, I think. Effectually frightened, she detains Pandarus, who had hastily started away, after making his threats of violence to himself. She now feels sorry for him and she begins to look at affairs squarely,

> And thoughte thus, ' unhappes fallen thikke
> Alday for love, and in swich maner cas,
> As men ben cruel in hem-self and wikke ;
> And if this man slee here him-self, allas !
> In my presence, it wol be no solas,
> What men wolde of hit deme I can nat seye.'

We are apt to laugh at the probability of self-violence as the result of love. And yet we know *at this day*, just as Criseyde thought, that " unhappes fallen thikke alday for love," and " unhappes " of the very kind Criseyde feared. She regains her coolness quickly, thinking,

> It nedeth me ful sleyly for to pleye.

Is there a tone of calculation about this line ? I cannot see it. Criseyde encounters a difficulty, and she faces it fairly and squarely. She is prudent and careful of her actions, and still cool-headed. Shall we, for this reason, call her " calculating " ? The truth is, she is here showing — what comes out more clearly later in the poem — one of her most noticeable traits, the ability and willingness to look at facts in the face. And so she succeeds in satisfying her crafty uncle, without at the same time committing herself to any course of action which will lead her into difficulty in the future. This done, she shows the womanly side of her nature in her desire to hear more of the new lover.

After Pandarus's departure, Criseyde considers the new turn that her affairs have taken. It is just now that Troilus comes riding by, and she sees him in his glory as a knightly hero. She remembers that this is the man who, her uncle swears, will die if she does not show him her pity. Naturally enough, she begins to consider the matter in all its phases. The lure of this new love which is just awaking in her is strong, but there are arguments against it.

> And, lord! so she gan in hir thought argue
> In this matere of which I have yow told,
> And what to doon best were, and what eschue,
> That plyted she ful ofte in many fold.
> Now was hir herte warm, now was it cold,
> And what she thoughte somwhat shal I wryte,
> As to myn auctor listeth for to endyte.

Then follows that remarkable soliloquy of the heroine. The arguments in favor of her loving him are strong : 1. The " person " and " gentilesse " make him a fit and attractive lover. 2. He is her king's son ; and since his delight is in seeing her, it would be very unwise, considering her " estat," to scorn him. 3. It is almost certain to her that Troilus " means well." 4. He is discreet ; he is no boaster. Of these four reasons, the first appeals to the distinctly feminine element in her. The other three are what might be called more practical considerations ; they concern more than her personal affections. Her position in the city was already not enviable, on account of the treason of her father ; it was the part of wisdom not to go too fast in

absolutely ignoring the wish of the son of the king, whom her
father had betrayed. As for the other considerations, they are
important for any sensible young woman to have in mind, before
going too far. The mediaeval love literature makes at least one
thing clear : that false lovers were as numerous as they are
to-day, and that the lady who was deceived by one of these had
every reason to cry, "Alas ! had I known ! " If Criseyde had
been an ultra-romantic young maiden, the thought of being loved
by a king's son might easily have set her heart in a flutter, and
have made her forget or neglect very practical considerations.
But she was not a maiden ; she had already been wooed and won.
Shall we call her " calculating " because she weighs every side
of this important question ? Why not rather call her wise ?

But there are other arguments in favor of the new love.
Troilus is " out and out " the worthiest man in Troy, save
Hector ; and he is fit to have for his love the very best lady,
in every respect, in all the " noble town " ;

> And yet his lyf al lyth now in my cure.

And then follows that remarkable example of her facing the
facts in the case, which is so noticeable in the heroine. She
realizes that she is the very fairest and " goodliest " woman in
all the town of Troy, and so everybody says. What wonder is
it that Troilus loves her ? She is her own woman, young and
free. She is not a nun. Why shall she not set her heart at
rest on this worthy Troilus, provided she can keep her name
unspotted ? We must answer for Criseyde that there is no reason for her not granting him her love, and every reason for her
doing so, if we decide the question from the only fair point of
view, — that of the courtly love ideas. One line in this soliloquy
should not be lost sight of. The poet is careful to have her say,
when she is considering her physical charms,

> Al wolde I that noon wiste of this thought.

This absolves her from the charge of immodesty. There certainly is nothing immodest in a woman's recognizing her own beauty, as long as she does not publish the fact that she recognizes it. Chaucer has here shown us the innermost workings of the mind of his heroine, as, indeed, he has with all the important characters of his drama. There is danger of our forming unfavorable opinions of these characters from our very intimacy with their private thoughts — thoughts which were perfectly natural and legitimate for them to have, but the publishing of which would be inexcusable. Critics would do well to bear this in mind, for instance, in speaking of Troilus as effeminate and unpractical. Certainly the people of Troy did not consider him in any such light, as he gave them no reason to do so. And so in this soliloquy, if we should lose sight of this principle, it would be possible for us to start with Criseyde's frank recognition that she is of an amorous disposition, and then, passing from this to her conclusion that there is no reason why she should not grant her love to Troilus, to make her out not only immodest but even brazen. Clearly, this would be absolutely the wrong impression of her, if we may judge her by her conduct in relation with Pandarus and Troilus. After coming to her conclusion, she still goes on to consider the arguments for and against it. There is the question of giving up her liberty, and of the "stormy lyf" that lovers lead, of the disadvantage a woman is at in a love affair, of the jangling of "wikked tongues," of the faithlessness of men in general. But after all, in accord with her strong practical bent, she decides to take chances in the matter, concluding that

> . . . he which that no-thing undertaketh,
> No-thing ne acheveth, be him looth or dere.

This soliloquy of Criseyde may rightly be considered as the poet's revelation to the reader of the character of his heroine. If we

can form an estimate of her from this scene, it will then be
possible to see whether the character remains constant throughout the poem.

Such an estimate is possible; for certain things come out
clearly in the first real presentation of the heroine. In the first
place, she is amorous. We have her own words for this:

> What shal I doon? to what fyn live I thus?
> Shal I nat loven, in cas if that me leste?
> What, par dieux! I am nought religious!

by which, of course, she means she is not the kind of woman to
be a nun. We also have Pandarus's testimony as to this characteristic of his niece:

> And for to speke of hir in special,
> Hir beautee to bithinken and hir youthe,
> *It sit hir nought to be celestial*
> *As yet.*

There is the element in her nature that makes her fond of the
opposite sex. It is well to observe that there is nothing improper
in this. We may accept Pandarus's observation as being true,
broadly speaking:

> Was never man ne woman yet bigete
> That was unapt to suffren loves hete
> Celestial, or elles love of kinde.

If some women are devoid of tendencies toward "love of kinde,"
there is nothing unnatural or in any way improper in such tendencies in other women. We must not assume that an amorous
disposition in Criseyde means a sensual nature.

Another thing that comes out clearly in Criseyde's soliloquy
is that she is not sentimental. The practical manner in which
she considers and weighs every side of the important question
of granting her love indicates this. Here was a love offered to
her, which might well sweep any young woman, too romantically

inclined, off her feet. But not Criseyde. She looks at things as they are, and as they may turn out to be. The poet has made her, in this respect, a foil to the sentimental Troilus.

Another characteristic of the heroine appears, not in the soliloquy, but in the interview with Pandarus : she is perfectly self-possessed and cool-headed under fire, so to speak. She has a quick wit, and when in her arguments with Pandarus she realizes,

It nedeth me ful sleyly for to pleye,

she puts her wits to work against her crafty opponent.

It is important to note some elements not found in her character. It has appeared, I trust, in the foregoing discussion, that Criseyde was not *designing and calculating ;* at least these words, with their present connotations, are not the correct ones to apply to her. Furthermore, there is nothing in all the first part of the poem to leave the impression that she is bold or immodest ; Chaucer's description of her while at the temple, as standing there

With ful assured loking and manere,

indicates no more than a modest, quiet self-control on her part, and agrees well with what we see of her later in the poem.

We have in Criseyde, then, a young widow of strongly amorous nature, but circumspect and modest ; of a quick and ready wit and a cool head ; without sentimentality, but with a marked ability to face facts which concern her and her welfare closely. This young woman is made the heroine of a poem, told in accord with the ideas of courtly love, — a love which in its essence is sensual, and which ultimately, as the heroine well knows, demands a complete yielding to the passion of the hero. How does this young woman conduct herself in the later parts of the poem ?

The next important appearance of Criseyde, after her soliloquy, is in the interview with Troilus at the house of Deiphebus.

Troilus is pretending to be sick, and at the approach of Criseyde he makes a movement to arise and " do [her] honor in some wyse." She gently stops him and reveals her purpose in coming to see him : first to thank him for his " lordshipe " in the past, and to beg a continuance of it. To Troilus, who was feeling the propriety of his beseeching her for favor, rather than of being besought by her, the situation was embarrassing, and he was unable to keep from showing his feelings in his blushes and confusion.

> Criseyde al this aspyede wel ynough,
> *For she was wys.*

It is possible to give these last four words in reading, a meaning that would be entirely wrong in the connection ; a knowing wink, a shrug, a peculiar inflection of the voice would easily enough convey the impression that Criseyde is here a designing and crafty adventuress. Taken as the poet evidently means them, the words mean no more than a statement of what is indeed true of most women in their love affairs. How many women, charming and innocent ones too, are unaware of the feelings of their lovers, even before such feelings have been declared ? Criseyde was " wys " in this manner ; and nothing more need be implied in the words. True to her feminine nature, however, she coyly leads Troilus on to declare his passion :

> . . . I wolde him preye
> To telle me the fyn of his entente ;
> Yet wiste I never wel what that he mente.

Then follow the lover's protestations of his desire to serve her patiently and humbly, in the genuine courtly fashion. The same Criseyde appears that we have seen before. She is cool and collected :

> With that she gan hir eyen on him caste
> Ful easily, and ful debonairly,
> Avysing hir, and hyed not to faste
> With never a word.

Quietly she tells him that she accepts him as a lover on the terms that he has just devised. And it must be noticed that the terms proposed were the most favorable ones possible to Criseyde. She expressly stipulates that

> A kinges sone al-though ye be, y-wis,
> Ye shul na-more have soverainetee
> Of me in love, than right in that cas is.

She is acting within her rights here ; for as her lover, Troilus could have no "soverainetee." Her discretion is manifest, in reminding him of the fact. She never forgets that in dealing with the sly Pandarus, and this young king's son hot with love for her,

> It nedeth me ful sleyly for to pleye.

Yet it must also be noted that the manner in which she promises her favor to Troilus is exquisitely charming and tender :

> And shortly, derë herte and al my knight,
> Beth glad, and draweth yow to lustinesse,
> And I shal trewely, with al my might,
> Your bittre tornen al into swetnesse,
> If I be she that may yow do gladnesse,
> For every wo ye shal recover a blisse ;
> And him in armes took, and gan him kisse.

At this point in the story we are to understand that Criseyde is fully decided in her mind to enter into this love affair with Troilus. True to the courtly ideas, the poet has kept her from granting her love, or even encouragement, too easily. He is very particular about defending her against any possible charge of lightness :

> For I sey nought that she so sodeynly
> Yaf him hir love, but that she gan enclyne
> To lyke him first, and I have told yow why ;
> And after that, his manhod and his pyne
> Made love withinne hir to myne,
> For which, by proces and by good servyse,
> He gat hir love, and in no sodein wyse.

And the poet has skilfully arranged it, so that we have seen the workings of her mind in considering all the arguments for and against this new love. It has become plain, I think, that she has been no easy wanton, simply waiting for the opportunity to give herself fully to Troilus. On the other hand, it is equally important to note that she has not been a prude. She has kept in mind her own interests in the matter and, when she decided to enter fully into this love, has done so with her eyes open. With his heroine in this state of mind, the poet is now ready for the climax of his story. This occurs in the meeting of the two lovers at the house of Pandarus.

The tender womanliness of Criseyde in this scene, in her endeavors first to satisfy the misgivings of Pandarus, and afterward to soothe Troilus, who, she is made to believe, is mad with jealousy; the pathos of her being accused of a fault of which she is entirely innocent; the delicacy of her nature which is revealed in her meeting the accusation, — all these things I pass over, important as they are in their bearing on the character of Criseyde. He who, in reading this scene, does not feel them, reads superficially, or with very little sympathy. Leaving these features, I wish only to look at one part of the interview in its relation to that side of Criseyde's character which has been under consideration. When Pandarus is arranging this meeting, and invites Criseyde to his house, the heroine's suspicions are aroused enough to make her inquire whether or not Troilus will be there. In his humorous, non-committal manner Chaucer declares:

> Nought list myn auctor fully to declare
> What that she thoughte whan he seyde so,
> That Troilus was out of town y-fare,
> As if he seyde ther-of sooth or no.

But, on the whole, the poet subtly makes us feel that Pandarus's reassurances are sufficient to allay the heroine's suspicions, and that she went to his house in innocence. Yet, after the scenes in which Troilus's feigned jealousy has been appeased, and he has been permitted to remain with her, we have the show of amorous violence on the hero's part, and his demand that she yield. To which she replies :

> Ne hadde I er now, my swete herte dere,
> Ben yolde, y-wis, I were now not here!

What shall we say to these words of Criseyde ? There is only one thing that can be said, — that they are a delicate way of stating the truth in the matter. If Criseyde had not already yielded in her mind, she certainly would not have been at the house of Pandarus. For, knowing, as she did, what was involved in her deciding to love Troilus *par amours*, the moment she decided to take him for " my knight, my pees, my suffisaunce," she had yielded then in her own mind. Let us, as Criseyde did, "set a cas." Suppose Criseyde had promised to marry Troilus in a legitimate fashion ; would she not have foreseen the events of her wedding night ? With equal clearness, in becoming the *amie* of Troilus, she saw that at some time there must follow the same events. The difference in the two cases lies in the uncertainty as to the time of the final adjustment of affairs. This very uncertainty as to events which Criseyde knew must come about some time or other, enables the poet to give the air of surprise which is about the story as he tells it ; for there is no doubt that the heroine is surprised in this scene, and Chaucer thus saves her from easy yielding. But with all this, there can be no doubt that she went to Pandarus's house feeling that possibly she might meet Troilus there, and matters would arrange themselves as they did. Before we condemn her for thus walking " with a hidden smile into the trap set by Pandarus with such needless craft," [1] we must remember once more that in making herself a party to the transactions of this night she is doing nothing

[1] Root, p. 114.

wrong according to the courtly ideas. Her honor has received no stain. Only by judging her and her actions by standards which have no place in this story, can we up to this point make her out a bad woman. She is amorous, and the poet intended to represent her so ; not cold and hard-hearted, but fond of men and at the same time conscious of the power of her beauty and wit over them. She is not light and easy in yielding herself, but ready to enjoy the extreme joys of love, when it is proper under the system for her to do so ; yet, up to this point of the story, she is true and faithful to one lover. To her amorous propensities she adds both the ability and the desire to look after her own welfare. She has also all the tenderness and the delicacy of womanly feeling which makes woman charming in the eyes of men. This is the Criseyde that Chaucer leaves with us at the close of the third book of the *Troilus*. Do we see the same Criseyde, or another, in the last two books ? Does her character undergo deterioration after her departure from Troy ?

We may note that from the time that the heroine first learns of the decision of the Parliament to exchange her for Antenor to the day of her departure there is no change in her character. Pandarus, who from the beginning has had the interests of the hero at heart, now appeals to Criseyde to use her womanly resourcefulness to relieve her lover of his bitter sorrow. This appeal is not in vain. Nowhere in the poem does the practical side of Criseyde's nature, and at the same time her tenderness, appear better than here, where she strives, though suffering quite as acutely as the hero, to forget her own sorrow out of consideration for her lover's feelings, and brings to bear all her womanly wit on the situation. She conveys to Troilus her reasons for thinking it best to accede to the wishes of the Parliament, and also her plan of action after reaching the Grecian camp. She feels confident that she can manage her father and handle the situation so that she shall be able to return to Troy within the ten-day limit. It is perfectly clear that in all this Criseyde is honest; she is yet true to her lover; and her sorrow at leaving is quite as poignant as that of the hero who remains behind. The poet is careful that at this point we do not get the wrong impression of her, and he assures us:

> And treweliche, as writen wel I finde,
> That al this thing was seyd of good entente;
> And that hir herte trewe was and kinde
> Towardes him, and spak right as she mente,
> And that she starf for wo neigh, whan she wente,
> And was in purpos ever to be trewe;
> Thus writen they that of hir werkes knewe.

There is every probability that Criseyde would have succeeded in managing things according to her plans, but for the fact that there now entered into the case circumstances which were too strong for her to cope with. She had stated to Troilus before leaving, her belief and hope that the war would soon end favorably to the Trojans; and, in such a case, she might easily return. When she gets to the Grecian camp, she finds that there is no foundation for this belief and hope. Her efforts to hoodwink her father also fail. In short, nothing turns out as she expected, and she is powerless to do anything but wait. In addition to this, Diomede, from the moment he met her on his way to the camp, began his wooing. But let us note that, while she was polite and courteous to him, she was, at least up to the tenth day, true to Troilus and fully determined to keep her promise. She realizes that she has acted imprudently in not taking Troilus's advice and fleeing with him; but she decides that she will on the morrow, "betyde what betyde," steal back to the city. But the morrow brought forth new reasons for not going. Diomede now begins his suit in earnest; and he shows himself a past master in the art of love-making. It is now that the very traits which we have seen in her character in the earlier part of the story, begin to appear again in her conduct and in her thinking. Already convinced that she shall not be able to manage her father as she had hoped, she comes to realize fully and unmistakably that the city of Troy is doomed, with all its inhabitants. Criseyde's tendency to look at things as they are and to determine her actions in accord with what seems her own best interests now exerts itself. She decides that it will be useless to go back to Troy and sacrifice herself in the destruction of the city. Besides, here is the powerful argument to keep her, that a dashing young man is offering himself as her lover. We do not trust this fine young Greek ourselves. His external brilliancy makes us feel that he is seeking only temporary pleasure in striving to win the heroine from her Trojan lover. Yet we feel that he is just the man to take her heart by storm. Knowing her amorous nature as we do, we are sure that she cannot hold out long against the seductive charms of this new hero. She must have a lover; indeed Criseyde without a lover is inconceivable. Love is happiness to her, and as she says,

> Felicitee clepe I my suffisaunce.

Since this is true, certainly had circumstances permitted her to remain in Troy, she would have been faithful to Troilus. As circumstances are, she realizes that the happy life in the city is a closed chapter. And so, true to her nature, she decides to act in accord with what she considers her best interests and her happiness.[1] She had done so before when she had given her love to Troilus. She does so now when she yields to Diomede. In the former case, though her action involved a surrender to

---

[1] Retorning in hir soule ay up and doun
The wordes of this sodein Diomede,
His greet estat, and peril of the toun,
And that she was allone and hadde nede
Of freendes help; and thus bigan to brede
The cause why, the sothe for to telle,
That she tok fully purpos for to dwelle (v, 147).

the passion of her lover, she did nothing wrong according to the code by which her actions were supposed to be governed. In the latter, she commits a definite and a heinous offense against that code. It is well to note that Criseyde herself realized the enormity of the offense. It never occurred to her, we may also observe, that she had done anything wrong in yielding to her amorous propensities in her relations with Troilus. Her sole sin was this particular, definite falseness in love, and it was this which caused her remorse.

> But trewely, the story telleth us,
> Ther made never wommen more wo
> Than she, whan that she falsed Troilus.
> She seyde, *allas ! for now is clene ago*
> *My name of trouthe in love, for evermo !*
> *For I have falsed oon the gentileste*
> *That ever was, and oon the worthieste !*

Her reproach was all the greater, because, at the very time she began to consider giving herself to Diomede, she was still in love with Troilus. To some men and women it is undoubtedly possible to love two persons at the same time. Criseyde was of such a nature ; for the poet makes it very clear that, up to the time that Diomede carried away her glove,

> . . . she . . . hadde hir herte on Troilus
> So faste, that ther may it noon arace.

Although it is pretty clear to us when she decides to give Diomede her heart, we must note that the poet, with a subtle touch, tries to save her from the charge of lightness by assuring us that it will be useless to consult the books to see how long it was after forsaking Troilus that she gave herself to Diomede. But he adds :

> . . . though that he [Diomede] began to wowe hir sone,
> Er he hir wan, yet was ther more to done.

Even after her decision to be true "algate" to Diomede, her
feeling for Troilus is still clear:

> But Troilus, sin I no better may,
> And sin that thus departen ye and I.
> Yet preye I god, so yeve yow right good day
> As for the gentileste, trewely,
> That ever I say, to serven feithfully,
> And best can ay his lady honour kepe:
> And with that word she brast anon to wepe.

Circumstances have so brought it about that henceforth Troilus
can be to her nothing more than a tender memory.

From the foregoing considerations it appears that in giving
her love to Diomede, Criseyde did nothing which was not in
accord with her nature and character as revealed in the first
part of the poem. She shows the same tendency to decide
matters in accord with her own interests. She grants her love
after deliberation, as she did when she decided to love Troilus.
If she is not so cool-headed in the latter case, it is because she
has her own conscience to reckon with, — an element which did
not enter into the former. There is the same strong appeal to
the amorous disposition as in the affair with Troilus. In short
the Criseyde of the latter part is the Criseyde of the earlier;
only circumstances are changed.

It is the fashion to say that the heroine's nature has deteriorated in her relations with Troilus.[1] Once more, we must recall
the fact that, according to courtly love ideas, such relations did
not degrade. On the contrary, they were supposed to ennoble
and uplift. The question as to the soundness of such philosophy
is aside from our consideration of Criseyde. Since, however,
her relations with her former lover may not be considered
wrong, it is clearly unjustifiable to say that her character had

---

[1] Dr. Root's statement (p. 115) may be regarded as typical: "Her poten-
tially sensual nature has inevitably deteriorated in her relations with Troilus."

undergone a gradual deterioration. It was circumstances, the poet makes clear, which led her to commit the sin for which her "belle" has been "ronge" from then till now. It was a definite, single offense; one that she committed deliberately, although she did it sorrowfully.

The charm and sweetness of this exquisitely feminine figure every sympathetic reader realizes. But it is well to keep in mind her faults; for there are some traits in her character which cannot be called admirable. She is far from being an-gelic. Angels, however, would make but poor lovers. In giving her faults the poet has made her a decidedly human creature, one that we can sympathize with and pity when she does not meas-ure up even to what might be regarded as a fair human standard. This is clearly Chaucer's own attitude toward her; and it will, I think, be the attitude of the reader who, like Chaucer, has a sympathetic appreciation of human frailty. Such a reader will gladly say with him:

> Ne me ne list this sely womman chyde
> Ferther than the story wol devyse.
> Hir name, allas! is publisshed so wyde
> That for hir gilt it oughte y-now suffyse.
> And if I mighte excuse hir any wyse,
> For she so sory was for hir untrouthe,
> Y-wis I wolde excuse hir yet for routhe.

If the foregoing conception of Criseyde's character be correct, we shall not have to assume that the poet has attempted to mis-lead us into believing that the heroine is a virtuous woman seduced by treachery, in order to shock and surprise us by her conduct with Diomede, and that in so doing he has resorted to an artistic duplicity.[1] It will be equally unnecessary to charge the poet with having left us in *Troilus and Criseyde* a "broken-backed" story, because of his failure to explain his heroine's

---

[1] Root, p. 115.

fickleness.[1] Unquestionably Chaucer fell in love with her, just as her first husband and Troilus and Diomede had all done before him. What charmed him was undoubtedly the same thing that charms us, — her absolutely human quality ; and not the least important element in her power to win the affections of four men was precisely that passionate nature which caused her to fall a ready victim to the charms of Diomede. The psychology of Criseyde is all right at this point, as it is before and afterward. If Chaucer fails to dwell upon her fickleness, it is not because he realizes that he cannot explain it,— that had already been provided for,— but because, loving her as he does and as we do, in spite of her frailty, to dwell upon her unfaithfulness gave him pain.

We turn to Pandarus. Of him Ebert[2] says, speaking of the unfavorable impression which he produces : " This is, however, somewhat softened by the fact that Chaucer makes this metamorphosed figure represent his own irony of the fantastical love of knighthood, the most decided and important feature of his work." Ebert's statement was challenged by Kissner in the following words : " Chaucer stand damals in seinen anschauungen noch ganz auf dem standpunkt des mittelalterlichen ritterthums, welches in der romantischen minne seinen mittelpunkt hatte ; er meint es mit seinem liebespaar durchaus ernst und sieht nicht moquirend auf sie herab ; sondern behandelt ihr schicksal mit wahrem herzenantheil. Vieles, was für uns den eindruck der ironie macht, hat seinen grund in der noch ungeschulten naïven ausdruckweise, oder ist, wie eben die figur des Pandarus, nur ein unwillkührlicher ausfluss der schalkhaften natur des dichters." [3]

Ten Brink, on the contrary, accepts Ebert's view. He says : " Ebert traf den nagel auf den kopf, als er — Pandarus den

---

[1] Oliver Elton, *Modern Language Review*, Jan. 1910, p. 115.

[2] *Review of Sandras's "Etude sur Chaucer*," Chaucer Society Publications, 1868, p. 13.   [3] Kissner, p. 53.

'träger der ironie des dichters der phantastischen liebe des ritterthums gegenüber' nannte." [1] And he asks Kissner the following questions :

1. "Konnte der übersetzer und schüler Jehan de Meungs noch auf dem standpunkt des mittelalterlichen ritterthums stehen ? "

2. "Meint nicht auch Cervantes mit seinem Don Quijote es durchaus ernst, ja hat er nicht sein eignes herz im character seines helden ganz anders offenbart, als Chaucer das seinige in der darstellung des Troilus ? "

3. "Ist bei wirklichen dichtern die ironie nicht immer (mehr oder weniger) auch ein unwillkührlicher ausfluss ihrer schalkhaften natur ? "

The remarks of Kissner show a curious combination of truth and error. The statement that Chaucer at the time of writing the *Troilus* held the point of view of the mediaeval knighthood with regard to love, is evidently extreme. And ten Brink's doubt with regard to this as shown in his first question is quite natural and reasonable. But of the truth of Kissner's statement which immediately follows, there can be, I think, no doubt ; the lovers had the poet's sympathy throughout, and he certainly expected both Troilus and Criseyde to have the sympathies of the reader. Of course, the implication in Kissner's statement, that inasmuch as the poet treated his lovers sympathetically, he could not therefore have satirized what they stood for, is erroneous, as ten Brink's second question shows. But I am inclined to feel that Kissner is not so far wrong in saying that much that appears to be irony is only the poet's humor. And while we may accept ten Brink's statement that all irony in true poets is more or less an involuntary outflow of their humorous nature, it would be illogical to assume, therefore, that all humor is ironical.

If Kissner makes an unwarranted assumption as the basis of his argument, Ebert, and after him ten Brink, is equally at

[1] *Studien*, p. 72.

fault. The statement made by the former that Chaucer makes Pandarus represent his own ironical mood toward chivalrous love is entirely gratuitous. And on this assertion ten Brink bases his argument. Moreover, the case of Cervantes and Don Quixote, while it serves well to rebut Kissner's statement, is hardly a parallel to Chaucer's case. Chivalry in Cervantes' day bore a very different relation to the life of the time from that which chivalrous love bore to the life of Chaucer's time; at least, to that particular phase of the life with which Chaucer was most intimately associated. Chivalry, when *Don Quixote* was written, was on its last legs; it had been practically dead for a century or more. On the other hand, love was a very vital question in all the higher circles at the time at which Chaucer wrote. From the early feudal days, love was the ruling spirit in courtly society. The opening lines of the *Chatelain de Coucy* tell us:

> Amours . . . est principaument
> Voie de vie honnestement.

And love-making was considered as the great business of social life.[1] That these ideas persisted to the later times in France is shown by the works of such writers as Machaut, Deschamps, and Froissart, in which no suspicion of burlesque may be found. In England at the court of Richard II, one form of entertainment was the division into the orders of the Flower and the Leaf, and the discussion of the qualities for which these emblems stood. All the members of this courtly group were supposed to be lovers, and were designated as "servants of love."[2] The fact that Chaucer was poet to this courtly society makes it seem highly improbable that he would deliberately set out to satirize the thing in which his patrons were highly interested — especially in a work with which he would be particularly anxious to please them.

[1] Wright, *Womankind in Western Europe*, London, 1869, p. 167.
[2] Kittredge, *Modern Philology*, I, 2.

But aside from these considerations, Chaucer, as an artist, was particularly interested, in the *Troilus*, in the portrayal of his actors as real people. He presents his figures dramatically, and their characters come out in their speech and their action. Critics cannot with right hold as Chaucer's own views what he puts into the mouths of the persons in the story. If this be done, where shall the process stop? We could just as fairly hear Chaucer speak through Troilus, on whom much of Pandarus's cynicism is vented, as through Pandarus himself. Criseyde expresses herself in a very pronounced manner to the effect that the gods are liars and were first made by men's fear.[1] Are we to infer then that Chaucer has in him a vein of skepticism, because this charming woman has? Manifestly such a process is all wrong.

But, assuming with Ebert and ten Brink that Pandarus does voice Chaucer's own opinions, let us see what Pandarus's love philosophy is. I shall take his expressions which bear on the subject of love in the order in which they occur. When he is trying to get Troilus to tell the name of the lady who has caused all his sorrow, he argues that it will be a wise thing for the lover to confide in some one whom he can trust (i, 98–99). This argument recalls the courtly love doctrine as expressed in the *Romance of the Rose*:

> Therefore I rede thee that thou get
> A felowe that can wel concele
> And kepe thy counsel, and wel hele,
> To whom go shewe hooly thyn herte
> Bothe wele and wo, joye and smerte.[2]

And in connection with this, we may observe Pandarus's argument: "Both thou and I complain of love; in truth I am so full of sorrow, that no more misfortune can sit on me for want of space. If thou art not afraid that I shall beguile thee of thy lady, tell me thy woe; for I am he whom thou trustest most"

---

[1] iv, 201–202.   [2] Eng. Trans., ll. 2856–2860.

(i, 102–103). In the same connection, Pandarus urges his friend to take some steps toward helping himself.

> For this nis not, certeyn, the nexte wyse
> To winnen love, as techen us the wyse,
> To walwe and wepe as Niobe the quene,
> Whos teres yet in marbel been y-sene.

He follows up his argument in great detail. But he makes it very clear that he recognizes that Troilus has just cause for his woe. As he says : " I grant well that thou endurest woe as sharp as doth Tityrus in hell, whose stomach the vultures devour. But I may not endure that thou persist in the unreasonable opinion that there is no cure for thy woe " (i, 113). " Many a lover has known his lady twenty years, and never kissed her " (i, 116). Should he therefore fall into despair, or slay himself ?

> Nay, nay, but ever in oon be fresh and grene
> To serve and love his dere herte quene,
> And thenke it is a guerdon hir to serve
> A thousand-fold more than he can deserve.

This is fine courtly love doctrine ; and it is interesting to note that it is just what Pandarus practised in his own love affairs. Pandarus's remarks are full of common sense ; but they are not directed against Troilus's being woeful ; the lover was expected to do that, and Pandarus recognized it. But his arguments are all against his friend's doing nothing to help himself ; and Troilus, who was a good courtly lover, saw the wisdom of his advice and decided to act upon it (i, 118).

Another point on which Pandarus is fully in accord with the courtly ideas is his belief that love comes to one from the god of Love, and at his whim. He says to Troilus :

> Love hath beset thee wel, be of good chere.
> . . . for nought but good it is
> To loven wel, and in a worthy place;
> Thee oughte not to clepe it hap, but grace.

Troilus has fallen in love entirely by the grace of his god, who arbitrarily makes whom he will to love. Pandarus's advice, immediately following, certainly does anything but satirize courtly love ; for he urges Troilus to repent of his sins against the god, and he reminds him that his most grievous sins consisted in making fun of courtly lovers (i, 131, 132, 133). To Troilus, at least, this advice was serious, for he acted upon it at once.

We may note, too, in this passage Pandarus's remark that " nought but good it is to love well," as a sample of courtly philosophy, which is everywhere found in the love literature. After the lover has made a confession of his sins, Pandarus advises him :

> Be *diligent and trewe, and ay wel hyde.*
> Be *lusty, free, persevere in thy servyse,*
> And al is wel, if thou werke in this wyse.

That is, he tells him to be just what the conventional courtly lover was expected to be : diligent, loyal, secret, lusty, generous, and faithful in his service of his lady.

Following up the counsel of Pandarus, we find that what he says on the subject of constancy accords well with courtly ideas :

> . . . he that parted is in every place
> Is nowhere hool, as writen clerkes wyse ;
> What wonder is though swich oon have no grace?

" It is just like planting a tree and then pulling it up the next day. No wonder it does not thrive. Therefore," he continues, " stand fast, since the god of Love has bestowed you in a worthy place " (i, 138–139).

When he begins to work with Criseyde, his whole argument is based on the courtly idea that beauty is the cause of love, and that a woman is entirely responsible for the love that her beauty inspires ; and he strengthens his case by reminding her that a man may be led to do desperate things because of love (ii, 16–50).

Wo worth the faire gemme vertulees!
Wo worth that herbe also that dooth no bote!
Wo worth that beautee that is routhelees!
Wo worth that wight that tret ech under fote!
And ye, that been of beautee crop and rote,
If ther-with-al in you ther be no routhe,
Than is it harm ye liven, by my trouthe!

Finally, when he is about to arrange the meeting between the two lovers at the house of Deiphebus, he gives this comfort to Troilus :

And certainly, I noot if thou it wost,
But tho that been expert in love it seye,
It is oon of the thinges that furthereth most,
A man to have a leyser for to preye,
And siker place his wo for to biwreye;
For in good herte it moot som routhe impresse
To here and see the giltles in distresse (ii, 196).

Other passages might be cited to indicate Pandarus's love philosophy, but these will suffice to show that if Chaucer intended to use him to satirize the courtly love, he puts into the mouth of his character strange doctrines for his purpose.

On the other hand, these doctrines are quite consistent with Pandarus, as he is portrayed in the poem. He himself is a lover, and a very sentimental one too. He himself tells us :

I love oon best, and that me smerteth sore;

and

So ful of sorwe am I, soth for to seyne,
That certeynly no more harde grace
May sitte on me, for-why there is no space.

The author informs us,

That Pandarus, for al his wyse speche,
Felte eek his part of lovers shottes kene,
That, coude he never so wel of loving preche,
It made his hewe a-day ful ofte grene;
So shoop it, that him fil that day a tene
In love, for which in wo to bedde he wente,
And made er it was day, ful many a wente (ii, 9).

Whatever conception we may have of Pandarus, at the bottom of it must be the fact that he is a lover. His words may be susceptible of different interpretations ; but, by his own testimony, by that of Troilus, of Criseyde, and lastly by that of the author himself, his sentimentality is a fact. This side of his nature is clearly indicated.

There is another side which comes out with equal clearness, and that is his cynicism. It is not at all an easy matter to reconcile these two phases of his character, nor shall I attempt to do so. This may be said, however, that if Pandarus does make fun of lovers and their actions, — and he really seems to do so in places independent of those passages which I have quoted to show his love philosophy, — Chaucer has made of him a splendidly human figure. For in laughing at the actions of another and then in going straight and doing, himself, the very things he laughed at, he behaves as many of us have often done. Nothing could be more natural, and it is in this very trait that much of the humor of this humorous character consists.

It should be remembered, however, that what is sometimes called cynicism in Pandarus, is not, or at least need not be, cynicism at all. A good example of this is found in what is regarded as his cynical attitude toward the virtue of women. It is clear from the story, and from Pandarus's own statements, that he had no reason to think that every woman was so easily accessible. Troilus says to him :

> Thou coudest never in love thy-selven wisse ;
> How devel maystow bringen me to blisse ?

Pandarus himself, after he has about arranged matters so as to bring the two lovers together, says (and this time he seems to be serious) :

> Have now good night, . . .
> And bid for me, sin thou art now in blisse,
> That god me sende deeth or sone lisse (iii, 49).

And another time, when Troilus is bewailing the loss of Criseyde, Pandarus remarks : "You have no right to sorrow in
this wise, since you have had all your desire.

> But I, that never felte in my servyse
> A frendly chere or loking of an yë,
> Lat me thus wepe and wayle, til I dye " (iv, 37).

Pandarus's remark to Criseyde, with regard to his speed in
love,
> By god . . . I hoppe alwey bihinde !

though spoken as a joke, was really the truth. We have already
seen the character of the love which Troilus and Criseyde felt
for each other ; and our acquaintance with Pandarus, who was
a courtly lover, does not lead us to think that his love was of a
different nature. So that Pandarus's theory that all women are
of easy virtue, if he really believed such a thing, was entirely a
theory, as far as his own lady was concerned.

The case of another woman may also be considered, — namely,
his niece Criseyde. He remarks that all women are apt to
suffer the heat of love, either celestial or natural. So far, he
has made an observation which comes near to being true. But
he continues that since Criseyde is far from being " celestial,"
it follows that she must suffer the other kind of love. From
what we have seen of Criseyde, Pandarus is quite right. So
that, if our observations with regard to the heroine are correct,
Pandarus's remarks show no cynicism at all ; but they do show
that he knew his niece well, — a fact which we might infer from
the manner in which he proceeded to win her love for Troilus.

Furthermore, we should note that Pandarus often talks for
effect, — " for the nones," as Chaucer tells us (iv, 62). His
genuine friendship for Troilus is one of the most noticeable
things about him ; and it really lies at the bottom of much of
his bantering talk. This is to be observed particularly in those

places where the ultra-sentimental Troilus is inclined to indulge himself in his grief, rather than to take any steps toward helping himself. For example, in the first book, Pandarus really sees the need of arousing his friend to some kind of action. It was a well-recognized principle in the courtly system that a man may either die or go mad for love. The literature is full of expressions of this idea. The author tells us that in spite of all Pandarus's coaxing and urging, Troilus would not reveal the name of the lady who was causing him all this sorrow, but lay there rolling his eyes and sighing. Pandarus really feared lest he should fall in a frenzy, or even die; and so he cried " 'awake' ful wonderly and sharp," and followed it up with rather biting words (i, 104–105). Pandarus recognizes the fact that his friend is in a bad state, and that any talk that will arouse him is better than to let him remain in a desperation that may lead him to some fatal act.

He follows the same tactics in the fourth book, when he finds Troilus in the depths over the recent decree of the Parliament. He immediately begins to propose measures which he does not believe in himself, and, I have no doubt, which he knows his friend will not adopt. He says : " This town is full of ladies, and much fairer ones, too, than Criseyde. Choose one of these for your love. ' The newe love out chaceth ofte the olde,' Zanzis tells us. It is your duty to save yourself, and the way to do it is by choosing another love. Absence of Criseyde shall drive her out of your heart " (iv, 58–61). Nothing more uncourtly than this advice could be imagined, and Pandarus knew it. But it does not represent Pandarus's feelings, for the poet tells us :

> Thise wordes seyde he for the nones alle,
> To helpe his freend, lest he for sorwe deyde.
> For doutelees, to doon his wo to falle,
> He roughte not what unthrift that he seyde (iv, 62).

And after Troilus has effectually answered these arguments, and, it seems, almost quieted him for once,

> . . . nathelees, thus thoughte he at the laste,
> ' What, parde, rather than my felawe dye,
> Yet shal I som-what more un-to him seye.'

And so he starts off again in his bantering style.

But even Pandarus's patience — and it has been great, we must acknowledge — is at last exhausted. And here a new side to his character is revealed. After setting forth every argument in favor of withholding Criseyde, he says to the lover : " Take heart and remember that every law is broken on account of love. Show your courage and your power ; have some mercy on yourself, and do not let this wretched woe gnaw your heart. Set the world, like a man, ' on six and seven.' " And then flash out the words :

> I wol myself be with thee at this dede,
> Though ich and all my kin, upon a stounde
> Shulle in a strete as dogges liggen dede
> Thourgh-girt with many a wyd and blody wounde.
> In every cas I wol a freend be founde,
> And if thee list here sterven as a wrecche
> Adieu, the devel spede him that it recche !

Here the valor of the man is speaking, and it is the only time in the poem that this side of him is revealed.

It is not intended here to make an exhaustive study of this great character delineation. The preceding paragraphs point out the important phases of Pandarus's nature. He is first of all a lover, and has therefore his sentimental side. He is loyal to his friend, sparing no effort to help him and promising desperate valor if the occasion demands it. And lastly, he is cynical ; although the foregoing remarks, if they are correct, show that his cynicism can easily be, and sometimes has been, overemphasized.

As for Chaucer's irony in treating the courtly love ideas, however certain we feel that he saw the extravagances of lovers and the absurdity in some of their actions, we cannot say that he satirizes that love in the *Troilus*. And further we have seen, I think, that even the satire of Pandarus himself, who has been supposed to express the poet's irony, is no more characteristic than is his sentimentality ; and that the inconsistency of the two elements in him helps to make him not only a delightfully humorous figure, but also, like Troilus and Criseyde, an eminently human one.

A very interesting feature of the *Troilus and Criseyde* is the author's treatment of the love divinity. The double personification of love noted in the earlier poetry appears here also. The deity is sometimes Cupid, sometimes Venus ; often simply Love. In many passages the personification does not admit of classification in categories which are exclusive ; for example, Criseyde revolves in her mind the wisdom and " gentilnesse " of Troilus,

> Thankinge Love he so wel hir besette.

Troilus also thanks " the heighe worthinesse of Love " that he is Criseyde's lover. The idea of the god as a benevolent lord in these passages might be applicable to any one of the three conceptions of the love divinity, the classical, the ecclesiastical, or the feudal. Similarly, the idea of service and obedience rendered the god, which appears in so many passages, is not inconsistent with either the ecclesiastical or the feudal figure. For example, Pandarus, when he persuades Criseyde to grant Troilus her love, swears by Minerva, by Jupiter,

> And by the blisful Venus that I serve.

Criseyde speaks of Pandarus as the one

> That alderfirst me broughte into servyse
> Of love.

Diomede assures Criseyde :

> And though ye Troians with us Grekes wrothe
> Han many a day be, alwey yet, pardee,
> O god of love in sooth, we serven bothe. . . .
> Eek I am not of power for to stryve
> Ayens the god of love, but him obeye
> I wol alwey.

And Troilus, who has come into such great happiness himself,

> lost held every wight
> But if he were in loves high servyse.

These last lines might be interpreted in the ecclesiastical sense, as if the idea were borrowed from the Church's doctrine that every man is in a lost condition who is not engaged in the service of religion.

Apart from such passages in which the figure is doubtful, there are many in the *Troilus* which illustrate clearly the three conceptions of the love divinity. The classical idea appears in the humorous description of the god's attack on the haughty Troilus :

> At which [i.e. at Troilus's words] the god of love gan loken rowe
> Right for despyt and shoop for to ben wroken ;
> He kidde anoon his bowe nas nat broken ;
> For sodeynly he hit him at the fulle ;
> And yet as proud a pekok can he pulle.

This delightfully fresh expression of an old conceit, the wound inflicted in a lover's heart by Cupid's arrow, is the only case in which the god appears with his weapons. The poet includes, however, " daun Cupyde, the blind and winged sone " of Venus, among those who had deigned to guide him to the end of his third book.

The feudal conception of the divinity, always a being of irresistible power, also appears in the *Troilus*. For example, the poet, digressing for a moment, moralizes with his inimitable humor on the foolishness of resisting Love as Troilus attempted to do: "As 'proude Bayarde' whose corn 'priketh him' is brought to endure horses' law by a lash of the long whip, so this worthy king's son,

> that now was most in pryde above,
> Wex sodeynly most subjet unto love.

"Therefore," continues the author, "all ye wise, proud, and worthy folks, beware of scorning Love,

> which that so sone can
> The freedom of your hertes to him thralle;
> For ever it was, and ever it shal bifalle
> That Love is he that alle thing may binde. . . .
> Refuseth not to Love to be bonde,
> Sin, as himselven list, he may you binde.

The feudal idea of the lover as a thrall or subject of Love, which is seen in these lines, appears also in the following, where the poet, in an interesting and effective manner, has mixed his metaphors, making Troilus subject to the fire of love:

> In him ne deyned sparen blood royal
> The fyr of love, the wher-fro god me blesse,
> Ne him forbar in no degre, for al
> His vertu or his excellent prowesse;
> But held him as his thral lowe in distresse,
> And brende him so in sondry wise ay newe
> That sixty tyme aday he loste his hewe.

But for the ecclesiastical figure Chaucer shows especial fondness in the *Troilus*. At the very beginning of the work, after announcing his purpose, he calls upon the Fury Tisiphone for her help; for, although he is a servant of those who serve the god of Love, on account of his unfitness to love he dares not pray to the god for speed in his task, so far is he from Love's help in darkness. "Yet," he says,

> "if this may doon gladnesse
> To any lover, and his cause avayle,
> Have he my thank, and myn be this travayle!"

He then calls upon all fortunate lovers, remembering their past sorrows, to pray for their unfortunate brethren like Troilus, that Love may bring them in heaven " to solas " ; to pray for those who are in despair in love and never will recover from it ; to pray also that God may permit all those lovers whose interests are wrongly injured by evil tongues, to leave the miseries of this world ; finally, to pray God that he continue his favor to all lovers who are now at ease, and send them might to please their ladies, so that it may be honor and pleasure to love. He asks also for their prayers in his own behalf, that he may show in his story such pain and woe as Love's folk endure ; for he hopes to advance the interests of his own soul by praying for Love's servants, by writing their woes, and by being charitably disposed toward them all, as toward his own dear brothers.

This passage is full of ecclesiastical ideas. In saying of himself,

> I that god of Loves servants serve,

Chaucer is either daringly or naïvely paraphrasing the official title of the Pope, used in the introductory greetings of all papal bulls,[1] in which the Pope speaks of himself as *servus servorum Dei*. The attitude of extreme humility which the poet assumes before the god of Love is noteworthy as a parallel to the self-abasement of many saints before the real God. He does not even dare to pray for help on account of his unfitness to love. In comparison with this humility, we may call to mind the attitude of John the Baptist, as shown in his words : " There cometh one mightier than I after me, the latchet of whose shoes I am not worthy to stoop down and unloose " ;[2] or that of Saint Paul,

---

[1] See Smith and Cheetham, *Dictionary of Christian Antiquities*, under " Briefs and Bulls." Thus the famous bull " Regimini militantis," confirming the order of Jesuits, issued by Pope Paul III in 1540, begins : " Paulus episcopus, servus servorum Dei, ad perpetuam rei memoriam. Regimini militantis ecclesiae, &c."

[2] Mark i, 7.

who says of himself : "Unto me, who am less than the least of all saints, is this grace given, that I should preach . . . the unsearchable riches of Christ." [1] The self-abasement of the old saints finds a striking and almost repulsive expression in the lines of the modern poet :

> Altho' I be the basest of mankind,
> From scalp to sole one slough and crust of sin,
> Unfit for earth, unfit for heaven, scarce meet
> For troops of devils, mad with blasphemy,
> I will not cease to grasp the hope I hold
> Of saintdom, and to clamour, mourn and sob,
> Battering the gates of heaven with storms of prayer,
> Have mercy, Lord, and take away my sin.

Yet the sentiments ascribed by Tennyson to St. Simeon Stylites are not at all exaggerated, as may be seen by comparing them with the following lamentation of Saint Augustine, one of the most elaborate of such self-derogatory expressions : " Quid sum ego, qui loquor tecum ? Vae mihi, Domine, parce mihi : ego cadaver putridum, esca vermium, vas fetidum, cibus ignium. . . . Quid iterum ego ? Abyssus tenebrosa, terra miseriae, filius irae, vas aptum ad contumeliam, genitus per immunditiam, vivens in miseria, moriturus in angustia. . . . Et quid sum ? Vas sterquilinii, concha putredinis, plenus fetore et horrore : caecus, pauper, nudus, plurimis necessitatibus subditus, ignorans introitum et exitium meum." [2]

We may compare Chaucer's statement that he is far from Love's help in darkness with the following prayer attributed to Saint Augustine : " O God our Father, . . . hear me, who am trembling in this darkness, and stretch forth Thy hands unto me ; hold forth Thy light before me ; recall me from my wanderings ; and Thou being my Guide, may I be restored to

---

[1] Ephesians iii, 8.
[2] *Liber Soliloquiorum ;* Migne, *Patrologia*, XL, col. 866–867.

myself and to Thee." [1] Another notable example from the same
saint is the following: " O Domini Verbum, O Deus Verbum,
. . . vae mihi misero toties obcaecato, quia tu lux, et ego sine
te ; . . . O Domine Verbum, O Deus Verbum, qui es lux per
quam facta est lux, . . . dic, Domine, ' Fiat lux,' ut videam
lucem et vitem tenebras. . . . Illuminare, Dominus lux mea,
illuminatio mea, illuminare huic caeco tuo qui in tenebris et in
umbra mortis sedet." [2] Such expressions from the saints of the
Church, who, oppressed with the consciousness of sin, felt that
they were in " outer darkness " away from the light of God's
countenance, seem to have been in Chaucer's mind when writing
the introductory stanzas to the *Troilus*.

In the last lines of the third stanza,

> if this doon gladnesse
> To any lover, and his cause avayle
> Have he my thank, and myn be this travayle!

Chaucer applies the ecclesiastical doctrine of merit to love — the
doctrine that the merit attaching to any good work may be im-
puted to the doer or to some other to whom he chooses to transfer it.[3] It is interesting to note the poet's clever use in the last

---

[1] Tileston, *Prayers Ancient and Modern*, New York, 1897, p. 344. See also
pp. 57, 75, 92, 138, 196, 312.

[2] *Liber Soliloquiorum ;* Migne, *Patrologia*, XL, col. 867–868.

[3] The following is St. Thomas Aquinas's statement with regard to " opera
supererogativa " ; quoting from the *Vitae Patrum*, he says : " quod propter
charitatem unius qui alterius fratris sui charitate ductus poenitentiam fecit pro
peccato quod non commiserat, alteri peccatum quod commiserat dimissum est "
(Migne, *Patrologia*, Supplement to Tertia Pars Summae Theologicae, Questio
XIII, art. ii, col.970). This same writer says elsewhere : "All the saints intended
that whatever they did or suffered for God's sake should be profitable not only
to themselves but to the whole of the church. And he further points out
(*Contra Gent.*, III, 158) that what one endures for another, being a work of
love, is more acceptable as satisfaction in God's sight than what one suffers
on one's own account, since this is a matter of necessity " (*The Catholic Encyclopedia*, article on " Indulgences," VII, 784). Applications of the doctrine
in prayers of Chaucer's time are frequent. Examples of such prayers may be
seen in the *Lay Folks' Mass Book*, pp. 65, 69, 78, Early English Text Society

line of a sentence addressed by Boccaccio to his mistress at the beginning of the *Filostrato*, and the shift of meaning to make it accord with the spirit of the rest of the passage and give it a religious significance.

In the following stanzas, the poet's call for the prayers of happy lovers in behalf of others less fortunate is phrased in ecclesiastical language and reflects the practices of believers in the matter of prayer. He asks for prayer in behalf of those who are in the unhappy condition of Troilus, that they may come to solace in heaven ; and for those who have despaired in love and never will recover. Chaucer here seems to have in mind the doctrine that despair damned the soul of him who gave away to it.[1] Further, he asks the prayers of lovers for those who are now at ease ; that is, he advises happy lovers to pray for themselves that God grant them perseverance in their good work of pleasing their ladies ; for this is honor and pleasure to the god of Love. The doctrine of perseverance was familiar to good Catholics before Calvin put forth his celebrated Five Points. The Church held that perseverance was the gift of God, and could be obtained by an appeal through prayer, not to the justice of God, but to his mercy and kindness.[2] Chaucer's line clearly applies this idea to love.

In the passage,

> For so hope I my soule best avaunce
> To preye for hem that Loves servaunts be
> And wryte hir wo, and live in charitee,

Publications, 1879. Note too the conclusion of the *Oratio ad Erasmum*, appended to his *Life :*

> Non noceat facinus : mihi, me iuvet almus Erasmus.
> O sacer Erasme : meritis precibusque regas me !

Horstmann, *Sammlung altenglischer Legenden*,
Heilbronn, 1881, p. 200.

[1] *Persones Tale*, sect. 56.

[2] " Hoc ergo (i.e. perseverance) Dei donum suppliciter emereri potest " (Saint Augustine, *Liber de Dono Perseverantiae*, Cap. vi).

the poet makes use of another theological idea. Good works held, and yet hold, an important place in the Catholic practice. By good works the Christian merits reward from God.[1] To read the life of a saint was an act of special merit.[2] To read the lives of the saints was not only to keep oneself from idleness, but to inflame oneself with the desire to imitate their virtues. For the same reason, to write the lives of saints was a meritorious act. Chaucer has in mind this method of acquiring merit in the lines quoted. Later, when he wrote the *Legend* of Cupid's saints, he elaborated very skilfully the same conception ; for in writing the *Legend of Good Women* he atones for his sins against the god of Love.

We pass to other examples of the use of ecclesiastical ideas. Troilus, overcome by Love, cries " with pitous voys " :

> " O lord, now youres is
> My spirit, which that oughte youres be.
> Yow thanke I, lord, that han me brought to this."

This is the language natural for a penitent sinner to use in the act of yielding his soul to God. It carries out the idea of the preceding passage, that Troilus has up to this point been a transgressor against the god of Love, but has been brought to see the true light through the operation of the god upon him, as the spirit of God works upon the heart of the sinner.

[1] See *Catholic Dictionary* under " Merit."

[2] Note the introduction to the *Vita Sancti Cristofori* (from MS. Cathedral, ca. 1430) : " Here bygynnes the lyffe of the Story of Saynte Cristofore, to the heryng or the redyng of the whilke storye langes . . . mede, & it be done with devocione " (Horstmann, *Altenglische Legenden*, Neue Folge, Heilbronn, 1881, p. 454); also the words of the teller of a saint's life :

> And ȝif ȝe wille ȝeve lestyng,
> Ȝe shollen here riȝt guod þyng
> Er ȝe hannes wende :
> Pardoun ȝe mowe þerwiþ wynne
> And þe betere ȝow kepe from dedly synne,
> ȝif ȝe wille have it in mende.
> Canticum de Creatione, st. 3, *Samml. alteng. Leg.*, p. 124.

Pandarus, attempting to move Criseyde to pity, invents a prayer which he pretends to have heard Troilus utter :

> " Lord ! have routhe upon my prayer,
> Al have I been rebel in myn entente,
> Now, *mea culpa*, lord ! I me repente."

" O god, thou that hast in thy power the death of every wight, hear my humble confession with favor, and send me such penance as is pleasing to thee ; but for thy goodness' sake, shield me from despair which would separate my soul from thee." The ideas of this passage are purely theological. Troilus uses the regular formula employed by penitents.[1] The idea is elaborated in his asking for penance. In the lines,

> but from desesperaunce,
> That may my goost departe awey fro thee,
> Thou be my sheld, for thy benignitee,

Chaucer has in mind the doctrine, already referred to, that despair damns the soul. Men were always falling into despair and, hence, according to the Church, into deadly sin. The Parson describes it as " wanhope, that is despeir of the mercy of god, that comth somtyme of to muche outrageous sorwe, and somtyme of to much drede : imagininge that he hath doon so much sinne that it wol nat availlen him, though he wolde repenten him and forsake sinne. . . . Which dampnable sinne, if that it continue unto his ende, it is cleped sinning in the holy gost. This horrible sinne is so perilous, that he that is despeired, ther is no felonye ne no sinne that he douteth for to do ; as shewed wel by Judas. Certes aboven alle sinnes thanne is this sinne most displesant to

---

[1] Note the following words from a mediaeval Order of Mass : " Confiteor Deo, beatae Mariae, et omnibus sanctis eius . . . quia ego peccator peccavi nimis corde, ore, opere, omissione *mea culpa*, &c." (*Lay Folks' Mass Book*, p. 90); also : " Confiteor Deo omnipotenti . . . quia peccavi nimis cogitatione, verbo et opere, mea culpa, mea culpa, mea maxima culpa " (Prayer Book of the Catholic Church, 1896).

Christ, and most adversarie." [1] Even in modern times men are not free from the sin of falling into despair. The most picturesque statement, perhaps, of the awfulness of the sin to be found in literature has been given us by Bunyan in the story of the encounter of Christian and Hopeful with the Giant Despair.

In the first stanzas of Antigone's song in the garden, both the feudal and ecclesiastical figures appear. The idea of paying tribute as a vassal to the god is seen in the lines :

> O love, to whom I have and shal
> Ben humble subgit, trewe in myn entente,
> As I best can, to yow, lord, yeve ich al
> Forever more, myn hertes lust to rente.

Antigone means that she will concentrate all the desires of her heart on love ; in so doing, she will be but rendering to the god of Love the service which is due him as her lord and master. Coleridge expresses, in effect, the same idea :

> All thoughts, all passions, all delights,
>   Whatever stirs this mortal frame,
> All are but ministers of Love,
>   And feed his sacred flame.

And we may further compare the biblical command: "Thou shalt love the Lord thy God with all thy heart, and with all thy soul, and with all thy mind." [2] Though the feudal idea is clearly present in the passage, the ecclesiastical is so closely blended with it that it is almost impossible to separate the two. The ecclesiastical feature is plainer perhaps in the lines immediately following, in which the Christian idea of grace is employed :

> For never yet thy grace no wight sente
> So blisful cause as me, my lyf to lede
> In alle joye and seurtee, out of drede.

Antigone's idea is that the god has bestowed upon her a special grace in inclining her heart to love, and in so ordering her life

---

[1] *Persones Tale*, 692–696.
[2] Matthew, xxxi, 37. Cf. Luke x, 27 ; Deuteronomy vi, 5.

that the object of her love is worthy. The rest of her song, in fact, is a hymn of praise and thanksgiving to the god who had her " so wel beset in love." Antigone's remarks should be interpreted in connection with Pandarus's comforting philosophy, addressed to Troilus :

> And for-thy loke of good comfort thou be;
> For certainly, the firste poynt is this
> Of noble orage and wel ordeyne,
> A man to have pees with him-self, y-wis;
> So oughtest thou, for nought but good it is
> To loven wel, and in a worthy place;
> *Thee oughte not to clepe it hap, but grace*[1] (i, 128).

To Pandarus, as to Antigone, falling in love was not an accident, but a manifestation of the special grace of the god of Love, who had a right arbitrarily to make one fall in love with anybody; and, in Pandarus's opinion, Troilus ought to believe this and thank the god for the experience. The doctrine is fully stated in the Proem to Book III, in the lines addressed to Venus :

> Ye knowe al thilke covered qualitee
> Of thinges which that folk on wondren so,
> Whan they can not construe how it may jo,
> She loveth him, or why he loveth here;
> As why this fish, and nought that, cometh to were.

Still another interesting illustration of the application of religious ideas to love is seen in Chaucer's use of Dante's lines addressed to the Blessed Virgin :

> Donna, sei tanto grande e tanto vali,
>   che qual vuol grazia ed a te non ricorre,
>   sua disianza vuol volar senz' ali.
> La tua benignità non pur socorre
>   a chi domanda, ma molte fiate
>   liberamente al domandar precorre.[2]

---

[1] Cf. for the same expression,

> Shal I clepe hit hap other grace
> That broghte me ther ? — *Book of the Duchess*, ll. 810–811.

[2] *Paradiso*, xxxiii, 13 ff.

The poet transfers the praise of the Virgin to Love :

> Benigne Love, thou holy bond of thinges
> Who so wol grace and list thee nought honouren
> Lo his desyr wol flee withouten winges.
> For noldestow of bountee hem socouren
> That serven best and most alwey labouren
> Yet were al lost, that dar I wel seyn, certeyn
> But-if thy grace passed our desertes.[1]

In Troilus's prayer to Venus, when he is about to go to Criseyde's bed, the idea of the goddess's intercession is probably borrowed from the worship of the Virgin as a mediator between God and man :

> And if I hadde, O Venus ful of mirthe,
> Aspects badde of Mars or of Saturne,
> Or thou combust or let were in my birthe
> Thy fader pray al thilke harm disturne
> Of grace.

This conception is so common in religious literature that a mere mention of it here is sufficient. As an example of Chaucer's own prayer for the Virgin's intercession, the following lines may be noted :

> O thou, that art so fayr and ful of grace,
> Be myn advocat in that heighe place
> Ther-as withouten ende is songe ' Osanne,'
> Thou Christes mooder, doghter dere of Anne![2]

After Pandarus had arranged the meeting of the two lovers at the house of Deiphebus, he hurried home with the news to Troilus, greeting him with the words :

> now is tyme, if that thou conne,
> To bere thee wel to-morwe, and al is wonne.
> Now spek, now prey, now pitously compleyne ;
> Lat not for nyce shame, or drede, or slouthe ;

---

[1] Compare Chaucer's use of the same passage in the *Invocacio ad Mariam* in his life of St. Cecilia (*Seconde Nonnes Tale*).
[2] *Seconde Nonnes Tale*, ll. 67-70.

> Som-tyme a man mot telle his owene peyne;
> Bileve it, and she shal han on thee routhe;
> *Thou shalt be saved by thy feyth, in trouthe* (ii, 214, 215).

The reference is clearly to the gospel stories, such as that of the woman who anointed the Master's feet with the precious ointment, and who received His commendation : " Thy faith hath saved thee ; go in peace." [1]

On this same occasion of the meeting at the house of Deiphebus, Criseyde accepted Troilus as her lover, under well-defined conditions. Whereupon Pandarus, in his exultation, fell upon his knees and, raising his eyes to heaven, cried :

> Immortal god! . . . that mayst nought dyen,
> Cupide I mene, of this mayst glorifye ;
> And Venus, thou mayst make melodye ;
> With-outen hond, me semeth that in towne,
> For this merveyle, I here ech belle sowne.

Pandarus's reference here to the bells ringing without hands is an expression of an idea not uncommon in mediaeval literature. To the simple-minded believer, the bell thus miraculously ringing was God's voice of approval of something done, or of protest against some wickedness committed or about to be committed. We read in the ballad of " Hugh of Lincoln "

> And a' the bells o merry Lincoln
> Without men's hands were rung,
> And a' the books o merry Lincoln
> Were read without man's tongue,
> And neer was such a burial
> Sin Adam's days begun.

Similarly, in the romance of *La Bone Florence de Rome*, we are told that on the heroine's approach to the city all the bells, of one accord, began to ring without the help of men's hands.[2]

---

[1] Luke vii, 50. Cf. also Mark v, 34 ; x, 52 ; Luke viii, 48 ; xvii, 19.
[2] On the miraculous ringing of bells see Child, *English and Scottish Popular Ballads*, I, 173, 231 ; III, 235, 519 ff.

And so, to Pandarus's mind, no occasion can be more fitting for the approval of the divine powers than that on which Criseyde agrees to become the love of Troilus.

The most elaborate use of the ecclesiastical figure in the poem is found in the instructions of Pandarus to Troilus after the youth had become a servant of the god of Love. Pandarus is surprised that such happiness has been bestowed upon Troilus. He could have sworn that such favor would never fall to one who had scorned Love and mockingly called him

> Seynt Idiot, lord of thise foles alle (i, 130).

Furthermore, Troilus had scoffed at those who were devout in the religion of Love. Pandarus therefore advises him to beat his breast [1] and call upon the god of Love with all his heart:

> Thy grace, lord! for now I me repente
> If I mis spak, for now myself I love.

Troilus obeys, and Pandarus hopes that the lover's tears of repentance and his confession have appeased the wrath of the god. He then instructs Troilus how to conduct himself in order to make a good end of all this affair, and he comforts the young neophyte:

> " I thenke, sith that love, of his goodnesse,
> Hath thee converted out of wikkednesse,
> That thou shalt be the beste post,[2] I leve,
> Of al his lay, and most his foes to-greve."

" Take, for example, these wise clerks who err most of all against religion: when once they have been converted from their

---

[1] Beating the breast was, of course, an outward manifestation of a penitential spirit, and the celebrant was directed to do this as part of the act of confession and at other times in the celebration of the Mass. For examples of such directions see Richard Rolle, *Prick of Conscience*, ll. 3400–3409; Caxton, *Book of Curtesye*, ll. 73–74.

[2] Unto his ordre he was a noble post.
Prologue to the *Canterbury Tales*, l. 214.

wicked works through the grace of God, they, more than any others, hold Him in awe, and are the more steadfast in the new faith for their former rebellion against it." Pandarus might have cited as an example of a sudden conversion, such as he mentions, that of Saint Paul, as one which would fit his observations exactly. Chaucer was probably thinking, however, of the case of Saint Augustine, whose zeal in the orthodox religion, after conversion from a worldly life and from the Manichean heresy, he has told in his *Confessions*. A very impressive instance of sudden conversion is told by Etienne de Bourbon.[1] On a certain occasion, a church was being consecrated in which the body of Count Raoul of Crépy had been interred. It became necessary to disentomb the body of the count, and his sepulchre having been opened, "there appeared a monstrous toad on his face, gnawing at it, also worms and serpents. From the sight of horror all recoiled. The son of the said count, however, a young man, hearing of this, approached; and having seen the corruption of his father's flesh and the horror of the worms, began to think of death, and of how vain are the riches of the world and its delights and honors. Wherefore, leaving all, he fled, thinking he should be happy if he should become poor for Christ." The story goes on to relate how he suffered hardships, hunger, and poverty and sickness until he "migrated to God."

It is interesting to note that the passages quoted to illustrate the different conceptions of the love deity are almost all Chaucer's own. With the exception of the lines borrowed from Dante's *Paradiso*, in only one of those passages which show the ecclesiastical idea is the language suggested by the Italian original. Chaucer's lines,

> O lord, now youres is
> My spirit which that oughte youres be,

[1] *Anecdotes, Historiques, Legendes et Apologues*, ed. A. Lecoy de la Marche, Paris, 1876, p. 66. Professor Kittredge calls my attention to this anecdote.

are taken from Boccaccio's

> Signore, omai
> L'anima è tua che mia essere solea.[1]

In the original, the ecclesiastical figure is carried out where Troilo prays :

> Perchè, se 'l mio servir punto ti piace,
> Da que' ti prego impetri la salute
> Dell' anima, la qual prostrata giace
> Sotto i tuoi piè.[2]

Chaucer here changes to the feudal idea, employing it, not to describe the relation of the lover to the god, but to his lady :

> Wherefore, lord, if my servyse or I
> May lyke yow, so beth to me benigne,
> For myn estat royal I here resigne
> Into her hond, and with ful humble chere
> Bicome hir man, as to my lady dere.

Then follows the passage already quoted, in which the power of love is figured as a flame. Boccaccio's words are :

> Non risparmiarono il sangue reale
> Nè d'animo virtù ovver grandezza
> Nè curaron di forza corporeale
> Che in Troilo fosse, o di prodezza,
> L'ardenti fiamme amorose.[3]

The feudal idea of the lover's thraldom to this powerful flame, which appears in the English poem, is Chaucer's own. In none of the other passages cited is the poet indebted for his ideas to anybody else. The telling use of "proude Bayard" and the accompanying stanzas, the fictitious prayer which Pandarus quotes to Criseyde, Antigone's song in the garden, Troilus's prayer to Venus, the stanzas in which Pandarus plays the high-priest of love and listens to Troilus's confession, are all the product of Chaucer's imagination. The raciness and fresh humor of these passages illustrate one of the distinctive qualities of the

---

[1] *Filostrato*, i, st. 38. [2] Ibid., st. 39. [3] Ibid., st. 40.

English poet's work, and the passages themselves furnish examples of his peculiar skill in the use of language to portray the passion of love.

In connection with Chaucer's references to the love deity two other passages must be noted. The first is the song which Troilus sings in praise of Love while in the garden with Pandarus. The poet here paraphrases one of the Metres of the *Consolation of Philosophy*.[1] The general idea of the passage is that all concord and harmony existing in the material universe is but a manifestation of the power of love ; and that if love ceased to operate, all things which now work together in harmony would be reduced to chaos. Love holds the seas in bounds and controls the movements of the heavenly bodies. This is the same Love

> that with an holsom alliaunce
> Halt peples joyned, as him list hem gye,
> Love, that knetteth lawe of companye,
> And couples doth in vertu for to dwelle (iii, 250).

The term "love" is here clearly used to designate the phenomenon of attraction, which must have been perfectly well known in the Middle Ages ; and this attraction is identified with the feeling which, either in the form of friendship or in the grosser form of physical passion, draws people to each other.

Boëthius derived the philosophy which Chaucer has here made use of, from Plato. In a passage of the *Timaeus*, the harmony existing in the world is explained as a manifestation of the spirit of friendship : " And for these reasons, and out of such elements, which are in number four, the body of the world was created, and it was harmonized by proportion, *and therefore has the spirit of friendship ;* and having been reconciled to itself, it was indissoluble by the hand of any other than the framer." [2]

---

[1] Bk. iii, metre viii.
[2] *The Dialogues of Plato*, trans. Jowett, New York, 1892, III, 451.

The Metre of Boëthius expresses more closely, however, Empedocles's doctrine of the working of Love and Strife in the universe; and the Latin poet may have had in mind some such passage as the following, in which the philosopher expressly identifies the love which operates in the natural world as the power of attraction, with love existing in human hearts : " At one time, it [i.e. the Universe] grew together to be one only out of many, at another it parted asunder so as to be many instead of one ; — Fire and Water and Earth and the mighty height of Air ; dread strife, too, apart from these, of equal weight to each, and Love among them, equal in length and breadth. Her do thou contemplate with thy mind, nor sit with dazed eyes. It is she that makes them have thoughts of love and work the works of peace. They call her by the names of Joy and Aphrodite." [1] Boëthius does not treat Love as a divinity, but merely personifies the abstraction. The song of Troilus does not differ greatly from the Latin Metre in this respect, although the general tone of the paraphrase, as well as the line,

> Al this doth Love ; ay heried be his mightes !

the second half of which is Chaucer's own, seems to indicate that the poet identifies personal love with the indefinite force of the philosophers, thinking of Love as a god.

In the Proem to Book III, which is the second passage to be noted, the love divinity appears. This invocation is addressed to Venus, goddess of Love, and is a glorification of her power and goodness which are felt through all the universe,

> In heven and helle, in erthe and salte see.

All nature, animate and inanimate, feels her influence at times ; she it was who first moved Jove to the creative act,

> Thorough which that thinges liven alle and be.

---

[1] *Early Greek Philosophy*, ed. Burnet, London, 1908, p. 242.

She ennobles those who come under her influence :

> Algate, hem that ye wol sette afyre,
> They dredden shame, and vices they resigne;
> Ye do hem corteys be, fresshe and benigne.

She binds together in harmony kingdom and family ; she is the·cause of friendship, and that mysterious power which draws people together in love emanates from her. This Proem is a close translation from the *Filostrato*, being taken from the song of Troilo,[1] which in Chaucer's work has been replaced by the paraphrase of Boëthius's Metre already mentioned. It may be regarded as a more detailed statement of the ideas of the Metre, the power and influence of love on humanity being emphasized, although the same identification of love with the phenomenon of attraction appears. We may end this consideration of the love deity in the *Troilus* by noticing the rather remarkable similarity between the ideas of Chaucer's Proem and those of the first part of the celebrated " Hymn to Venus " of the poet Lucretius :

" Mother of the Aeneadae, darling of men and gods, increase-giving Venus, who beneath the gliding signs of heaven fillest with thy presence the ship-carrying sea, the corn-bearing lands, since through thee every kind of living things is conceived, rises up and beholds the light of the sun. Before thee, goddess, flee the winds, the clouds of heaven ; before thee and thy advent ; for thee earth manifold in works puts forth sweet-smelling flowers ; for thee the levels of the sea do laugh and heaven propitiated shines with outspread light. For soon as the vernal aspect of day is disclosed, and the birth-favoring breath of Favonius unbarred is blowing fresh, first the fowls of the air, O lady, shew signs of thee and thy entering in, throughly smitten in heart by thy power. Next the wild herds bound over the glad

[1] *Filostrato*, iii, st. 74–89.

pastures and swim the rapid rivers : in such wise each made prisoner by thy charm follows thee with desire, whither thou goest to lead it on. Yes, throughout seas and mountains and sweeping rivers and leafy homes of birds and grassy plains, striking fond love into the breasts of all, thou constrainest them each after its kind to continue their races with desire." [1]

The Legend of Good Women

Near the end of the *Troilus and Criseyde*, in a passage in which the author shows that he is profoundly moved by the seriousness of the story he has been writing, he beseeches all gentle women not to be angry with him on account of Criseyde's unfaithfulness.

> Ye may hir gilt in othere bokes see;
> And gladlier I wol wryten, if yow leste,
> Penelopeës trouthe and good Alceste.[2]

> Ne I say not this al-only for these men,
> But most for wommen that bitraysed be
> Through false folk ; god yeve hem sorwe, amen!
> That with hir grete wit and subtiltee
> Bitrayse yow! and this commeveth me
> To speke, and in effect yow alle I preye
> Beth war of men, and herkneth what I seye! [3]

In view of the facts that in the *Legend of Good Women* the poet writes of the falseness of men towards women, and that, had he finished his work, he would not only have written of " Penelopeës trouthe," [4] but he would have crowned the *Legend*

[1] *De Rerum Natura*, I, 1–20, translated by Munro.

[2] *Troilus*, v, 254. On the significance of this passage in connection with the *Legend* see ten Brink, *Studien*, p. 120, Skeat, Oxford Chaucer, III, xviii, and Lowes, Pub. Mod. Lang. Assoc., XX, 820.   [3] Ibid., 255.

[4] Note the god of Love's words to the poet:

> Thise other ladies sitting here arowe
> Ben in thy balade, if thou canst them knowe . . .
> Have hem now in thy Legende alle in minde,
> I mene of hem that ben in thy knowinge. — B-Prol., ll. 554–558.

with the story of Alceste, — " Kalender to any woman that wol lover be," [1] — in view of all this we may infer that the poet had already in mind the writing of the *Legend*. At the least, a very close connection between the two works is indicated. This closeness of connection is made clear by certain other features found in the two works.

One of these features which is very noticeable is the attitude which the poet assumes with regard to love. We have already seen what this is in the *Troilus*. He professes to be only a servant of lovers.[2] He declares to all lovers that he does not write this story out of his own feelings, and says :

> Eek though I speke of love unfelingly,
> No wonder is, for it nothing of newe is ;
> A blind man can nat juggen wel in hewis.[3]

He urges those who understand love to do as they please with any words that he, out of reverence to Love, may have added to his author's story,[4] for he speaks all his words " under correccioun" of those that have feeling in love's art.[5] In another place, he professes to be the clerk of those who serve Venus, and begs her help in writing the joys of lovers.[6] This attitude of Chaucer as " an outsider in the affairs of love " — which has already been noted [7] — was consistently maintained by him,[8] and

---

[1] But now I charge thee, upon thy lyf,
   That in thy Legend thou make of this wyf
   Whan thou hast other smale ymaad before.

> B-Prol. ll. 548–550 ; A-Prol. ll. 538–540.

[2] *Troilus*, i, 3.   [3] Ibid., ii, 3.   [4] Ibid., iii, 190.
[5] Ibid., iii, 191.   [6] Ibid., iii, 6.
[7] By Mr. Lowes, in his explanation of Chaucer's failure to utilize the opening stanzas of the *Filostrato* in his *Troilus*, Pub. Mod. Lang. Assoc., 1904, p. 622.
[8] Cf. also,
   For al be that I knowe not love in dede,
   Ne wot how that He quyteth folk hir hyre,
   Yet happeth me ful ofte in bokes rede
   Of his miracles and his cruel ire.— *P. of F.*, ll. 8–11.

he assumes it in the Prologue to the *Legend*. In imposing upon
him the penance of writing the *Legend*, Alceste says :

> And thogh thee lyke not a lover be
> Spek wel of love ; this penance yive I thee.

In all her defense of the poet before the god, she speaks of him
as one who was, as Chaucer calls himself,[1] the "clerk" of lovers.

> The man hath served yow of his conning
> And forthred wel your lawe in his making.

And the tone of the poet's own attempted defense of his conduct
is the same. Again he calls on

> lovers, that can make of sentement

to help him in praising the daisy aright, and asks their forbear-
ance if he does not do it as well as they :

> Sin that ye see I do hit in the honour
> Of love, and eek in service of the flour,
> Whom that I serve as I have wit or might.

The closeness of connection between the *Troilus* and the
Legend indicated by this similarity of attitude, is emphasized by
the spirit which, as an outsider, the poet exhibits. We have
already noted the almost abject humility which the writer professes to feel at the opening of the *Troilus*. He is only a servant
of those who in truth serve the god of Love. His unfitness for
loving is so great that he does not even dare to pray for help in
his work ; he is in outer darkness, far from the help of the god.[2]
Much the same humility, and realization of his poor standing
with the god, is displayed by the poet in the *Legend*. He reports
that the god of Love spoke to him :

> For it were better worthy, trewely,
> A werm to comen in my sight than thou. . . .
> My servaunts been alle wyse and honourable.
> Thou art my mortal fo, and me warreyest.

---

[1] *Troilus*, iii, 6.   [2] Ibid., i, 3.

He prays God's blessing on Alceste ;

> For ne hadde confort been of hir presence,
> I had be deed, withouten any defence,
> For drede of Loves wordes and his chere.

Indeed the idea at the basis of the whole Prologue is that the poet has sinned against the god and must do penance for it.

We may note further, as an indication of the close connection between the two works, what may perhaps be called a similarity of method. We have already seen how Chaucer, in the case of the *Troilus*, evinces a great fondness for using ecclesiastical ideas and phraseology. Examples were cited of the classical conception of the god of Love ; and a somewhat larger number of instances in which the feudal character of the god was shown. But the conception of the love divinity, which is by far the most prominent, is, as we have seen, the ecclesiastical; and the same preference for the ideas of the church appears, not only in the actual account of the love of Troilus and Criseyde, but also in other passages, which have nothing to do with this story itself.[1] Now if we consider the *Legend of Good Women* as a whole, we see a continuation of this method.

The ecclesiastical figure that describes human beings who have suffered and died for love as martyrs to their religion, of which Cupid was the divinity, needs only be mentioned. The fact that Cupid appears with a halo, as the B-version tells us,

> His gilte heer was corouned with a sonne,
> In-stede of gold, for hevinesse and wighte,

makes the conception more vivid than usual.[2] The ecclesiastical idea is fundamental in the *Legend*, and the corresponding

---

[1] An instance of the latter is the Proem to the first book, a part of which has been cited above.

[2] Professor Neilson, who has made a wide study of the Court of Love poems, states that this is the only instance of the god's wearing a halo which he has found (Neilson, *Origins*, p. 145).

conception of the love deity is therefore the prevailing one in the Prologue. The god is given his classical equipment of wings [1] and fiery darts but, as we have noted, this is not inconsistent with the ecclesiastical figure. The references which Alcestis makes to envious tattlers and flatterers in the court of the god, and her argument that a king or a lord should be just to high and low, and especially should "han of pore folk compassioun," [2] reflect the feudal characteristics of the god. But clearly the larger conception in the Prologue is the ecclesiastical. The charge against the poet is that he was guilty of spreading heresy against the religion of the god, in translating the *Romance of the Rose*, [3] and of encouraging schism. [4] The god refers to Criseyde's faithlessness as "wickkednesse" [5] and demands of the poet why he could not just as well have "seyd goodnesse of wemen." [6] He swears by "Saint Venus" that although the poet has renounced the religion of love, he shall repent it. [7] Alcestis pleads that he has furthered the god's "lawe" with his poetry, [8] and she asks the god "right of [his] grace" not to hurt the poet. Later, when she bids the culprit leave off his arguing, she states

> Thou hast thy grace, and hold thee right ther-to.

She follows this declaration by imposing upon him for his trespass the penance of spending the greater part of his life

> In making of a glorious Legende
> Of Gode Wemen, maidens and wyves
> That were trewe in loving al hir lyves.

There is yet one detail, which is a part of this large use by Chaucer of ecclesiastical ideas in the *Troilus* and the *Legend*, and which is significant as regards the connection of the two

---

[1] A. 142–169.   [2] A. 376; B. 390.   [3] A. 256; B. 330.
[4] And (thou) makest wyse folk fro me with draw (A. 257; B. 331).
[5] A. 209.   [6] A. 268–269.   [7] A. 313–316; B. 336–340.   [8] A. 399.

poems. Near the end of the Proem to Book I of the *Troilus* Chaucer, after admitting his own unworthiness to be a lover and calling for the prayers of various kinds of lovers in behalf of their less fortunate brethren, says :

> For so hope I my soule best avaunce,
> To preye for hem that Loves servaunts be,
> And wryte hir wo, and live in charitee,
> And for to have of hem compassioun
> As though I were hir owene brother dere.[1]

The poet, in the spirit of humility which characterizes this whole Proem, declares that he hopes to advance the interests of his own soul by doing a work which has merit attached to it, and this work is to write the woes of Love's servants. Of course, the statement is made primarily with reference to the *Troilus*, which he is just beginning. But when we remember that the writing of a saint's life was an act of peculiar merit, and when we consider that that is precisely what he is doing in the *Legend*, except that he is writing of Cupid's saints, the connection between the statement and the *Legend* seems inevitable ; so clear is it that one might almost feel confident that the statement suggested to the poet the plan of the *Legend* itself.

We have noted in the preceding pages instances in which Church ideas were used for secular purposes, particularly in the love literature. The *Concile de Remiremont* affords an early example of this.[2] In *Li Fablel* the feature of the tomb, over which the birds were singing for the soul of the lover buried there, is another case in point, as is the funeral of the young man who had died in the service of Love in *Venus la Deesse*. Examples have also been cited from Andreas Capellanus, in his use of the Paradise and Purgatory of lovers ; and traces of the use of ecclesiastical ideas were pointed out in the *Romance of the Rose*. Perhaps the most elaborate employment

---

[1] *Troilus*, i, 7, 8.   [2] See p. 18, above.

of such ideas for setting forth a story of love is to be found in *La Messe des Oiseaus*, written by Jean de Condé.[1] This story relates the author's dream, in which he saw in a beautiful meadow a court presided over by Venus, attended by numerous birds. Before proceeding to the work of administering justice, she orders the nightingale to sing mass. Here the feudal character of the story changes to the ecclesiastical. The service which is sung by the birds is an elaborate parody of the service of the Mass as celebrated by the Church. The Confession, the *Introit*, the Litany, the *Gloria*, the Collect, the Epistle, the *Alleluia*, the Gospels, the Creed, the Offertory, all follow in due order. A sermon on the virtues of Obedience, Patience, Loyalty, and Hope in lovers is delivered by the parrot, after which absolution is granted. The *Sanctus* is sung; the *Paternoster* and the *Agnus Dei* follow, and the service in which the bird congregation have participated closes with the Collect, the *Ite missa est*, and the Benediction. After the service the poet proceeds with the story of the feast of lovers, followed by an account of the judgment rendered by the goddess in the complaint made by the white canonesses against the gray nuns.

Other less elaborate uses of the ecclesiastical phraseology for the language of love could be pointed out.[2] Those here noted are sufficient to show that in equating the worship of God with the worship of Love Chaucer was following an old literary tradition. Such a process of equating would find many different manners of expression. The particular form which the poet here uses we may assume is original with him, and possibly it grows out of the passage in the Proem to Book I of the *Troilus*.

[1] *Dits et Contes*, ed. A. Scheler, Brussels, 1866, III, 166 ff.

[2] For a discussion of this feature of the love literature of the period, see Neilson, *Origins*, pp. 220–226. It may be said that no other author handled these ideas so cleverly or in so masterly a fashion as Chaucer, with whom the device was a great favorite.

Notwithstanding the fact that Chaucer was thus following in the *Legend* a well-defined plan based on the mediaeval ecclesiastical ideas, we are struck at once with what appears to be the unsuitableness of some of the individual legends to the plan adopted. This may possibly be explained by conjecturing that Chaucer did not write all the legends with such a series in mind, but that some of them were written before he conceived the general plan, and were utilized by him afterward. At the same time, even if this conjecture be correct, the *Legend*, as we have it, is as the poet left it, and the separate stories as they stand he regarded as suitable for

> a glorious Legende
> Of Gode Wommen.

The difficulty in understanding Chaucer's use of these stories is, I believe, apparent rather than real. At any rate, it is easy to see how the poet's mind was working. The unfitness of certain of the women for the *Legend* appears the greater to us, because we do not easily forget our habitual way of regarding them, and do not, therefore, look at them as Chaucer wished us to do in this particular poem. For it is clear that the poet has adopted a definite mode of procedure in treating the stories; and this is nowhere more evident than in the very one of all the legends which seems to us the least adapted to his purpose, the story of Cleopatra.

Certainly, as we know her history, Cleopatra is a strange example of those that were true in loving all their lives. Are we to infer that the poet did not know the true account of her life, and the scenes which he here describes? He himself assures us that the tale as he tells it is "storial truth, hit is no fable." Or shall we say that his sources misled him, or that he only vaguely remembered what he had read?[1] Thus far scholars have

---

[1] As Professor Lounsbury intimates, *Studies*, II, 186.

found no sources which will account for the version of the story which Chaucer gives. Or yet again, shall we say that the poet took liberties with the facts in order to meet the exigencies of his *Legend*, — a license which is allowable in any writer of fiction ? So long as the truth is not known, the reader is free to choose whichever of these alternatives pleases him best ; and the last of the three will be, perhaps, the easiest to accept. For it is clear that, as we have the story, the poet has intended to make, and has succeeded in making, the Egyptian queen a martyr to her love. As he says :

> And she hir deeth receyveth, with good chere,
> For love of Antony, that was hir so dere.

Professor Lounsbury remarks on this point,[1] " Even in the story as told by Chaucer, Antony is not only the more in earnest of the two, he is much more of a martyr." I cannot at all agree with this statement. To me Cleopatra cuts the better figure throughout. It should be remembered that to tell the story of women who were true in love was only part of the duty imposed upon the poet by the good Alceste ; he must also

> telle of false men that hem bitrayen ;

and although he recognizes the worth of Antony as a lover, his " persone," " gentilesse," " discrecioun," and " hardinesse," the effort to make the hero appear at a disadvantage, however slight, as a lover, is quite as apparent as the desire to exalt the heroine. He very carefully inserts near the beginning the detail that Antony had already been false in love :

> And over al this, the suster of Cesar,
> He lafte hir falsly, er that she was war,
> And wolde algates han another wyf.

The insertion of this detail is especially significant, if we assume that the poet was familiar with the history of Antony's and

[1] *Studies*, II, 185.

Cleopatra's lives. To include this point from Antony's life, and to omit the unsavory love experiences of his heroine previous to her affair with Antony, must have been part of a well-defined purpose of the poet to make the lady appear in the better light.

Furthermore, the death of Antony is not at all that of a martyr to love. The cause of his suicide, as Chaucer tells us, was despair at the thought of having lost his " worshipe " in the day's fight. Here again if Chaucer *really knew* the facts of history in the case of the battle here described, his purpose in suppressing the detail of Antony's flight becomes clear. To give up honor and everything for love, as Antony did, would be the part of a martyr. It seems clear that in omitting the detail, if he really knew it, Chaucer has intended to reserve this great honor of sacrificing all for love to his heroine. At any rate, as he tells the story, this is reserved for her ; and in so doing, the poet makes it stand out as boldly as he can. Of the one hundred and twenty-six lines contained in this *Legend*, forty-one — that is, almost one third — are devoted to the death of the love-stricken queen. Nor do we find in the account of the queen's sacrifice anything suggestive of lightness or frivolity. Furthermore, if we allow ourselves to forget the true character of the queen which we learn from history, it is possible for us to feel the pathos of the tale as Chaucer tells it, — particularly of that part in which Cleopatra addresses her lover, while preparing for death.

The introduction to this scene is noteworthy, when considered in relation to the general plan of the *Legend*. The poet says : " Ye men, who are always falsely swearing that you shall die, if your ladies be angry, listen and I will tell you of a woman who really did what you pretend to do." Both in this and in the humorous lines with which he concludes his story the poet keeps before us his purpose in the *Legend*, — to exalt the constancy of women in love and to deprecate the falseness and fickleness of men.

In view of these facts, I do not see how we can say with Professor Lounsbury that in Chaucer's tale Antony is more of a martyr and more in earnest than Cleopatra; much less can we say with a recent writer that the story as Chaucer tells it is ironical, a travesty in which the poet satirizes the inconstancy of women.[1]

The conjecture that Chaucer deliberately changed the appearance of the historical facts in the *Cleopatra* will seem to do less violence to the truth when we consider that he has consistently manipulated his sources to suit the needs of his *Legend* in the accounts of the other women.[2] Not all of them, however, demand that such liberties be taken as in the *Cleopatra*. For example, in the classic story of Pyramus and Thisbe, Chaucer found material particularly well suited to his purposes. The object ever to be kept before him was to tell of women who were true in loving all their lives, and who, if need were, willingly and gladly suffered death on account of their love. In Thisbe he found just such a woman, and her story was already made for him in the works of his favorite author Ovid. Accordingly we have in Chaucer's version, on the whole, a faithful reproduction of the Latin narrative. Yet there are some changes, the purpose of which is unmistakably to make the tale fit in better with the plan of the *Legend*. Note, for example, the interpolations which our poet makes in Ovid's version. The words

> Callida per tenebras . . . Thisbe
> Egreditur fallitque suos,[3]

---

[1] H. C. Goddard, "Chaucer's Legend of Good Women," *Journal of English Philology*, VII, 87 ff., and VIII, 47 ff. See also Professor Lowes's reply in the same periodical, VIII, 513 ff.

[2] For the sources of the legends see Skeat, *Works*, III, xxxiv–xl; Bech, *Anglia*, V, 313–382.

[3] *Metamorphoses*, iv, 93–94.

Chaucer interprets thus :

> For alle her friendes — for to save her trouthe —
> She hath forsake.

And then he remarks :

> and that is routhe
> That ever woman wolde be so trewe
> To trusten man, but she the bet him knewe !

The object of this observation is, of course, to keep before the mind of the reader the proposition at the basis of the *Legend :* that women are for the most part true in love ; that they will usually go to greater lengths than men to remain true ; and that many will suffer death rather than be untrue.

To emphasize this thought, Chaucer has made one other very noticeable change in the Latin poem. This is the omission of all reference to the mulberry tree, which has a rather prominent place in Ovid's account. In omitting this, he has not only greatly improved the story as a story, but he has got rid of material which for his purpose is irrelevant. Accordingly, where in the Latin Thisbe addresses the tree, Chaucer has the opportunity to make her speak these words :

> And rightwis god to every lover sende,
> That loveth trewely, more prosperitee
> Than ever hadde Piramus and Thisbe !
> And lat no gentil woman her assure
> To putten her in swich an aventure.
> But god forbede but a woman can
> Been as trewe and loving as a man !
> And, for my part, I shal anoon it kythe ;

whereupon she stabs herself.

The story of Pyramus and Thisbe offers some difficulty, however, happy illustration of woman's loyalty as it is. For, as we have noted several times already, part of the poet's purpose in the *Legend* was to show man's unfaithfulness in love ; yet,

Pyramus is quite as true as Thisbe herself. Chaucer slyly apologizes for having told the tale at all :

> Of trewe men I finde but fewe mo
> In alle my bokes, save this Piramus,
> And therfor have I spoken of him thus.
> For hit is deyntee to us men to finde
> A man that can in love be trewe and kinde.
> Heer may ye seen, what lover so he be,
> A woman dar and can as wel as he.

Of course this apology in reality strengthens the poet's case ; for here, as usual, the exception proves the rule.

Yet it is quite clear that Chaucer is not content with such proof. We have already seen, in the legend of Cleopatra, how the heroine was allowed the centre of the stage ; the same is true in the account of Pyramus and Thisbe. Pyramus is given enough prominence to make perfectly clear the part he enacted in this tragedy of love. Yet, as the story is here told, what is said of the hero is evidently designed to bring into greater relief the part played by Thisbe. This favor shown the heroine by the poet is all the more noticeable when the version is compared with Ovid's ; for in the latter greater prominence is given to neither character; it is the unusual love of the two, and the unhappy end to which their love brought them, which interests the Latin poet, and which he makes the theme of his story.

The story of Dido furnishes Chaucer with material really better suited to his purpose than the tale of Pyramus and Thisbe. Dido is an actual example of a woman who sacrificed all for love ; Aeneas, Chaucer uses as an example of the false lover. It is in the latter respect that the poet departs from his source ; for it is very clear that Virgil exonerates Aeneas from any blame for his treachery to the queen, and considers the command of Mercury as sufficient excuse for his forsaking her. As the hero of the epic, Aeneas is made to appear in the most favorable light. Not so in the version of Chaucer, who gives all his sympathy to the queen, and makes the Trojan maliciously false.

A successful carrying out of the purpose in the individual legends requires a strongly pathetic element in them. Accordingly, as we have seen in the case of the *Cleopatra* and *Thisbe*, the poet spares no pains to make them effective in this respect. The same is true of the *Dido*. One means of gaining this effect is a close attention to details in the earlier part of the story. Care is taken to show the depths to which Fate had reduced the hero, and the magnificence to which he was raised by the generosity of the queen.

> This Eneas is come to Paradys
> Out of the swolow of helle, and thus in joye
> Remembreth him of his estat in Troye.

Then follows a long list of the presents the queen had made Aeneas. All this helps to emphasize the treachery of the Trojan, and to increase the pathos of the latter part of the tale.

Another means the poet employs for the purpose of pathos is the apostrophe to women who trust themselves to men.

> O sely womman, ful of innocence,
> Ful of pitee, of trouthe, and conscience,
> What maketh yow to men to trusten so?
> Have ye swich routhe upon hir feined wo,
> And han swiche olde ensamples yow beforn?
> See ye nat alle, how they been for-sworn?
> Wher see ye oon, that he ne hath laft his leef,
> Or been unkinde, or doon hir som mischeef,
> Or pilled her, or bosted of his dede?

This utterance, while it is, I believe, the sincere expression of the poet's feelings, as were the similar utterances in the *House of Fame* version, has its artistic value, and plays its part in heightening the pathetic effect of the tale.

Yet another means employed for this purpose is the speech of Dido near the end. This speech, as was the case in the *House of Fame*, is different in spirit from Virgil's. In the Latin, the queen calls down curses upon the departing Aeneas:

> I, sequere Italiam ventis, pete regna per undas.
> Spero equidem mediis, si quid pia numina possunt,
> Supplicia hausurum scopulis et nomine Dido
> Saepe vocaturum. Sequar atris ignibus absens
> Et, cum frigida mors anima seduxerit artus,
> Omnibus umbra locis adero. Dabis, improbe, poenas.
> Audiam et haec manis veniet mihi fama sub imos.[1]

In Chaucer's poem, anything harsh is omitted from the queen's speech, and only her tender and pathetic supplications are given.

Lastly, the poet has with fine instinct seized upon the words of Ovid to close his story:

> Sic ubi fata vocant, udis abiectus in herbis
> Ad vada Maeandri concinit albus olor;
> Nec quia te nostra sperem prece posse moveri,
> Adloquor (adverso movimus ista deo),
> Sed merita et famam corpusque animumque pudicum
> Cum male perdiderim, perdere verba levest.
> Certus es ire tamen miseramque relinquere Didon,
> Atque idem venti vela fidemque ferent?[2]

The pathos of these lines in the original is unmistakable; as rendered by Chaucer, they add distinctly to the pathetic effect of his poem.

In the legend of *Hypsipyle and Medea*, Chaucer is concerned more with making known the treachery of Jason than with showing the unhappy plight of the two women. True to his purpose, he devotes the greater part of his poem to the lover, painting him as all that a lover should be, except for want of truth and loyalty, and showing what a villain he was "with feyning and with every sotil dede." He prefaces his

---

[1] *Aeneid*, iv, 381–387.   [2] *Heroides*, vii, 3–10.

narrative with one of those expressions, frequent in the legends, in which he laments the faithlessness of men. After his challenge to the " rote of false lovers, duk Jasoun," and his threat to publish his treachery, he remarks :

> But certes, hit is bothe routhe and wo
> That love with false loveres werketh so ;
> For they shul have wel better love and chere
> Than he that hath aboght his love ful dere,
> Or had in armes many a blody box.
> For ever as tendre a capoun et the fox,
> Thogh he be fals and hath the foul betrayed,
> As shal the good-man that ther-for hath payed ;
> Al have he to the capoun skille and right,
> The false fox wol have his part at night.

This is in the same spirit as the similar utterances noted from time to time in the *House of Fame* and in the other parts of the *Legend*. With this introduction, Chaucer proceeds to the tale, following in the main the version as Guido delle Colonne gives it in the first book of the *Historia Trojana*,[1] but omitting all of Guido's account that is irrelevant to the love story, or that is not necessary for a swift presentation of the events in which the love story is set.

Chaucer does not tarry long over the account of Hypsipyle, which is hardly more than an introduction to the tale of Medea. It is in the latter that the poet's most interesting and significant departures from Guido's narrative are to be seen. For example, the long description of Medea's powers of necromancy, obviously unsuited to a portrayal of a fond and trusting maiden, he omits, as he does the account of how the heroine takes especial pains to adorn herself for the feast given to Jason, although she was naturally very fair. This action of Medea's is the signal for

---

[1] For the references to Guido it proved convenient to use a MS. copy of the Strassburg edition of 1494, made by Mr. G. B. Weston in Dresden in 1897 and now in the Harvard University Library.

Guido to launch out into a long diatribe against woman's inconstancy and lustful seeking after men, with special application of
his remarks to Medea. He tells how, as she sits at the feast
between her father and Jason, she is so overcome with love-
longing that she cannot eat nor drink : " Est enim sibi tunc
cibus et potus Jasonis dulcis aspectus, quem totum clausum
gestat in corde, et in cuius amore libidinis repletus est sto-
machus saturatus."

It is in this part of Guido's story that Chaucer sees fit to
make another very interesting change. Guido, in his scathing
remarks on woman, declares : " Scimus enim mulieris animum
semper virum appetere, sicut appetit materia semper formam, et
turpe bonum. O utinam materia transiens semel in formam
posset dici suo contenta formato. Sed sicut ad formam de
forma procedere materiam notum est, sic mulieris concupiscentia
dissoluta procedere de viro ad virum utique esse creditur sine
fine, cum sit quedam profunditas sine fundo, nisi forte pudoris
labes aliqua abstinentia laudanda concluserit sub terminis hon-
estatis." These ideas Chaucer is pleased to use as follows :

> As matere appetyteth forme alwey,
> And from forme into forme hit passen may,
> Or as a welle that were botomless,
> Right so can fals Jasoun have no pees.
> For, to desyren, through his appetyt,
> To doon with gentil wommen his delyt,
> This is his lust and his felicitee.[1]

The manner in which Chaucer has here applied to Jason in
particular Guido's words directed against women in general,
illustrates his whole treatment of the story as told by Guido.
For, according to the latter, the entire disgrace in this affair of
Jason and Medea attaches to Medea. Chaucer not only paints

---

[1] The connection between the first two lines of this passage and Guido's
words has already been noted by Bech, *Anglia*, V, 329–330.

the man as black as possible, but he dwells upon those qualities in him which were likely to make him attractive to the feminine nature :

> Now was Jaoun a semely man withalle,
> And lyk a lord, and had a greet renoun,
> And of his loke as real as leoun,
> And goodly of his speche, and famulere,
> And coude of love al craft and art plenere
> Withoute boke, with everich observaunce.

The impression the poet wishes to make is that such a man no woman could resist ; hence he says,

> And, as fortune oghte a foul meschaunce,
> She wex enamoured upon this man.

On the other hand, in Guido all the advances come from Medea.

The pathetic element in neither the *Hypsipyle* nor the *Medea* is as large as in the other legends already considered ; yet there are in both pathetic passages which are very effective. In the former, for instance, there is the letter which Hypsipyle sent to Jason ; for the substance of this the poet is indebted, of course, to Ovid's sixth Epistle. There is something very touching, too, in the simple statement with which the story ends :

> And trew to Jason was she al her lyf,
> And ever kepte her chast, as for his wyf;
> Ne never had she joye at her herte,
> But dyed, for his love, of sorwes smerte.

In the *Medea* a fine effect is gained by using the truly pathetic lines of Ovid,

> Cur mihi plus aequo flavi placuere capilli
> Et decor et linguae gratia ficta tuae?

and Chaucer has made the original still more moving by his fine translation :

> Why lyked me thy yelow heer to see
> More then the boundes of myn honestee,
> Why lyked me thy youthe and thy fairnesse,
> And of thy tonge the infinit graciousnesse?

In the legend of *Lucretia* we have a tale of a somewhat different nature from those already considered; different in that it does not deal with love at all. But it fits well enough into the general plan. In the Prologue to the *Legend*, the petulant god had blamed the poet for not telling in his writings, instead of the stories of Criseyde and faithless women, the stories of those heathen women who were glad to suffer tortures and even death, rather than lose their fair name and be untrue. Lucretia was such a woman; and we find her mentioned in the *Balade* which included the names of women noted for their faithfulness. The poet's purpose in telling of her is, as he says at the beginning,

> to preise and drawen to memorie
> The verray wyf, the verray trewe Lucresse.

And at the end he informs us,

> I telle hit, for she was of love so trewe,
> Ne in her wille she chaunged for no newe.

But this latter, if we consider the story alone, is a bit far-fetched, and Chaucer's real application of the tale is rather to be found in the lines following:

> And for the stable herte, sad and kinde,
> That these women men may alday finde; . . .
> And as of men, loketh which tirannye
> They doon alday; assay hem who so liste,
> The trewest is ful brotel for to triste.

That is, using Lucretia as a particular example, he places her faithfulness over against the fickleness and falseness of men in general.

Of the poet's manner of treating his sources in carrying out his purpose, there is little to say. He professes to follow Ovid and Livy; in reality, he adheres closely to Ovid's account,[1] and finds it necessary to depart very little from the Latin version. In accordance with his usual practice, however, he introduces

[1] Skeat, Oxford Chaucer, iii, 330.

some observations of his own, which serve to make the story more suitable to the *Legend*. To emphasize his purpose, he relates how Lucretia fainted for fear of shame and death; and then he adds the apostrophe to Tarquin:

> Tarquinius, that art a kinges eyr,
> And sholdest, as by linage and by right,
> Doon as a lord and as a verray knight,
> Why hastow doon dispyt to chivalrye?
> Why hastow doon this lady vilanye?
> Alas! of thee this was a vileins dede.

These lines, which "breathe the spirit of chivalry," [1] are doubtless, as others already noted, to be taken as the sincere sentiment of the poet himself. One characteristic touch in the story is interesting to note. Ovid in telling of Lucretia's discretion, even after stabbing herself, says:

> "Tunc quoque, iam moriens, ne non procumbat honeste,
> Respicit. Haec etiam cura cadentis erat. [2]

Chaucer makes the matter more concrete in the lines:

> And as she fel adoun, she caste her look,
> And of her clothes yit she hede took;
> For in her falling yit she hadde care
> Lest that her feet or swiche thing lay bare;
> So wel she loved clennesse and eek trouthe.

Another observation which the poet volunteers is found in the lines:

> Ne never was ther king in Rome toun
> Sin thilke day; and she was holden there
> A seint, and ever her day y-halwed dere
> As in hir lawe.

Professor Skeat remarks on this: "This canonization of Lucretia is strikingly mediaeval. It was evidently suggested by the fact that Ovid gives her story under a particular date, so

---

[1] Skeat, Oxford Chaucer, iii, 333.   [2] Ovid, *Fasti*, ii, ll. 833–834.

that she seemed to have *her own day*, like a saint." The interesting feature of Chaucer's remark, from the point of view of the present study, is the manner in which it fits in with the use of the religious convention in the *Legend* as a whole.

Of the pathos of the tale, little need be said. In Ovid's version, the story throughout is pathetically told. Chaucer's rendering, though itself not lacking, certainly adds nothing to the Latin in this respect.

It seems superfluous even to consider Chaucer's purpose in the *Ariadne*. He himself tells us that he writes

> to clepe agein unto memorie
> Of Theseus the grete untrouthe of love.

With this purpose in view, he swiftly narrates the events up to the story of Theseus and Ariadne in such a manner as to make Theseus's treachery as black and Ariadne's plight as pathetic as possible. The part played by the heroine in rescuing Theseus is therefore given prominence. In connection with this, the poet's words are interesting :

> Wel maystow wepe, O woful Theseus,
> That art a kinges sone, and dampned thus.
> Me thinketh this, that thou were depe y-holde
> To whom that saved thee fro cares colde !
> And now, if any woman helpe thee,
> Wel oughtestow her servant for to be,
> And been her trewe lover yeer by yere !

These words, taken in connection with Theseus's false love-making further on, greatly increase the irony of the situation.

In the latter part of the story, Chaucer chooses such incidents from Ovid's tenth Epistle as will heighten the pathetic effect. The desertion of the sleeping heroine, her groping in the bed, her walking barefoot on the sands, her display of the kerchief on the pole, her swoon, her kissing the footprints of the treacherous lover, and lastly her words to the bed, which formerly held two lovers, but which now has only one, — all these arouse our sympathy. Throughout all, the poet never lets us forget the baseness of the betrayer.

> Hadde he nat sinne, that her thus begylde?

he asks ; and again he remarks :

> Me list no more to speke of him, parde ;
> Thise false lovers, poison be hir bane !
> But I wol turne again to Adriane. . . .
> Allas ! for thee my herte hath now pite !

His plan here again is what we have seen it to be in the preceding legends : to engage our sympathies for the woman, and to make the man appear in as bad a light as possible.

If the tale of Lucretia was a little out of the poet's province in writing the *Legend*, the *Philomela* was still more so. This is no story of love ; nor does the lady, as did Lucretia, show any nobility of action as a result of her shame. It is simply the account of man's baseness in seeking the gratification of his sensual nature. It really lies entirely outside the scope of Chaucer's plan in the *Legend*. He undoubtedly feels this ; for the conclusion is forced and far-fetched :

> Ye may be war of men, yif that yow liste.
> For al be that he wol nat, for his shame,
> Doon so as Tereus, to lese his name,
> Ne serve yow as a mordrour or a knave,
> Ful litel whyle shul ye trewe him have,
> That wol I seyn, al were he now my brother,
> But hit so be that he may have non other.

The tone of this is indicative of the poet's purpose : to paint the blackness of Tereus's deed. To this purpose he adheres strictly. The first sixteen lines of the poem are a denunciation of Tereus ; and at times, the poet stops in the narrative to express his abhorrence of the villain ; for example, in the line :

> For I am wery of him for to telle.

Contrary to his usual practice in the legends, Chaucer devotes but little space, comparatively, to his heroine. The effort on his part to heighten the pathetic effect of the tale by dwelling on the woman's situation is far less conspicuous than in the legends so far considered. Indeed, the pathos attaching to Progne's sorrow is almost as strong as that of Philomela's plight.

Chaucer, in following his author Ovid,[1] succeeds in telling an interesting and effective story. But considered in its relation to the general purpose of the *Legend*, the tale must, I think, be accounted one of the least appropriate of all.

In the last two stories of the series the poet has made a happier choice. The *Phyllis* is of the same kind as several other stories in the *Legend:* the *Dido*, the *Hypsipyle and Medea*, the *Ariadne*, — in all of which the lover gains his will by a promise of marriage, and then deserts the trusting woman. Little need be said of the *Phyllis*. The method of treatment is the same as that we have noticed in connection with the poems just mentioned : the actions of the lover are made to appear more despicable because of the generosity of the heroine in raising him from the depths of misfortune to a position in which he is prosperous and happy. The sorrow of the woman is made more conspicuous by the addition of lyric expressions (mostly taken from Ovid) in which she laments her sad plight, and implores the pity of the false lover.

In the *Hypermnestra* we have a tale of wifely devotion, which fits in well, as such, with the scheme of the *Legend*. It is difficult to see what the poet can say against the husband in this case. Chaucer has left the poem unfinished, but he has given us a hint of his feelings toward Lino, in the lines :

> Allas ! Lino ! why art thou so unkinde ?
> Why ne haddest thou remembered in thy minde
> To taken her, and lad her forth with thee ?

[1] *Metamorphoses*, vi, 424–605.

In both the *Phyllis* and *Hypermnestra* the poet has succeeded in treating the heroines with genuine pathos ; in them, as usual, he has adhered closely to Ovid's Epistles.[1]

The foregoing considerations show with sufficient clearness, I think, that in handling the tales which make up the individual legends, Chaucer was following a definite plan, which was a part of the larger plan of the *Legend* as a whole. This plan demanded a similar treatment for each of the separate stories ; a treatment in which the loyalty of woman would be exalted and the falsity of men would be decried. Anything in his sources which would in any way emphasize either of these features, the poet would be careful to utilize. With equal care he would avoid any details which would tend to lessen this impression of the woman's faithfulness and of the man's disloyalty. This plan the poet studiously adhered to throughout ;[2] and doubtless the sameness of treatment which it involved made the whole task wearisome and led to the abandonment of the scheme.

Certainly Chaucer was in earnest in what he wrote, as far as he went. At some time or other in his poetic career, the plan of telling stories of women who were faithful in love doubtless appealed to him. But at the time when the poem was put in the form in which we have it, the love theme could have had but little attraction for him. He had reached the high-water mark in his treatment of love in *Troilus*. After such a superb effort, anything in the nature of the *Legend* must have seemed tame. Besides, the lure of a larger representation of life was before him, in the already projected plan of the *Canterbury Tales*. When the poet laid aside the *Legend*, he gave up for good and all the handling of love in and for itself. Wherever

---

[1] For the *Phyllis*, *Heroides*, ii ; for the *Hypermnestra*, *Heroides*, xiv.

[2] Except, of course, in the *Pyramus and Thisbe*, and then he apologizes for having to speak of the hero as he does.

the theme is found in the *Canterbury Tales* it is subservient to some other purpose, and love appears only as an aspect of the larger life with which the *Tales* deal.

The Canterbury Tales

In the *Canterbury Tales*, two types of love are prominent. One of these, the courtly love of the higher classes, we have seen to be abundantly illustrated in Chaucer's earlier works. The other type is found in those tales in which Chaucer in his masterly fashion portrays the life of the lower classes — the love of the *fabliaux*. This is solely and entirely carnal in its nature. We have seen that the courtly love itself was often sensual; but along with the sensualism, there was found a refinement and often a nobility of sentiment which went far toward lessening the repulsive effect of the baser element. The love of the *fabliaux*, on the other hand, is all grossness without any of the refinement.

With this lower type of love we shall not deal here. We shall take the attitude, for this study, that the courtly classes of the poet's own time would have assumed, — that, although the " hende Nicholas," January and May, and that splendid animal, the Wyf of Bath, dignified their passion with the name of love, they were incapable of experiencing real love, or even of comprehending its nature. We shall confine our discussion to what would have been deemed love by those people for whom Chaucer wrote; that is, in accordance with the plan followed so far, we shall direct our attention to the courtly love element in the *Canterbury Tales*.

The Prologue

Of the company of pilgrims pictured for us in the Prologue, two are of especial interest to us in the present study; these are the Knight and his son the Squire,

> A lovyere and a lusty bachelere.

Of the Knight it is said that he was worthy, wise, meek, and that he loved,

> Trouthe and honour, fredom and curteisye.

These are the qualities which we have found to be requisite in the model courtly lover back to the time of Andreas Capellanus. The characteristics, indeed, of the knight and the lover in mediaeval times were identical, since every knight was supposed, when young, to be in love; and since the great majority of lovers were knights.

The description of the Squire agrees well with our ideas of lovers as derived from the courtly literature. He is said to be courteous and humble. His love was so "hot" that it kept him awake at night. He had travelled far on military expeditions and had conducted himself well, in the hope of standing high in his lady's favor. He was accomplished in riding, song-making, writing, drawing, jousting, and dancing. He was merry all the day with his singing and his "fluting."

> He was as fresh as is the month of May,

and the garments he wore were a symbol of the freshness of his nature.

It is noticeable that the Squire meets all the requirements with regard to character, behavior, dress, and accomplishments, which the god put before his lover in the *Romance of the Rose*. As for his military expeditions, and his desire to stand well with his lady, this, as we have seen in the preceding part of this study, is in accord with ideas commonly held, that the young lover must perform deeds of prowess, so that his fame may come to his lady's ears, if he wishes to gain her favor.

Two other characters of the Prologue are brought into relation with this study by what the poet says of them; these, strangely enough, are the Prioress and the Monk. The Prioress wore a brooch on which was written the motto, *Amor vincit omnia*. Similarly, the Monk wore a pin, the larger end of which was fashioned like a love-knot. Of course, neither of these characters was a lover ; but the devices which they wore show the prevalence of love ideas at this time. " Chaucer's Prioress and Monk, whose lives were devoted to religious reflection and the most serious engagements, and while they are actually travelling on a pilgrimage to visit the shrine of a sainted martyr, openly avow the universal influence of love. They exhibit on their apparel badges entirely inconsistent with their profession, but easily accountable for from these principles. The Prioress wears a bracelet on which is inscribed, with a crowned A, *Amor vincit omnia*. The Monk ties his hood with a true lover's knot." [1]

The Knight's Tale

It seems hardly necessary, after showing the large use, by Chaucer, of conventional ideas in his erotic work, to point out such features in the *Knight's Tale*. Yet, following our usual plan, we may note such employment of the stock ideas of love literature as the poet has here made. In so doing, we shall see once more that Chaucer in his love stories never tried to avoid the conventional ideas. On the contrary, he used them freely ; but, as a poet of genius, he managed them and never allowed them to manage him.

Love is conceived as a god whose power is absolute. Nowhere may a better expression of the courtly idea of the god of Love be found than in the words of Theseus :

> The god of love, a ! *benedicite*,
> How mighty and how great a lord is he !
> Ayeins his might ther gayneth none obstacles,
> He may be cleped a god for his miracles ;
> For he can maken at his owne gyse
> Of everich herte, as that him list devyse.

[1] Warton, *History of English Poetry*, London, 1871, III, 3.

He has shown his power on Palamon and Arcite, for he has, Theseus says,

> maugree hir eyen two
> Y-broght hem hider bothe for to dye! . . .
> Thus hath hir lord, the god of love, y-payed
> Hir wages and hir fees for hir servyse!

Theseus himself was a servant of the god and had been "caught ofte in his las."

Although the god appears often, Venus is prominent as a love deity. In this capacity, she requires absolute devotion ; nothing is of avail against her might :

> wisdom ne richesse,
> Beautee ne sleighte, strengthe, ne hardinesse,
> Ne may with Venus holde champartye ;
> For as hir list the world than may she gye.

References to Cupid with his arrows appear in the poem. Arcite complains :

> And over al this, to sleen me utterly,
> Love hath his fyry dart so brenningly
> Y-stiked thurgh my trewe careful herte,
> That shapen was my deeth erst than my sherte.

In the description of the Temple of Venus, too, Cupid is pictured as an attendant of Venus :

> Biforn hir stood hir sone Cupido,
> Upon his shuldres winges hadde he two ;
> And blind he was, as it is ofte sene ;
> A bowe he bar and arwes brighte and kene.

In fact, in this Temple, everything incidental to the passion of love is pictured on the walls.

Venus in her capacity as the goddess of carnal love is referred to in the words spoken by Palamon while praying in the Temple :

> I shal for evermore,
> Emforth my might, thy trewe servant be,
> And holden werre alwey with chastitee.

The lady in the *Knight's Tale* has the characteristics, physical and spiritual, common to ladies in the courtly poetry. Her position with regard to her lovers is the usual one of superiority. Arcite determines to return to Athens,

> To see my lady that I love and serve.

Elsewhere he declares :

> Only the sighte of hir, whom that I serve,
> Though that I never hir grace may deserve,
> Wolde han suffised right y-nough for me.

Similarly, Palamon is a servant of Emilia. Theseus says of him, addressing Emilia :

> That gentil Palamon, your owne knight,
> That serveth yow with wille, herte, and might,
> And ever hath doon, sin that ye first him knewe,
> . . . ye shul, of your grace, upon him rewe,
> And taken him for housbonde and for lord.

The attitude of the lady toward the lovers is the usual one of indifference; at least, it seems to be that to the lovers themselves. Arcite, in praying to Mars, says of Emilia :

> For she, that dooth me al this wo endure,
> Ne reccheth never wher I sinke or flete.
> And wel I woot, er she me mercy hete,
> I moot with strengthe winne hir . . .

The lovers themselves are portrayed in accordance with the conventional ideas. They suffer torments and woe, and show all the customary symptoms. The changes in mood caused in Arcite by his love are thus described :

> Whan that Arcite had . . .
> . . . songen al the roundel lustily,
> Into a studie he fil sodeynly,
> As doon thise loveres in hir queynte geres,
> Now in the croppe, now doun in the breres,
> Now up, now doun, as boket in a welle.

And again :

> His sleep, his mete, his drink is him biraft,
> That lene he wex, and drye as is a shaft.
> His eyen holwe, and grisly to biholde ;
> His hewe falwe, and pale as asshen colde,
> And solitarie he was, and ever allone,
> And wailing al the night, making his mone.
> And if he herde song or instrument,
> Then wolde he wepe, he mighte nat be stent.[1]

The touch in the last two lines is interesting, and, so far as I know, it is original with Chaucer. I have not met in my reading with any passage in which weeping at the sound of music was a symptom of love.

Finally, the conventional idea that love is caused by beauty is employed. Beauty wounds the heart of the lover through his eyes. Palamon declares :

> But I was hurt right now thurgh-out myn ye
> Into myn herte, that wol my bane be.

He is " stung " by the sight of Emilia's beauty :

> He caste his eye upon Emelya,
> And therwithal he bleynte, and cryde ' a ! '
> As though he stongen were unto the herte.

Arcite has the same experience :

> And with that sighte hir beautee hurte him so, . . .
> And with a sigh he seyde pitously :
> ' The fresshe beautee sleeth me sodeynly
> Of hir that rometh in the yonder place ;
> And, but I have hir mercy and hir grace . . .
> I nam but deed.'

The instances given above are not all the examples of Chaucer's employment of conventional ideas in the *Knight's Tale*. They will suffice, however, to show that in the framework of

---

[1] With these symptoms may be compared the list of the pictures of sighs, broken sleeps, etc., on the walls of the Temple of Venus.

his love story he made the same large use of these ideas that he was accustomed to make when he wrote of love elsewhere.

Chaucer's purpose in the *Knight's Tale*, it is generally held, is to show the conflict between love and friendship. Indeed, this must have been no small part of Boccaccio's purpose in the *Teseide*. But as he manages his narrative, the friendship of the two cousins is given such prominence, is kept so constantly before the reader as almost to make him feel the possibility of friendship's triumph over love in the long run. Not so in Chaucer, whose aim seems to be to show

> that love ne lordshipe
> Wol noght, his thonkes, have no felaweshipe.

With this end in view, the English poet has made some significant changes in his original, the most important of which we may note as follows:

1. He has greatly abridged Boccaccio's version of the story.

2. From certain hints in Boccaccio, he has developed the character of Palamon, thus making an extremely effective contrast with the character of Arcite.[1]

---

[1] This feature of Chaucer's poem is brought out with considerable detail by Mr. Tatlock (*Chron. and Dev.*, Appendix C, pp. 231–232); and need not be further set forth here. I agree, for the most part, with Mr. Tatlock's statements. I do not think, however, that he recognizes sufficiently the prominence given by Boccaccio to Arcite over Palamon. Mr. Tatlock remarks: " In the *Teseide*, though Arcite cuts slightly the better figure, they are hardly distinguished, and both are valorous and honorable young knights, full of all worthy emotions " (pp. 231–232). This, to my mind, is a little misleading. Arcite, it seems to me, cuts decidedly the better figure throughout the tale. He is, up to the time of his death, constantly in the limelight. Note, for instance, the manner in which he holds the center of the stage in the combat scene; how he stops to take a breath, and catches a glimpse of Emily, the sight of whom restores his vigor, and he returns to the fight, fiercer than ever (viii, 78–80).

> E vie più fiero ritornò a fedire
> Che prima, si e' lo spronò il desire (viii, 80).

It seems to me, too, that Arcite has the author's sympathy throughout, much more than Palamon. This may account, perhaps, for Boccaccio's disregard of

3. He has made Emilia almost characterless, though he presents her as a charming picture, the object of the love of the two cousins. A recent writer says of her : " Emelye is, within her limits, as beautiful and touching a figure as any in poetry ; but her limits are those of a figure in a stained-glass window compared with a portrait of Titian's." [1] This is quite true, and in the portrayal of Emilia Chaucer perhaps made his greatest change. To make this matter clear, I must give, at some length, an outline of Boccaccio's account of his heroine.

Not until the third Canto does Emilia make her appearance. Then we see her, a simple, innocent girl, going alone every morning into the garden, singing songs of love to divert herself. But, the poet assures us, she was not in love ;

> A ciò tirata da propria natura ;
> Non che d'amore alcun fosse costretta.

It was while she was singing in the garden that she heard the " Alas ! " of Palamon. At this, looking over her shoulder, she turned her eyes to the window and blushed ; then arising, she

poetic justice in having Arcite see Emilia first, though Palamon finally possesses her. A passage, in which the author seems to show his sympathy for Arcite, is that hero's soliloquy, in which he gives his reasons for expecting to win in the fight with his cousin :

> Poi potete veder ch' i' ho ragione
> Di tal battaglia ; onde avremo il favore
> Del forte Marte, e 'n la nostra questione
> Il cor mi dice i' sarò vincitore.
> Perocch' io volli già con Palemone
> Participare, amando, quanto amore
> Con pace, ed e' non volle ; ond' io son certo
> Che degl' Iddii n' avrò debito merto (vii, 136).

I cannot read this passage without the feeling that the author sanctions Arcite's words, — indeed, that he puts this speech into his hero's mouth in order to justify his taking part in a contest with his cousin. There is in this speech, too, a hint of the petulance of Palamon's disposition, and of his jealousy. Such hints, doubtless, Chaucer seized upon, in building up the character of Palamon, as it is presented in the *Knight's Tale*.

[1] Coulton, *Chaucer and His England*, p. 222.

went away (iii, 18). But as she went, she thought of the
" Alas "; and although she was a young girl, too young, indeed,
for Love to claim, still she understood what the " Alas " meant;
and she was pleased with herself and counted herself beautiful.
Therefore, she adorned herself the more when she returned
into the garden (iii, 19). And so she continued to go, always
keeping her eyes on the window.

> Non che a ciò Amor la costringesse,
> Ma per vedere s'altri la vedesse.

And if she saw that she was being watched, as if she were not
aware of it, she began to sing, gathering the flowers meanwhile,
and humbly and in a womanly fashion (*donnescamente*) she
tried to make herself pleasing to whoever saw her.

> Nè la recava a ciò pensier d'amore
> Che ella avesse, ma la vanitate
> Chè innato è alle femmine nel core
> Da fare altrui veder la lor biltate (iii, 30).

The next glimpse we get of the maiden is when, Arcite being
about to leave Athens at the command of Theseus, she appears
on a balcony with her maid, and looks at the exiled hero and
feels sorry for him.

We see her again for a moment at the feast which Theseus
made shortly after Arcite, now disguised as Pentheus, took service with him. She was invited, along with the other ladies, and
her beauty was the marvel of all ; so great was it that all said

> Che veramente ell' era Citerea.

But Arcite most of all was charmed by the sight of her. And
it happened too, that Emilia recognized him, though he was
unknown to all the others (iv, 53–56). The author reminds us
later (iv, 56) that Emilia was so young that she had not felt
the sting of love when Arcite had gone. So when she saw him,
she remarked within herself, all innocently: " This is that

Arcite, whom I saw grieving. What does he here? Does he not realize that if he should be recognized, he would have to die, or return to prison (iv, 57)?" Still, she was discreet and said nothing to any one (iv, 58).

The next appearance of Emilia in the story is on the occasion of the duel in the wood. She is riding on the hunt with the royal party, and suddenly she comes upon the two lovers fighting, and is at once known by each of them (v, 80). At first she is so astonished that she neither goes forward nor turns back; she neither moves nor speaks. But after a while, coming to herself, she calls some of her party and has Theseus summoned to witness the duel (v, 81). After the strange case has all been explained to Theseus, he addresses her : " Young damsel, do you see what love does on your account, since you are more beautiful than any other creature? You ought to consider it a sovereign honor."

> Nulla rispose Emilia, ma cambiossi
> Tutta nel viso, tanto vergognosi.

As they all return to the city, Emilia rides between the two lovers, greatly to their delight, being made to do this by Theseus (v, 104).

In the following canto, she appears only for a moment, when she with her sister, queen Hippolita, receives graciously the many warriors who came to Athens to fight in behalf of Palamon and Arcite. They are all struck by her beauty, and are not surprised that one of the cousins broke out of prison, and the other, contrary to command, came back to Athens to gain such a treasure (vi, 66, 67).

The next canto tells of Emilia's preparations for the sacrifice to Diana to whom she is devoted; and of her prayer to the goddess so to order things that she may remain a maiden, and to turn the hearts of the two lovers away from her. But if her destiny be such that she must become the wife of one, she prays the goddess that she will send that one to her arms that most desires her.

> Che io nol so in me stessa nomare,
> Tanto ciascun piacevole mi pare.

The reply to her prayer comes at once, when the goddess appears and tells her that it is already decided among the gods that she must marry one of the two, but which one cannot now be disclosed. The goddess then disappears and Emilia returns home (vii, 95–109). In this scene for the first time, Emilia is something more than a picture.

We next see the heroine as a witness of the fight. She inclines to neither party, but is very much troubled that she should be the cause of all this conflict. She pathetically chides Love and Fortune for making her the object of this strife (viii, 96). She laments that mothers, fathers, friends, and brothers of those in the combat will curse her, and before the altars of the gods will call for vengeance upon her. And further, if she must be the wife of one of the lovers, she does not know which she would choose. Both are the same to her. The god of Love has disposed her heart to love, but where to place her affections she does not know (viii, 109). The heroine's perplexity and her pathetic utterances appeal strongly to our sympathies. She is here, for the second time, something of a character.

Palamon's misfortune in being seized by the savage horse loses the day for him. And now suddenly we see Emilia's love directing itself to Arcite. Knowing the conditions of the fight,

> Già d'Arcita credendo veramente
> Esser l'animo suo, senza dimoro
> A lui voltò, e divenne fervente
> Dall' amor d'esso ; e già per suo ristoro,
> Per lui vittoria pietosa chiedea,
> Nè più di Palemon già le calea.

She praises his fairness and noble bearing, his prowess and daring. Whereas the lovers appeared equal before, now they appear entirely unequal (126). She already considers herself espoused to Arcite, and prays the gods for her lord, looking at him with a new desire, and praising his works above all (127).

> E sol d'Arcita l'immagine prende,
> E sè lascia pigliar, nè si difende.

The ninth canto tells the story of Arcite's falling under his horse. In this book, Emilia appears more as a character than she has yet done in the story. She sees the unfortunate accident from where she is, and is stunned and terrified, — pale as one who is carried to his bier (ix, 10). She laments to herself the brevity of her happiness (11, 12) but she, along with the queen and others, goes into the lists and tries to comfort and aid Arcite (16). Moved by the pitiable sight, she can scarcely restrain her grief, and within herself she curses Love, who has placed her in such sorrow (18). She cannot keep back the tears and her visage changes (19).

After Arcite has been brought to himself, at the solicitation of Theseus, Emilia modestly tries to console the wounded hero, tenderly assuring him of her sorrow and of her affectionate regard for him (27). As Arcite rides back to the city in triumph, she sits beside him (32), conducting herself with modesty, her beauty being praised by all (40). After the triumphal procession reaches the palace and Arcite is placed on a bed, Emilia, together with Hippolita and the other ladies, exerts herself in comforting the stricken man (49).

According to the agreement before the fight, the conquered rival was to place himself at the mercy of Emilia. It now becomes her duty to pass judgment upon Palamon. As he kneels before her (63), he begs her to condemn him to death (64). She listens, moved with pity, and with difficulty refrains from weeping (65). She appears here to the best possible advantage, — tender, delicate in feeling, and lovable. She assures Palamon gently but firmly that, if the gods had decreed that she should love him, she would have done so with true devotion (66). But since she is Arcite's alone, she can give no comfort to his rival's amorous pains (67, 68). She begs him to look for another love (69) and she assures him that she feels no inclination to condemn him to death. She then gives him a ring, a sword, a new horse, and other gifts, and bids him win glory with them (75).

In the death scene of Arcite, Emilia is a touching and pathetic figure, in her genuine grief and despair. She reproaches herself as the cause of all this woe, since she is the object of the god's wrath (xi, 67), which had been shown before in the death of Achates (a former suitor). Why do they not visit their wrath upon her rather than upon Arcite? She curses the day she was born (70), and declares that she will not remain in life long after Arcite (71). Now she understands the unfavorable omens which she saw while sacrificing to Diana (72). And now Arcite asks her, after his death to marry Palamon — this is too much to think of ; rather will she serve Diana the rest of her days (76–79), for she has brought nothing but sorrow, first to Achates and then to Arcite himself. If Theseus will have her marry, let him send her to one among his enemies, in order that the disasters that attend her may fall upon them (80). Then, weeping, she kisses Arcite for the last time, and falls in a swoon (83). The whole scene is one of the most genuine in the work in its pathos and tenderness.

In the eleventh canto we see Emilia lamenting for the dead hero (5), and later applying the torch to the funeral pile.

The twelfth tells how, at the command of Theseus, Emilia marries Palamon, although she mildly protests that she feels bound to serve Diana, since vengeance had been brought upon Arcite on account of her not remaining true to the goddess, as she had promised. We see her for the last time at the wedding, in all the glory of her heavenly beauty.

From this synopsis it is apparent that Chaucer, in his presentation of Emilia, has sacrificed much in his original that is beautiful and attractive. We may feel certain that Chaucer himself appreciated the beauty of Emilia's character as Boccaccio portrays her; we may be sure, too, that as an artist he deemed it necessary to make the sacrifice he did. In fact, it is clear that all three of the changes enumerated above, which the poet has made in his original, and not the least, the change in the character of Emilia, conduce to one end. By the abridgment of the tale, Boccaccio's diffuseness is avoided; by the sharp distinction drawn between the characters of Palamon and Arcite, attention is directed to them; and by leaving Emilia a bright and lovely picture, yet on the whole characterless, the same effect of concentrating the reader's mind on the two cousins is obtained. The total result is that which Chaucer was, doubtless, aiming at: namely, to heighten the impression that the love passion of the two heroes was not only earnest but absolutely genuine.[1]

---

[1] Perhaps no other poem of Chaucer's shows the poet's ability to infuse life into commonplaces more than the *Knight's Tale*. We have seen above the large number of absolutely conventional ideas which he employed in telling the story. We may note, too, that as far as concerns the love language of the poem, little else but conventional language has been used. Notwithstanding this, and notwithstanding the fact that his purpose is not to treat the subject of love for its own sake, he has contrived to leave the reader with the impression that both the lovers were burning with a fervent passion for Emilia. This impression is heightened, of course, by the events in the narrative, — the risks run by Arcite in returning to Athens, the combat in the wood, and other details of the story. But it is by the judicious combination of conventional ideas with such incidents, and with remarks and comment, that the poet displays his genius and vitalizes the dead conventions of love poetry. That the author of the *Canterbury Tales* should show such ability is not astonishing. But the failure of many contemporary poets, who were using the same conventions, to get into their poetry any effect of genuineness, brings into bolder relief the genius of Chaucer.

In this feature it must be acknowledged, I think, that the English poet has improved greatly upon the Italian original. While passion, and that in abundance, is not wanting in Boccaccio's poem, there is about this passion an evenness, a certain lack of warmth, one might almost say a placidity, which make it seem artificial.[1] Such an impression Chaucer has entirely overcome; and in so doing, he has accomplished in a much more effective manner his purpose of showing the conflict between the love and the friendship of Palamon and Arcite.

The Nonne Preestes Tale

We have already had examples in this study in which Chaucer employed the conventions of the courtly love poetry for humorous purposes. In the *Nonne Preestes Tale* we find the same clever use of these ideas. The poet ascribes to Pertelote those qualities and characteristics which were expected of the lady in conventional love affairs :

> Curteys she was, discreet and debonaire,
> And compaignable, and bar herself . . . faire.

She was also fair, so fair, indeed, that

> she hath the herte in hold
> Of Chauntecleer loken in every lith.

The most interesting use of conventional ideas in the poem is found in the words of Pertelote, in which she tells Chauntecleer what kind of a husband a woman likes :

> For certes, what so any womman seith,
> We alle desyren, if it mighte be,
> To han housbondes hardy, wyse, and free,
> And secree, and no nigard, ne no fool, . . .
> Ne noon avauntour . . .

---

[1] For a judicious criticism and comparison of the two versions, Italian and English, as regards this point, and as regards the improvement made by Chaucer throughout, see Warton, *History of English Poetry*, III, 308–310.

These were the qualities demanded of courtly lovers from the time of Andreas on. Considering the connotations of the words " secree " and " avauntour " in the courtly love, it is a delightful bit of humor in the poet to have Pertelote demand of her husband (!) that he be *secret* and that he be not a *boaster of favors received*.

The Squieres Tale

In the early part of this tale where is described the merriment at the house of Cambinskan, the poet makes some use of conventional love language. For example:

> Now daunïen lusty Venus children dere.

The line contains the idea that Venus is the goddess of Love and of lovers; and " lusty Venus children " means nothing more than " lovers." Reference to the service of the love deity, and to the gaiety which was demanded of a lover, is found in the lines:

> He moste han knowen Love and his servyse,
> And ben a festlich man as fresh as May.

Secrecy in love affairs is hinted at in the lines:

> Who coude telle yow the forme of daunces,
> So uncouthe and so fresshe countenaunces,
> Swich subtil loking and dissimulinges
> For drede of jalouse mennes aperceyvinges?

We have already had instances of Chaucer's portrayal of false lovers; for example, in the *Anelida and Arcite* and in several of the individual poems of the *Legend*. In every case the deceiver, who pretends to be in earnest, acts in all respects the courtly lover's part. *The Squieres Tale* furnishes one more example of this type. Though he was a hypocrite, yet to the falcon the pretender appeared to be true. She tells Canace of the impression he made upon her when he came a-wooing. He seemed to

her a " welle of gentilesse " ; he showed " humble chere " and
a "hewe of trouthe," " plesaunce," " busy peyne."

> Right so this god of love, this ypocrite,
> Doth so his cerimonies and obeisaunces,
> And kepeth in semblant alle his observaunces
> That sowneth into gentillesse of love.

In the lines quoted it is interesting to note once more, along
with the conventional love ideas, the transfer of terms of religion
to love.

In the further description of their relations, the falcon tells
of the tercelet's " service " (524), of his humility (544), of his
reverence for her (545), of his obedience, and of his " truth,"
— all of which characterized the courtly lover in his position
of inferiority before the lady.

Finally, she speaks of the tercelet as being " gentil born, fresh,
and gay, goodly for to seen, humble and free," all of which
were the regular qualities ascribed to the courtly lover.

The Franklin's Tale

The situation in the love affair of the *Franklin's Tale* is precisely that of the accounts of many of the troubadours. Here
is a woman who is married, and happily married too, to a knight ;
but her beauty inflames another man with passion. He suffers
in silence as long as he can bear it ; then he mentions his love
to her and begs for her favor. The end of his love is purely
physical gratification, and she recognizes the fact and listens
patiently to his requests. But unlike the ladies in most of the
early stories Dorigen does not grant the desired favors to the
importunate lover. This feature may have been in the original
" lay " from which Chaucer professes to have taken his story.
If it was not, the poet has departed from what may be called
the more usual plan of such stories for the special purpose of
putting before the reader a picture of the ideal love of man and

wife. For the real interest in the tale is not in the love story of Aurelius, or in the wooing of Dorigen by Arveragus, but in the discussion of the question of "sovereignty" which the Wife of Bath had started a short time before.

In those episodes which deal with love the usual conventional ideas are employed. The familiar winged god is mentioned in the lines :

> Whan maistrie comth, the god of love anon
> Beteth hise winges and farewel! he is gon!

The conventional secrecy in love affairs is observed by Aurelius.

> Of this matere he dorste no word seyn.
> Under his brest he bar it more secree
> Than ever dide Pamphilus for Galathee;
> His brest was hool, withoute for to sene,
> But in his herte ay was the arwe kene.

The lover, as usual, is his lady's servant. Arveragus, it is said,

> loved and dide his payne
> To serve a lady in his beste wyse;

and at last, this lady for his "worthinesse" and for his "obeysaunce" had pity on him and accepted him as her husband. Whereupon he swore that he would never take upon himself the "maistrye" over her,

> But hir obeye, and folwe hir wil in al
> As any lovere to his lady shal.

The idea of the lover's fear to speak his love to his lady appears in the lines :

> For she was oon the faireste under sonne,
> And eek therto come of so heigh kinrede,
> That wel unnethes dorste this knight, for drede,
> Telle hir his wo, his peyne, and his distresse.

Similarly, though Aurelius loved Dorigen better than any other creature for two years,

> never dorste he telle hir of his grevaunce;
> Withouten coppe he drank al his penaunce.

As the love of Aurelius for Dorigen was unsuccessful, there are many statements devoted to this lover's woes and sorrows and amorous pains. He made songs, complaints, roundels, and virelays in which he lamented

> that he dorste not his sorwe telle
> But languissheth as a furie dooth in helle;
> And dye he moste, . . . as dide Ekko.

He addresses his lady :

> Madame, reweth upon my peynes smerte
> For with a word ye may me sleen or save.

When she puts on him the task of removing the rocks along the shore, recognizing the impossibility of his performing it,

> He to his hous is goon with sorweful herte;
> He seeth he may nat fro his deeth asterte.
> Him semed that he felte his herte colde ;
> For verray wo out of his wit he breyde.

His brother puts him to bed, where

> In languor and in torment furious
> Two yeer and more lay wrecche Aurelius
> Er any foot he mighte on erthe goon.

Here again, in the case of the *Franklin's Tale*, the examples quoted do not comprise all the conventions of which Chaucer has made use. But they are enough to show that, as a basis for the love stories involved in the narrative, he has employed nothing but ideas which had been long familiar in love literature. Further comment on the tale seems unnecessary. Working with the courtly commonplaces, the poet has so managed them as to make the story real. Aurelius's passion appears as genuine and earnest as is the grief which Dorigen feels at being forced to be untrue to her husband.

CHAPTER V

CONCLUSION

With the *Franklin's Tale*, Chaucer's employment of the courtly-love ideas ceases. One question now suggests itself, an answer to which would be very interesting, were it possible to get it : " What was Chaucer's own attitude toward these conceptions, of which he made such a large use in his poetry ? " The writer wishes to state frankly that he does not believe it is possible to answer this question finally and definitely. It is difficult to tell what Chaucer's ideas are on any subject, so predominantly dramatic is his poetic work. Indeed, the question just stated would not be raised, were it not that others have felt that they could see in the poet's works evidence of a spirit of irony and satire against the courtly ideas. We have already, in connection with our study of Pandarus, considered the opinions of Ebert and ten Brink upon this subject. Another expression, more recent, and more cautious, is the following : " His [Chaucer's] attitude towards the chivalric ideal of love was, upon the whole, a critical one." [1] Still later, certain remarks of Mr. Tatlock [2] seem to indicate that he sees in the *Knight's Tale* a tendency on the part of the poet to poke fun at the courtly love therein portrayed. But all such statements seem to be unwarranted, and Mr. Tatlock, oddly enough, himself supplies the corrective for them. He says, in the connection just noted : " Satire is easier to suspect than to prove, especially in a poem written when ideas of what is ludicrous and the connotations of words were so different from

[1] Billings, *Middle English Metrical Romances*, New York, 1901, p. xxxi.
[2] *Chron. and Devel.*, Appendix C, pp. 232–233.

what they are now." [1] We cannot say that Chaucer did not laugh to himself at some of the vagaries of lovers of his time. But we may suspect that the actions of courtly lovers then were no more ridiculous than are the actions of lovers of our day to people with a lively sense of humor. Extravagant as the courtly love may seem to us, this was the only kind of love there was at that period (except the grosser passion of the *fabliaux* which we do not consider here). Only in so far as love is always a fit subject for satire, was the chivalrous love ridiculous in an age when chivalrous ideas obtained.

But, aside from the question as to Chaucer's inclination to display levity at the extravagance of lovers, the most casual consideration of his poems will show the improbability of his deliberately satirizing the courtly love. In all the early lyric poems, which are purely conventional in both sentiment and language, there is nothing that remotely suggests satire or irony. And the same is true of those later lyric poems, where there is indeed fun in full measure. The *Book of the Duchess* abounds, as we have seen, in the courtly ideas and sentiments. Yet far from satirizing these ideas, the poet uses them to pay a graceful and delicate compliment to his patron. Consider again the *Parlament of Foules*. Here, if anywhere in the whole range of Chaucer's poetry, we might feel justified in saying that the courtly ideas were being satirized — if we judge entirely from the contents of the poem. Nothing can be plainer than that the goose and the duck openly ridiculed the courtly sentiments of the royal tercelet. But are we to identify Chaucer with the goose and the duck? Clearly not. The occasion which the poem was written to celebrate (and scholars agree that it has reference to the courtship of the royal couple) precludes the possibility of any satirical purpose on the part of the author. We have already examined the sympathetic treatment of the chivalrous love in

[1] *Chron. and Devel.*, Appendix C, p. 233.

the *Troilus*, and there is no more indication of satire in the *Knight's Tale*. Levity there may be ; of fun there is plenty. But to say that there is irony in the description of the courtly love of Palamon and Arcite is unwarranted by anything in the poem itself.

What then is Chaucer's attitude toward this love, judging from his poetry? All we are justified in saying is that he used the courtly ideas, as he used every element of the life about him, for artistic purposes. If love is ridiculed anywhere, it is done by some one of the poet's characters. And we have no right to say that the sentiments expressed by any character are those of the poet himself. We cannot justly say even, as one writer above quoted has said, that Chaucer's attitude toward the chivalrous love is a critical one. It is enough to say, and it detracts nothing from the glory of our poet, that in treating this material he has maintained the detachment of a poetic artist, and has been unconcerned about giving his own opinions.

A recognition of this makes short and easy the task of summarizing the results of this investigation. We have observed that both Gower and Chaucer in their treatment of love employed ideas which had been present in erotic literature from the time of the troubadours. These ideas Gower took as he found them, as many another poet did before him, and lacking the ability to impress them with his own individuality he left them unchanged. The language employed to set them forth was conventional throughout. The figures of the lovers whom Gower wishes to portray he does succeed in endowing with some degree of life and human quality. But his lack of imagination impoverishes his poetry, and his tendency to moralize has the grotesque result of making Gower the man elbow out of place Gower the artist. With Chaucer, the opposite of all this is true. In his hands, in some manner which defies analysis, the old love conventions become the poet's own. The language he uses to give expression to the passion of love is clever, forceful, and inevitable. His characters live before us as real people. In his maturity, he shows himself always the poet of genius, under whose magic touch commonplaces are transformed and become alive. In a word, in his use of the courtly-love ideas, as in all his work, Chaucer the artist is brilliantly revealed, even though we see but little of Chaucer the man.

INDEX